THE
MOUNT SHASTA
MISSION

THE MOUNT SHASTA MISSION

MACHAELLE SMALL WRIGHT

PERELANDRA

CENTER FOR NATURE RESEARCH
JEFFERSONTON, VIRGINIA

The Mount Shasta Mission

Machaelle Wright

FIRST PRINTING

Copyright © 2005 by Machaelle Wright

This book is manufactured in the United States of America.
Designed by James F. Brisson and Machaelle Wright
Cover design by James F. Brisson, Williamsville, VT 05362
Naked Man, Bag Lady and other artwork by James F. Brisson
Front cover image copyright © Jane English, Mt. Shasta, CA 96067
Copyediting: Elizabeth McHale, Readsboro, VT 05350
Photos: Jenny Durrant and Clarence Wright
Formatting, page layout and computer wizardry: Machaelle Wright
Quark Rescuer and Photoshop Queen: Jenny Durrant
Proofreading and GROMs extraordinaire: Amy Shelton,
Jenny Durrant and Jeannette Edwards
Food: Maria Gabriel

This book was formatted, laid out and produced
using QuarkXPress 6.5 software.

Published by Perelandra, Ltd.,
P.O. Box 3603, Warrenton, VA 20188

Library of Congress Control Number: 2005905284
Wright, Machaelle
The Mount Shasta Mission

ISBN: 0–927978–60–1

2 4 6 8 9 7 5 3 1

*To all who worked on
the Mt. Shasta Mission*

To protect the innocent (as they say), I have changed the names of the Foot People and Foot People wannabes except for Peter Caddy and Clarence Wright. They're the two brave ones. Since the Mt. Shasta Mission, Peter Caddy has died. But prior to his death, I asked permission to use his name. Without hesitation he said, "Of course."

Contents

THE
MOUNT SHASTA
MISSION

Introduction

BACK IN 1971, I MET Ben Hunt. He was the Philosophy of Science professor at St. Paul's College, a Catholic seminary in Washington, D.C., and he was a priest. Outside the college the students referred to him as "Ben Hunt" rather than Father Hunt. In my opinion, he was one of those truly brilliant people who also happened to be eccentric. For one thing, he always wore an overcoat, indoors as well as outside—throughout the entire year. The overcoat in winter made a lot more sense to me than the overcoat during the brutally hot, humid, Washington summer days.

His classes were legendary. On the first day of one semester, he came into the classroom, opened a book of nursery rhymes and read aloud, "Twinkle, twinkle little star." Just that line. Nothing else. He then closed the book and said to the students, "Now, let's examine that." I'm told they spent the rest of the semester discussing that one line: What does that sentence mean? What are these things called "stars"? What does "twinkle" mean? And why does it say these things called "stars" are little? What does it mean by "little"? Throughout the semester, the seminarians had to observe the night sky and, without making assumptions based on anything they had learned in their lives up to that point, they had to describe what they saw as if each was the first man on Earth to observe the sky.

Ben Hunt began another semester with the biblical line, "O Lord, Thou hast made the cliff for the rock badger." For the rest of the semester they discussed. What does it mean to say that God made the cliff for the rock badger? Did He? Or is this our definition because we see rock badgers on cliffs? Does the original definition of "cliff" mean that it was made for the rock badger, or did we decide that later? Like "Twinkle, twinkle little star," the purpose of studying the biblical quote was to examine how we define things and how we assign purpose and meaning for things.

The students I knew who took his class said that they never knew what he was getting at until the very last day. And then, all the semester's classes would fall into place and suddenly make sense. It was the "Ben Hunt Aha Moment" that they all looked forward to.

A friend of mine, who was a former student, asked Ben Hunt if he would read a book review my friend had written for publication. Later, he showed me the copy of the review Ben Hunt had read. At the top of the first page, Ben had written, "This is interesting." Now, normally that kind of comment would be a kiss of death to a writer. But along with this terse three-word review, Ben Hunt had written a page and a half on what he meant by the word "interesting." Trust me. It was well beyond any definition from a dictionary, and it made his comment not only reasonable but highly complimentary.

Which reminds me. I'm told that if you passed Ben Hunt in a hallway on a beautiful day, you did not want to say, "Nice day!" to him because he'd ask you just what you meant by "nice" and "day." Really.

Probably the most wonderful Ben Hunt story I ever heard had to do with his trip to California to teach a summer semester at the University of California at Berkeley. So many students had registered for the class that they had to hold it in the auditorium. So there Ben Hunt was on this big stage with a dog named Diane that he had borrowed from a friend for the class. The place was packed. Ben sat in a chair with Diane at his feet. And he began to talk to her. Actually, he held a Socratic discussion with her—for the entire period. He would say something and then ask Diane what she thought. The next class, he did the same thing. By the end of the third class, Ben Hunt was still talking to Diane. She would sometimes look like she was listening (or maybe she was), or she'd spend the time sleeping. He never stopped talking to her, and he never addressed anyone else in the auditorium. This was when the class started thinning out. Still he kept talking to Diane. Halfway through the semester, there were only about twenty students coming to the auditorium to listen to this man in an overcoat talk to a dog. According to the story, about three quarters of the way through the semester, a few students figured out what he was doing (the renowned Ben Hunt Aha Moment) and returned to class to listen to Ben talking to Diane. The next week, more students trickled in. By the last few weeks of the semester, the auditorium was once again full, with standing room only. And Ben Hunt, not missing a beat, continued talking to his friend Diane through the rest of the semester.

Don't ask me what he was talking about or what the students finally understood. I don't know. A number of seminarians told me this story, but they didn't know what he was doing either—except having a Socratic discussion with a dog. The dictionary states that a Socratic discussion centers around Socrates' "philosophical method of systematic doubt and questioning of another to elicit a clear expression of a truth supposed to be implicitly known by all rational beings."...It makes you appreciate Diane, doesn't it?

I suspect that right about now you're wondering why in the world I'm telling you about Ben Hunt. If you're thinking this, you are having the other kind of Ben Hunt moment—confusion with the promise of leading to purpose and reason. And this brings me to *The Mount Shasta Mission.* Whenever I have talked about the Mt. Shasta Mission, I've felt that it is truly a Ben Hunt class. Because I'm presenting the story sequentially, there are a lot of what seem to be disconnected pieces that will weave together, if you hang in there and get all the way to the end of the book. And there you'll have it, your very own "Aha" moment.

I am presenting the Mt. Shasta Mission sequentially because this is how I experienced it. I want you to see how the mission came together from my perspective. And I'd like you to know only what I knew at each step of the way. If you feel lost or confused, that's fine. I had those feelings too—a lot. That's the way these big, multilevel events feel when you're actually experiencing them, and I think it's only fair that I share the pain of confusion. (Oh, okay…Every once in a while I'll throw you a bone and give you information just to keep you from screaming and pulling out your hair.)

And, speaking of pain—one of the things I'd like to accomplish with this book is to dispel those obnoxious, cutesy, all-is-perfect, no-hair-gets-messed-up myths and rumors about these kinds of large multilevel events. People think it's like a Steven Spielberg movie where everything happens on cue and it all looks beautiful, with John Williams orchestral music playing in the background. Well, not only does hair get messed up, but clothes get torn and hands get dirty. Sometimes it's just not pretty. And that's the truth about big events like the Mt. Shasta Mission.

❦

Finally, and this is the most important suggestion I can make to you for when you are reading this book:

Eat chocolate!
Good chocolate. Not the crappy, cheap stuff.
It helps. Honest.

Chapter 1

Your Anchor

I SAID I'D MAKE YOU GO through this story knowing only what I knew at each step of the way. Well, this is your lucky day. I'm going to throw you a bunch of those bones that I promised and give you a break now. Prior to the Mt. Shasta Mission, there were key principles and concepts I didn't know or understand but were important to the mission. I'm not going to make you wait until the end of the book to give you that information. I know you may be tempted to skip this chapter and go right to the story. Don't do that… No, really… It's not a good idea. This chapter will help you understand the story and catch the lessons that are there for you to consider and learn. In short, let this chapter be your anchor throughout the rest of the book.

AQUARIAN ERA

"Aquarian Era" is the name given for the coming phase of evolution facing not only those of us on Earth but those throughout the universe and beyond as well. Although it is termed "Aquarian" because of its loose connection to the astronomical alignment of Aquarius, it is more importantly a term that connotes a specific emphasized pattern and rhythm in life behavior and social structures — equality, cooperation and teamwork.

AQUARIAN LEADERSHIP AND TEAMWORK

There are three key elements of Aquarian leadership and teamwork that were critical to the Mt. Shasta Mission:

- Leadership recognition
- Service without a personal agenda
- Flexibility and factor-x

Leadership recognition: The position of the leader of the Mt. Shasta Mission was understood, accepted and respected by all who helped put this mission together. Those involved in the planning and execution stages of the mission were peers, each with a high level of expertise. They chose their leader and, without hesitation, they deferred to that one person throughout the entire mission. (In other words, there were no meetings around the water cooler to carp and gripe about the leader.) The leader's strength, efficiency, organization, coordination and vision were the bonds that held the team together. An example of his leadership style: He established a free-flowing relationship between the different areas of expertise, making it possible for problem solving and ideas for one part of the mission to come from anyone on the team.

Service without a personal agenda: Another way of saying this is that the team members did not allow personal ego to cloud or get in the way of the leader's role, their jobs or the mission's goals. You will see throughout the story that there are a number of examples where people (from our Earth level) complicated or compromised their participation because they could not put their egos aside for something larger.

Flexibility and factor-x: Sometimes something suddenly comes into our lives that we were not expecting, and we have no plans for dealing with it. I dare say we've all experienced that kind of moment. This is a factor-x. It can be part of whatever project or goal we are working with that we simply didn't know existed until it popped up. Or it can be an accident. Something has happened that was not only unexpected but was never meant to be part of our project or goal. Wherever a factor-x originates, we have to deal with it.

The mission's leader had strong feelings about factor-x and the need for flexibility. He said, "A plan is only as strong as its ability to cope with factor-x." Sometimes the guiding force of a plan can arise from a factor-x, and success often hinges on the plan's ability to cope with and adjust to the factor-x. A plan is weak and rigid if it has no structure built in to accommodate this. But there also must be a sense of appropriateness when considering a factor-x. Sometimes the flexible response, the correct response, is for the leader to say no. Just because something unexpected has occurred doesn't mean it was meant to be part of the plan for achieving a specific goal.

BALANCE

Balance is relative and measured by the demonstration of the laws of nature in each element of life, including all that we humans do and create. Imbalance occurs when there is distortion between the laws of nature and an element of life, including what we humans do and create.

I was able to maintain balance for the Mt. Shasta Mission work that I did by working with nature—i.e., nature intelligence. (See "What Is Nature Intelligence?" on p. 28.) I presented nature with the mission's goals, and nature, in turn, gave me the information on the matter, means and action needed to best achieve those goals. By doing this, we were able to ensure that the laws of nature were reflected in the mission goals, thus demonstrating balance. (See "What Do I Mean When I Say, 'Working with Nature'?" on p. 33 for more information on this concept.)

CONINGS

A coning is a balanced vortex of intelligent energy that includes nature and humans. The simplest way to explain a coning is to say that it is a multilevel conference call. With a coning, we are working with more than one intelligence (human and nature) simultaneously. The information each member of a coning can offer will mix within the coning vortex and become available to the human who is operating the coning as a single, unified body of information. If you have four members of a coning, each with different information about a subject or situation, the person who activates that coning will not hear "four voices" all "talking" at once. They will hear one, unified body of information that contains all the information each coning member can offer.

A coning is needed for multilevel work such as the Mt. Shasta Mission because of the greater stability, clarity and balance it provides. With multilevel processes, we are working with many different facets and levels of intelligences at one time. Consequently, it is better to work with an organized team (a coning) made up of all those involved in the issue we are focusing on. I always activated specific conings for my work in the mission. In general, the coning was comprised of the nature intelligences specifically connected with the Mt. Shasta Mission, specific members of the White Brotherhood involved in the planning and implementation of the mission, and myself.

Another advantage to a coning is that it has a high degree of protection built into it. Because of the larger scope of multilevel work, it is important to define exactly who and what are involved in that work. All others are excluded by the mere fact that they have not been included in the coning, thus eliminating all irrelevant information. In essence, a coning creates not only the team but also the "safe room" in which the team is meeting.

CONSCIOUSNESS
DEFINED BY NATURE

NOTE: Several years ago, I presented nature with a list of terms on which I wanted their understanding and perspective. I found their information to be much deeper and more useful than anything we humans have come up with when considering these terms. Where I have "Defined by Nature" with the terms in this chapter, I am letting you know that the information is from those definitions I received from nature.

The concept of consciousness has been vastly misunderstood. To put it simply, consciousness is the working state of the soul. In human expression, as one sees it demonstrated on the planet Earth, the personality, character, emotional makeup, intellectual capacity, strong points and gifts of a human are all form. They are that which give order, organization and life vitality to consciousness.

We say "working state of the soul" because there are levels of soul existence that are different than the working state and can best be described as a simple and complete state of being.

Humans tend to think of the soul as being something that exists far away from them because they are in form. This is an illusion. The core of any life is the soul. It cannot exist apart from itself. Like the heart in the human body, it is an essential part of the life unit. A human in form is, by definition, a soul fused with nature. Personality and character are a part of the nature/form package that allows the soul to function and to express itself in form. Personality and character are not the soul; they are part of the order and organization of that soul.

Consciousness physically fuses into the body system first through the electrical system and then through the central nervous system and the brain. This is another aspect of nature supplying order, organization and life vitality. Consciousness itself cannot be measured or monitored as a reality. But what can be measured and monitored is the order, organization and life vitality of consciousness....

We wish to add a thought here so that there will be no confusion about the relationship between nature and the soul. Nature does not, with its own power, superimpose its interpretation of form onto a soul. We have said that nature and soul are intimately and symbiotically related. This implies a give and take. No one consciousness group operates in isolation of the whole or of all other parts of the whole. When a soul chooses to move within the vast band of form, it communicates its intent and purpose to nature. It is from this that nature derives the specifics that will be needed for the soul to function in form. It is a perfect marriage of purpose with the order, organization and life vitality that is needed for the fulfillment of that purpose. Nature, therefore, does not define purpose and impose it on a soul. It orders, organizes and gives life vitality to a soul's purpose for expression in form.

EXPANSION

A person undergoes expansion when an experience or event affects the electrical, central nervous and sensory systems *in new ways,* thus making it difficult to sort, identify and integrate accurately what is being experienced.

Everything in our immediate environment affects us physically. We experience outside stimulus first in our electrical system, a complex electrical grid that is located within and surrounding the body. The electrical system responds to the stimulus, and its impulses are immediately shifted to the central nervous and sensory systems for identification, sorting and integration. All of this happens within a nanosecond.

There are two main areas of difficulty in an expansion experience. The first area is physical. Because an expansion experience affects these three body systems (electrical, nervous and sensory systems) in new ways, they often are unable to adjust immediately to the new input, and they may become over-energized, over-loaded and, as a result, nonfunctional as far as the new experience is concerned. As a consequence of this physical breakdown, the person feels confused and is unable to discern what he is actually experiencing. What a person intellectually perceives is a direct result of the function of and interaction between the electrical system, central nervous system and sensory system. Sometimes an experience is so far beyond a person's present ability to sort, iden-tify and integrate within these three systems that he is not even conscious of being influenced by it at all. It is as if the experience never happened.

The second area of difficulty is intellectual. During expansion, our intellectual understanding of what we are experiencing is chal-lenged because it is new to us. What is occurring is not founded in what is already familiar. If we try to force understanding, we shove the experience through the framework of what we already know. An expansion renders that framework obsolete as far as this ex-perience is concerned. If we persist in trying to push the experi-ence through the old framework, we end up confused and we misinterpret the experience.

We can actually distort an expansion by forcing it through our old intellectual framework. In essence, we experience what we *think* we are experiencing. I have met a number of people who have described some pretty frightening "sixth-sense" events to me. While I listened to them, I saw that their ordeals were actually benign in nature, but because it was new to them, they quickly shoved it through their already-existing intellectual framework. Invariably, these were people who had read a lot about other peo-ple's frightening tales or black magic stories. So they pushed their benign new experience into a frightening framework and literally forced themselves into having a frightening experience that they could describe, even "understand." In the process of finding intellectual satisfaction, they managed to scare the bejeebers out of themselves.

The way I've been taught to deal with my own intellect during expansion is to suspend the intellect and be patient: I just focus on the experience and what I'm doing in the moment, let it integrate—and *observe,* sometimes for days or weeks and sometimes for years. This enables the organic formation of a new logic or intellectual framework. As a result, I gain a completely different understanding. Before an expansion, I don't have the ability to understand because the new pieces aren't yet in place. The step-by-step experience itself builds the new logical framework. By approaching expansion in this manner, I allow my intellect to work for me and not against me.

EXPANSION: HOW WE
PHYSICALLY SUPPORT EXPANSION
PERELANDRA CONING SESSION

An expanded experience does not by definition mean it is nonphysical or beyond five-senses form. It simply implies that the experience is beyond that which the person has experienced prior to that time—thus, the sense of expansion…

The laws of form are much broader than what is encompassed when one thinks of the five-sense sensory system. In fact, an expanded experience is simply learning or allowing the sensory system, as most individuals know it, to operate in a fuller capacity. The problem is that individuals tend to see the five-senses system as one range of function, and anything beyond or outside this basic functioning as being something entirely different. In fact, they are both functions of the same system.

When a child is born, its sensory system is quite sensitive and expanded. It is, after all, just moving from a state prior to birth in which the sensory system naturally functions in a broader state. If left on its own, the child would continue to develop its sensory system from the point of this broader perspective. And what others might call "expanded experiences" would be the norm for this child. Societal preconceptions are what encourage the child to limit the sensory range, and the development of the sensory system throughout childhood then takes place from this more limited perspective. Along with this, the limited definition of the sensory system and its scope of discernment becomes the rule of thumb by which to judge experience.

Now, if the sensory system is naturally capable of operating in a much broader scope than most individuals can at present imagine, it follows that the physical body must respond to and support that expanded operation. The sensory system itself is a part of that overall body response and support system. Everything works as a team, ideally. Consequently, one cannot have what is known as an expansion experience without the sensory system and the physical body as a whole responding to and attempting to support it. So, one may see entering a meditative state as an expanded experience, but, in fact, it is a broader use of the sensory system and draws appropriate response and support from within the physical body itself. Just as one cannot move a finger or toe without the entire body's muscular and skeletal systems responding, one cannot shift from one state of mind to another without a similar physical response and shift.

There is a saying many on the Earth level use: "If you don't use it, you lose it." Normally, this refers to muscle and body tone. When a child limits the scope of operation within the sensory system, the complementary scope of physical response and support is no longer needed or utilized. In those areas, a person stiffens and atrophies. Then, later on, when the individual is an adult and consciously chooses to reactivate the sensory system in a broader range, the physical body no longer "knows" how to respond and support that expansion. The person will experience nothing, no matter how much willpower he musters, or the experience will be partially perceived and most likely distorted, as well.

Let's address the body system itself and what happens when the human sensory system responds to an experience. Any experience initially impacts the human body through its electrical system. This occurs whether the *experience is easily perceived or not. The initial receptor of experience is not the brain or the senses but the electrical system. The impact immediately, almost simultaneously, shifts and translates into the nervous system and routes itself throughout the nervous system appropriately as it begins its identification and experience process. This includes activating the sensory system in an appropriate manner. (All this occurs within a split second.) The point to remember is that the initial level of impact is electrical, followed by an impact on and within the nervous system. If the experience is within the individual's perceived notion of "acceptable," the person probably knows how to perceive the experience on all levels operating within the physical body.*

Two things can occur if the individual does not know what to do with the experience. Either the physical body does not know how to respond and support the experience and is in need of assistance, or the experience itself is so beyond the person's operating range of reality that it takes on an intensification that literally overwhelms the body and requires of it a level of operation well beyond its present capability.

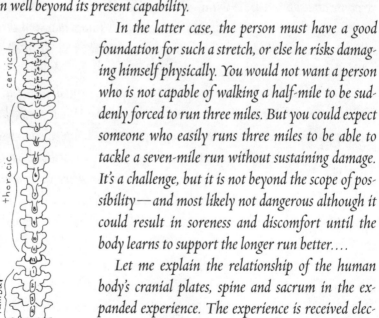

In the latter case, the person must have a good foundation for such a stretch, or else he risks damaging himself physically. You would not want a person who is not capable of walking a half-mile to be suddenly forced to run three miles. But you could expect someone who easily runs three miles to be able to tackle a seven-mile run without sustaining damage. It's a challenge, but it is not beyond the scope of possibility—and most likely not dangerous although it could result in soreness and discomfort until the body learns to support the longer run better....

Let me explain the relationship of the human body's cranial plates, spine and sacrum in the expanded experience. The experience is received electrically and shifted to the central nervous system for sorting and identification. At this point, the physical

Human Spine

body moves to support what is being identified. If the body cannot adequately respond, the electrical system will overload or break, and the corresponding vertebrae, sacrum or cranial plates will most likely react by misaligning. Hence, you have the sensation of trying to catch six balls all at once while only being able to catch four.

Human Cranial Plates

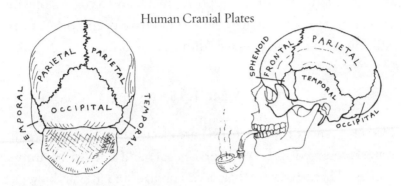

A special note about the cranial plates: An expanded experience carries with it an intensity that registers through the electrical system, moves into the nervous system and continues its impact into the cerebrospinal fluid (CSF). Then the brain is impacted by both the nervous system activity and the CSF pulse response. The cranial plates must respond accordingly to accommodate this two-pronged impact. The range of plate movement will be affected. If the cranials have lost their knowledge of how to move within the new range or if they are three-milers stretching for the seven-mile run, they run the risk of jamming or misaligning. This is when you have head pain associated with expanded experience. Cranial adjustments may be necessary over a period of time in order to allow the plates to adjust properly to and move in a more expanded range.

Just as the leg muscles need to adjust to the seven-mile run, the cranial plates need time to adjust to expansion. Because of the close working proximity with the electrical and nervous systems, the cranials must be considered one of the primary areas for assistance during times of expansion. In a relatively short period of time, the cranials, as well as the rest of the physical body system, will learn how to operate within the expanded range of experience with ease, accuracy and efficiency.

FAITHFULNESS TO JOB

This concept proved to be critical for the mission. If we accept the responsibility for doing a job, we also accept the responsibility for completing that job, even if it means waiting thirty or forty years—or longer—for the opportunity finally to come along that enables us to complete it. There would have been no Mt. Shasta Mission had there not been faithfulness to job.

FLOWER ESSENCES

Flower essences (or "essences") are electrical patterns infused in water, preserved in brandy (or vinegar) and bottled in dropper bottles. These patterns balance, stabilize and repair biological electrical systems, as well as the electrical systems connected with all form. In the Mt. Shasta Mission, essences were used to balance, stabilize and repair human electrical systems. They were also used in my work with nature as stabilizers for the different processes and environmental work.

FORM AND ENERGY
DEFINED BY NATURE

We consider reality to be in the form state when there is order, organization and life vitality combined with a state of consciousness. We do not consider form to be only that which can be perceived by the five senses. In fact, we see form from this perspective to be most limited, both in its life reality and in its ability to function. We see form from the perspective of the five senses to be useful only for the most basic and fundamental level of identification. From this perspective, there is very little relationship to the full understanding and knowledge of how a unit or form system functions.

All energy contains order, organization and life vitality; therefore, all energy is form. If one were to use the term "form" to identify that which can be perceived by the basic five senses and the word "energy" to refer to that aspect of an animal, human, plant or object's form reality that cannot be readily perceived by the basic senses, then one would be accurate in the use of these two words. However, if one were to use the word "form" to refer to that which can be perceived by the basic five senses and assume that form to be a complete unit of reality unto itself, and use the word "energy" to refer to a level beyond form, one would then be using these two words inaccurately. From our perspective, form and energy create one unit of reality and are differentiated from one another solely by the individual's ability to perceive them with his or her sensory system. In short, the differentiation between form and energy within any given object, plant, animal or human lies with the observer.

On the planet Earth, the personality, character, emotional makeup, intellectual capacity, strong points and gifts of a human are all form. They are that which gives order, organization and life vitality to consciousness.

Order and organization are the physical structures that create a framework for form. In short, they define the walls. But we have included the dynamic of life vitality when we refer to form because one of the elements of form is action, and it is life vitality that initiates and creates action.

FORM AND ENERGY: BAND OF FORM

At some point in my early twenties, I heard or read that Earth was the only planet that existed in form, and souls on Earth were the only souls operating in form. Since I saw no evidence to the contrary, and since I really didn't care anyway, I didn't bother to question this piece of information—for years. Even after I began to work directly with nature in 1976, I still didn't challenge it. Although nature was teaching me a lot about form and the underlying dynamics of form, I continued to assume that what I was learning applied to my Earth reality only.

It was evident that I had to learn something new about this form business. I learned that form as I experience it on Earth is

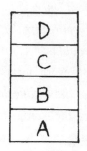

One reality unit showing
four of its dimensions.

not the only form experience there is. In fact, there is a complex and broad "band of form" made up of many different dimensions—some of which we on Earth are capable of seeing and some of which we can't see or experience in any of our usual ways. I eventually learned that no matter how "unique" the dimension, it operates with the same universal laws of form (the laws of nature) as every other dimension within the band of form. Only the way those laws are demonstrated are different.

I learned there are many realities in the universe and beyond. Each reality has other dimensions or "sister dimensions" that correspond in every way to what we are experiencing on Earth. This does not mean that each reality's "Earth" dimension is the mirror image of everything that exists on our planet. Rather, it means that our many sister dimensions have a planet *similar* to ours. People live on those planets in dwellings similar to the ones we use. The planets have trees, mountains, deserts, rivers and oceans. There are animals and plants that we would recognize. There are also some we wouldn't. The people wear clothes, have jobs and travel by means similar to ours. Their social structures are comparable. And they live in cities, towns, suburbs and rural areas similar to ours.

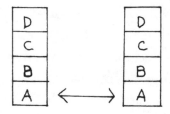

"Sister Dimensions": Comparable dimensions within two different realities.

An expansion may occur if you *consciously* begin to perceive and experience a sister dimension. In fact, this is a common expansion. Although rare from our Earth's perspective, you may also undergo expansion if you consciously begin to perceive and experience another reality that is not a sister dimension to Earth. In either case, the level that you live on remains your "home base." It functions as your foundation. You aren't released from it. The new level that you consciously begin to perceive and experience is an expansion of your perceived reality as lived out on your home base, and what you learn from the experience becomes integrated into your home-base life. As you might imagine, this adds a whole new meaning to "life on Earth as we know it"!

FREE WILL, OPTION, SYNCHRONICITY, ACCIDENTS

Our lives operate on free will. Conscious free will is the dynamic that allows us freedom of choice in all that we do and how we develop within a lifetime. In order to participate fully in the bigger picture, we must learn to function responsibly, intelligently and ethically in ways that are consistent with the universal dynamics of that larger picture—and we must choose to do this consciously and freely.

Some people like to think that we enter a lifetime not only with direction and purpose, but also with the game plan we need to execute to fulfill that direction and purpose. If you think about this for a minute, you'll see that this preset game-plan idea eliminates conscious free will. Our participation in the larger picture is so important that we simply cannot sidestep our growth and development in the vast area of conscious free will. It seems like everyone in the universe and all the intelligences in nature know this—except us. Some of us work awfully hard to sidestep our responsibility in this matter. We must learn to weigh situations and issues consciously, and to say "yes" and "no" and "maybe." In this way, we learn to choose options deliberately that are consistent with universal dynamics and law and to participate consciously in the larger picture. Our participation implies free and knowledgeable participation. The only way we can learn this is through conscious growth and development around free will.

At any given point along the way, we are faced with many options for accomplishing direction and purpose. Some options are harmonious with our direction and purpose—and the larger picture. Some are not. We have to learn to discern and choose. We choose one option over the others for various reasons. It's the one that we find most attractive or exciting. It's the one that seems easiest. Perhaps it's the option that seems most efficient. Maybe it's the one we have the strongest gut reaction to. Or perhaps it's the option that seems the most difficult out of all the others, and, for whatever reason, we feel it's important for us to take that one. As we choose each option along the way, we begin to weave a unique pattern based on who we are and our ability to use free will to make choices. Over time we learn the formula for choosing what works best for us.

Two issues tend to come up whenever I have talked about free will. The first is synchronicity. Usually people use synchronicity to describe an event where one's need or desire is suddenly and unexpectedly met by the perfect opportunity. There is a sense that "someone has heard them" and magically met their need.

In actuality, this kind of synchronicity is an illusion. They have simply chosen the option out of all the different ones available to them that allowed for their need to be met in this particular way. They could have chosen another option that was equally available to them that would have also met their need, but in a different and less "magical" manner.

At any given point along the way, we are surrounded with a

number of options for meeting need and desire. Most of them are positive in nature, and can meet need and desire quite well. If we choose one of these, we experience our lives moving easily—even magically. This causes some to think that they "received" the one and only option for fulfilling need and desire. In fact, they chose one of several options. And had they chosen one of the difficult options or one of the options that was not consistent with their direction and purpose, their tough experiences might become labeled "bad luck."

Both concepts—synchronicity and bad luck—distance us from our personal responsibility in life and complicate our growth and development in the area of conscious free will.

The second issue generally raised centers around accidents. Many feel that there are no accidents in life. Every event and opportunity is in right timing or predestined—i.e., synchronistic. Although this concept can be comforting at times—especially when dealing with what we call someone's "untimely" death—it eliminates free will. You simply cannot have over five billion people running around the planet exercising free will and not have accidents occur.

The Mt. Shasta Mission is a complex weave of option, free will, synchronicity and even accidents.

GROUNDING
DEFINED BY NATURE

Quite simply, the word "grounded" is used to acknowledge full body/soul fusion or full matter/soul fusion. The word "grounding" refers to what must be accomplished or activated in order both to ensure and stabilize body (matter)/soul fusion. To be grounded refers to the state of being of a fused body (matter)/soul unit. To achieve this fusion and to function fully as a fused unit is the primary goal one accepts when choosing to experience life within five-senses form. Functioning as a grounded body (matter)/soul unit is a goal on all levels and dimensions of form, whether the form can or cannot be perceived by the five senses.

Nature plays two key roles in grounding: First, it is through and with nature that grounding occurs. Nature, which organizes, orders and adds life vitality to create form, is what creates and maintains grounding. Second, nature knows what is required to fuse the soul dynamics within form. Nature provides the best examples of body (matter)/soul fusion. Humans have recognized the form or matter existence of nature on the planet, but they have only recently begun to understand that within all form there are fully functioning soul/intelligence dynamics. On the other hand, humans acknowledge or concentrate on their personal soul dynamics but have little understanding as to how they, in order to be functional within form, must allow the soul to fuse with and operate through their form body. Humans do not see the examples or learn the lessons of the master teachers of body (matter)/soul fusion that surround them in all the kingdoms of nature. Humans also deny the fusion within themselves. The relative extent of this denial interferes proportionately with the quality and stabilization of their body/soul fusion.

HORIZONTAL COMPATIBILITY PRINCIPLE

Horizontal compatibility is one universal principle that occurs within our Earth reality and between "sister dimensions" where the laws of form are demonstrated in a similar manner. For example, we on planet Earth live out and experience life that is horizontally compatible with every level in all other realities that live and experience life in comparable five-senses ways.

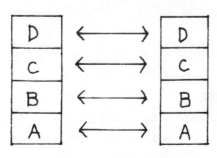

Horizontally compatible dimensions between two different realities.

The Horizontal Healing Principle that is referred to in this book is part of the Horizontal Compatibility Principle. In short, the easiest, most efficient and effective means of repairing and healing are horizontally compatible with the object or person in need of healing. *Like healing like.* For example, flower essences are electrical patterns that balance, stabilize and repair biological electrical systems: Electrical patterns used to heal electrical systems. That's horizontal compatibility.

To take this a step further, because of the Horizontal Compatibility Principle, what constitutes quality health practice on Earth can have a similar positive health impact for those living in a "sister dimension" in another reality and vice versa.

INTENT
DEFINED BY NATURE

Intent refers to the conscious dynamic within all life that links life vitality (action) with soul purpose and direction. When an individual uses free will to manipulate what he or she willfully desires instead of what is within the scope of higher soul purpose, then intent is combined with the manipulative power of free will and this combination is linked with life vitality. Life vitality adds action to order and organization. It both initiates and creates action. To maintain harmonious movement with soul purpose and direction, life vitality must be linked with the soul dynamics. This linkage occurs on two levels. One is unconscious, allowing for a natural patterning and rhythm of action through form that is consistent with soul purpose. As the body/soul fusion moves through its evolutionary process as a functioning unit, it takes on a greater level of consciousness and an expanded level of awareness and knowing. As a result, the unconscious link between soul dynamics and life vitality takes on a new level of operation, thus shifting it into a state of consciousness. The shift is a gradual, step-by-step evolutionary process in itself. Intent is therefore defined as conscious awareness of soul purpose, what is required within the scope of form to achieve soul purpose, and how the two function as a unit. Consequently, when one wishes to express soul purpose, one need only consciously fuse this purpose with appropriate form and action. That act is what is referred to when one speaks of intent.

Intent as a dynamic is an evolutionary process in itself and, as we have said, does not suddenly envelop one's entire life fully and completely. Intent is only gradually incorporated into one's everyday life. Therefore, one does not suddenly and immediately function within the full scope of the dynamic in those areas of life where intent is present. Intent as a dynamic is as broad a learning arena as life itself. And in the beginning, intent can often be confused with or intermingled with free will. However, as it is developed, it becomes the cutting edge of the body/soul unit and how it operates. Intent is the key to unlimited life within the scope of form.

INTUITION
DEFINED BY NATURE

Intuition, as it is popularly defined, relates to a sixth sense of operation. This is false. It is not a sixth sense. When individuals experience a phenomenon that they consider to be beyond their five senses, they tend to attribute this experience to another category, the sixth sense, and call it "intuition." The fact is that the phenomenon is processed through their five senses in an expanded manner.

Intuition, in fact, is related to and linked with intent. It is the bridge between an individual's conscious body/soul fusion—that state in which he knows and understands the body/soul fusion and how it functions—and the individual's unconscious body/soul fusion. Intuition bridges the unconscious and the conscious. This enables what is known on the level of the unconscious body/soul fusion to be incorporated with and become a part of the conscious body/soul fusion. Intuition is the communication bridge between the two that makes it possible for the conscious body/soul unit to benefit from those aspects of the unconscious body/soul unit. This benefit

results when the conscious unit opens to and moves through the lessons surrounding intent. Where intent is functioning fully, these two levels, the
unconscious and the conscious, are no longer separate but have become
one—the expanded conscious level. Consequently, there is then no need for
the bridge known as intuition, and intuition as a dynamic will evolve into
a new function within this expanded conscious level.

However, lest you think otherwise, intent is not considered greater than
intuition; rather, they are two excellent tools utilized equally by the highest
developed souls functioning within form. We say this to caution those who
read this not to think intent is "greater" than intuition and to be aimed for
at the exclusion of intuition. Evolution as seen from the highest perspective
is endless. Therefore, discovery of all there is to know about both intuition
and intent is endless. For all practical purposes, an individual can safely
consider that there will never be a time in which the development of intuition will be unnecessary. As we have said, the highest souls who function to
the fullest within the scope of form do so with an equal development and
expansion of both intent and intuition.

LEYLINES

Leylines are electrical "lines" or circuits that create a complex grid
located within and surrounding a planet. They are sometimes used
for shifting, releasing and making available information to those
inhabiting the planet. These particular leyline properties were key
elements for the Mt. Shasta Mission.

MOVING ENERGY FROM
POINT A TO POINT B

One of the fundamental characteristics of energy is that we may
move it from Point A to Point B using our focus. To understand
and experience what I mean, do the following exercise:

I.   Picture a white ball the size of a baseball in your left hand. If you can't see it, just stay focused on it and feel its presence in your hand. Or trust that it's there.

2.   Maintaining focus on the ball, slowly roll it up your left arm. See it pass over your wrist, your lower arm, the bend at the elbow and your upper arm. Again, if you see nothing, just sense the ball moving on your arm.

3.   At the shoulder, see the ball change direction and roll slowly across your chest. Stop it at the top of your right arm. To do this, just see it stop.

4.   Now, slowly roll the ball down your right arm, seeing or feeling it pass over your upper arm, the bend at the elbow, your lower arm, your wrist and into your right hand.

5.   Stop the ball in your right hand and spend a moment seeing or feeling its presence.

6.   Focus on the ball and throw it softly from your right hand to your left hand. See or feel the ball leave your right hand and see or feel the ball land in your left hand. Throw the ball back between your two hands a few times just to get the feel of this energy moving. If you "lose the ball," see step 8.

7.   Now it's time to "dismantle" the energy that created the ball. Say, "Release the ball energy," and throw the ball straight up in the air. See or sense the energy disperse in the air.

8.   If you had trouble holding your focus on the ball, refocus yourself, see the ball again right where you lost it, sense or see its presence, then continue with the exercise. If this has been a challenging experience for you, you might want to consider working with the exercise regularly to develop your ability to focus and maintain that focus.

NATURE
DEFINED BY NATURE

In the larger universe and beyond, on its many levels and dimensions, there are a number of groups of consciousnesses that, although equal in importance, are quite different in expression and function. Together, they make up the full expression of the larger, total life picture. No one piece, no one expression, can be missing or the larger life picture on all its levels and dimensions will cease to exist. One such consciousness has been universally termed "nature." Because of what we are saying about the larger picture not existing without all of its parts, you may assume that nature as both a reality and a consciousness exists on all dimensions and all levels. It cannot be excluded.

Each group of consciousnesses has what can be termed an area of expertise. As we said, all groups are equal in importance but express and function differently from one another. These different expressions and functions are vital to the overall balance of reality. A true symbiotic relationship exists among the groups and is based on balance—universal balance. The human soul-oriented dynamic is evolution (a process of change in a forward direction) in scope and function. Nature is a massive, intelligent consciousness group that expresses and functions within the areas of involution, that is, moving soul-oriented consciousness into any dimension or level of form.

Nature is the conscious reality that supplies order, organization and life vitality for this shift. (Life vitality initiates and creates action.) Nature is the consciousness that is, for your working understanding, linked with form. Nature is the consciousness that comprises all form on all levels and dimensions. It is form's order, organization and life vitality. Nature is first and foremost a consciousness of equal importance with all other consciousnesses in the largest scheme of reality. It expresses and functions uniquely in that it comprises all form on all levels and dimensions, and is responsible for and creates all of form's order, organization and life vitality.

NATURE: EXCERPT FROM "WHAT IS NATURE INTELLIGENCE?"
DEFINED BY NATURE

All form has its intelligence in common. By this we mean that the organizing dynamic between all form may be viewed as similar. This is critical for humans to understand because it is the reason they may interface and interact with the intelligence of anything around them. You may say that the intelligence of something operates with a universal framework, thus allowing for full and complete interchange. Nature intelligence is the organizing dynamic between the package of nature and its multitude of varying form. Consequently, when one connects with this intelligence flow, one accesses the full reality, potential and possibility of all of nature.

With each major classification of form there is a key element within its intelligence that defines it, making it unique with respect to every other classification. With human form, the key element is free will. With nature, the key element is inherent balance. Nature reality does not contain free will, and human reality does not contain inherent balance. The organization flow (intelligence) of nature's soul dynamic moves through its various forms reflecting inherent balance—always.

When humans impact nature adversely, they do not disrupt nature reality on its intelligence level. They interfere with its reality on the form level. An out-of-balance condition within nature is a balanced nature form that has been altered by humans. Fused with that form is its intelligence level that still maintains inherent balance. Humans cannot impact this level. They may only access it.

When humans consider solutions for restoring balance to an out-of-balance world, they need only access the intelligence of nature involved for answers. That intelligence contains inherent balance and is fully capable of defining all that is required for reflecting that inherent balance through specific form.

The biggest hurdle for humans in understanding nature intelligence is their habit of using human intelligence as the defining yardstick for the different intelligences in the rest of reality. Human intelligence is but one expression of intelligence. It is defined by the unique physical facility of human form through which human intelligence generally functions (brain, central nervous system and sensory system) and the overall driving dynamic of free will. Free will requires the development of intellectual characteristics such as the ability to think, consider, debate, argue, observe, develop opinions, educate and inform oneself, believe, daydream, fantasize, understand, define and hypothesize. Within nature intelligence—where there is not free will but inherent balance—these characteristics are not needed. Nature intelligence operates in a state of being and within present time. Because of inherent balance, nature intelligence does not need to develop the same characteristics as humans. Nature simply knows. It does not need the facilities for understanding what it knows and why.

In order for man to acknowledge and interface directly with nature intelligence, he must put aside the criteria that make up human intelligence and create bridges through which the two different intelligences may directly interface. Man must understand something about his own intelligence, how it operates, the range of its operation and what must be supplied in order to meet the needs of that range. He must then extend himself out to an intelligence with a different operation, range and need, and discover together a common meeting ground in which both may communicate. At Perelandra, examples of this are the use of kinesiology as a communication tool between both intelligences and the various processes that have been developed for mutually beneficial work to be done together. Kinesiology and the various processes create a common framework through which the human and nature intelligences may work.

From the human perspective, accessing nature intelligence is a mystery. It does not respond to the kind of research that humans use in order to learn about and understand their own intelligence. For a human, nature intelligence is like a 5,000-piece puzzle that has been dumped in a great heap on the table before him. He has no idea what the picture is or how and where to begin to access it. Nature, of course, knows the picture and has its copy of the puzzle already put together. From nature's perspective, everything is in order. To work with nature intelligence, as we have said, man must learn to access it in an orderly fashion that meets the needs of his own intelligence. For example, he must devise mutually agreed upon "codes." A language must be developed that contains mutually agreed upon definitions.

Nature does not use or need words. At all times, nature knows. It does not need words to convey within nature what it knows. Language becomes the bridge between the two intelligences. It succeeds when the differences between the intelligences are recognized and addressed. It fails when humans expect nature to understand and use language as humans do.

One example of the language bridge is the widespread use by humans of the words "deva" and "nature spirit." "Deva" generally applies to that area of nature intelligence that operates in its architectural or creative mode. Because nature knows the intent and definition of this word when an individual uses it, its use allows that individual to access the devic area or level of nature's intelligence. The word is automatically matched with that area of nature intelligence that corresponds with its agreed upon definition. "Deva of Broccoli" connects the person with that area of nature intelligence that deals with the creative elements of the plant known as broccoli. Connecting with the Deva of Broccoli will not give you access to the creative level of intelligence that addresses kumquats. Nature always responds in inherent balance. "Broccoli" does not equal "kumquats." Therefore, the two words are not interchangeable and, therefore, do not reflect inherent balance. Connecting to the area dealing with kumquats when you request broccoli cannot be nature's response.

"Nature spirit" generally applies to the action and implementation functions of the intelligence that is unique to and addresses individual form within its (form's) regional context. The intelligence input about the fertilizing needs of broccoli growing in Kansas, Brazil and Israel will differ because the broccoli in each location is in a different context. The creative devic scope of nature intelligence is universal in its function. The nature spirit aspect focuses that intelligence on specific form within individual context and is, consequently, regional.

Because of the mutual understanding of the terminology by so many people, humans may use these two terms to access areas of nature intelligence that operate within the definitions of the terms themselves. The terms "deva" and "nature spirit" allow an individual to link in an organized manner different pieces of the puzzle that have been heaped on the table before them. However, if a person chooses to switch the definitions— "nature spirit" would mean creativity and universality, and "deva" would address implementation and action within context—nature's intelligence would not be accessible because there is no mutual agreement about changing the definitions. Someone may also wish not to use these two terms at all. Perhaps he would prefer to use the word "plipcock" to refer to the creative areas of the intelligence and "mangoby" to refer to action and implementation in context. He cannot assume that nature intelligence automatically acknowledges and "records" these changes simply because he has thought of them and/or written down the new words and definitions. All this is an exercise of human intelligence. To create a language bridge using these two new words, he must directly address nature intelligence and "enter" the new terminology and definitions. He must then make sure nature accepts the new words.

Nature does not make judgments regarding specific words. It does not say, "Gee, we would have preferred 'mango' and 'persimmon.'" This kind of preference is demonstrated within human intelligence. Nature needs to know what humans mean when they use their own terms. If nature "rejects" the new words, it is not because of preference. It is because the definition is not clear enough for nature to know what humans mean when they use those words. It requires humans to be clearer than they have ever been. In short, words such as "deva" and "nature spirit" are used by humans to access and address specific levels and areas in those levels within nature intelligence. They are mutually agreed upon accessing codes. When speaking about nature intelligence, these kinds of words do not refer to individual, independent beings within nature.

This brings us to the issue of elves, faeries, gnomes and devic angels. Nature intelligence does not include these types of beings. It is a massive intelligence, a dynamic. It is not made up of individual life forms. This intelligence dynamic flows through form. It is not made up of these forms. One may look at beings such as elves and devic angels more as communication bridges between man and nature intelligence. If nature is to communicate what it knows to an individual, it may create form through which this communication can flow. Nature is, after all, the order, organization and life vitality of all form. At any time, it may create, modify and utilize form in response to the moment. The "appearance" of a nature spirit is a response to the inherent balance of the moment that includes an individual human being. More often than not, the nature-spirit form used is seen only within the mind's eye of the person with whom nature wishes to communicate. However, whether seen within the mind's eye or by the individual's outer sensory system, the form is equally real. But it is a communication bridge in the form of an elf, not an elf with an independent life of its own. The nature spirit level of nature's consciousness does not need elves and gnomes to function. That level simply flows through all existing form directly. When such an event occurs, many humans unfortunately tend to overlay it with expectation and definition that is unique to human intelligence rather than understand that this is a bridge from nature intelligence. It has different dynamics and has been initiated and activated for a specific purpose. If humans could focus on the communication surrounding such an event rather than get lost in the excitement of the event itself, more would come of the experience, and it would be more useful to them, as well.

Pan

The word "Pan" is used by humans to access and work with the part of nature intelligence that bridges the creative activity (devic) with the action and implementation activity (nature spirit) of the intelligence. The Pan function of nature intelligence also bridges these two activities with the overall soul dynamics of nature. Humans call these soul dynamics "natural law" or "laws of nature." The Pan function is critical because it operates as a switching station for the various levels of nature intelligence to "meet and mix." The Pan function organizes the flow in ways that are not found elsewhere in the larger nature intelligence. Because of its unique qualities within the overall dynamic flow, the Pan function may be accessed independently by humans, and it may create a bridge on its own to communicate its unique knowledge to humans—hence, the experiences and sightings people have had with the forms they call "Pan."

It is through the Pan function that one finds the "heart of nature." This is because the Pan function mixes all levels of nature creativity and action/implementation, and then combines this mixture with its soul dynamics. In essence, by combining the soul dynamics, it provides the foundation for all nature intelligence—that is, inherent balance—as a result of its unique function. It is the action of bridging the combined levels with the soul dynamics that creates a different reality referred to as Pan, the heart of nature.

When an individual connects with the Pan function within nature intelligence, he is linked with a most vibrant and comprehensive knowledge that is a result of this mixing and bridging activity. It is not the pure knowledge of the creative devic functions, nor is it the pure knowledge of the action and implementation functions. It is the knowledge that is created when these two functions are combined creating a new, more complex reality; then they are bridged to nature's soul dynamics, creating an even more complex reality.*

NATURE: WHAT DO I MEAN WHEN I SAY, "WORKING WITH NATURE"?

I don't mean I'm just observing something in nature or reading what the experts say about this thing and, from that information, figuring out how best to work with the thing. I mean:

---

* See our web site (www.perelandra-ltd.com) for the complete paper, "What Is Nature Intelligence?"

1. I'm literally accessing the intelligence that is inherent in anything that has order, organization and life vitality (i.e., all form).

2. I am literally asking this intelligence specific questions. (Do you need to be fertilized?)

3. Then, I literally get the answer to my question(s) directly from that intelligence (usually the Pan level because of this level's exceptional connection and function within nature's intelligence) by testing using kinesiology or, for the lengthy information, by getting a direct translation from nature on the subject.

PC PAT ON THE BACK

This is a concept I use to honor my friend, Peter Caddy (hence the "PC"). Peter was one of the three co-founders of the Findhorn Community in Scotland. We met after I visited that community for four months in 1977, and we have been friends ever since. Sadly, he died in a car accident several years ago. Peter was a proper English gentleman. In this era of jeans and t-shirts, he wore trousers, sport coat and turtleneck—or tie. He abhorred the American custom of drinking coffee out of a mug. He liked a proper cup and saucer. We won't even discuss his feelings about serving milk or cream on the table in its carton.

But Peter had another side, and this is where the pat on the back comes in. Early on in life, he had a spiritual teacher who had a lot of drill-sergeant qualities about her. She taught him to act immediately on intuition and guidance: Never stop to question it. Just do it. Peter listened and learned well. As a result, he went through one crazy, totally insane adventure after another—all because of acting immediately on his intuition or someone else's guidance. When he was on the move—and he traveled a lot—it was as if the whole world would reposition itself to accommodate whatever he needed to do. His adventures were amazing, and his stories were magical.

As I have moved through the years since meeting Peter, I've been challenged to do some pretty outrageous things myself—as this book will attest to. Whenever I have hesitated moving forward into what looks to be absurdity, I have thought of Peter. And I'd say to myself, "Peter wouldn't even blink an eye at this." Then I'd go ahead, knowing that I'm not the only person who would be crazy enough to do that thing. In this way, he's given me terrific support. But the Mt. Shasta Mission was particularly special for me because Peter participated and was with me at key times to give me his PC pat on the back personally.

PERELANDRA LEVEL
AND COTTAGE LEVEL

These are the names I have given to two sister dimensions from two separate realities. The Perelandra level refers to the planet where you and I are currently residing—assuming you are presently residing on planet Earth. The Cottage level is a five-senses sister level and planet in a different reality. It is within the band of form that is identical to our own in how it lives out the principles of form. It is a planet that is as large and as complex as Earth, but it is not our Earth. At this point, don't despair. I describe the Cottage level in more detail in Chapter 2.

PISCEAN ERA

"Piscean Era" is the name given to that period of time, roughly 2,000 years long, out of which planet Earth, the universe and their inhabitants are presently passing and during which specific universal laws were grounded. In a broad overview, one may say that the Piscean Era explored, developed and demonstrated the dynamics of parent/child, higher/lower and masculine-dominate relationships, and demonstrated these principles in both action and social structure throughout all levels of form.

REALITY
DEFINED BY NATURE

From our perspective, reality refers to all levels and dimensions of life experience within form and beyond form. Reality does not depend on an individual's perception of it in order to exist. We call an individual's perception of reality his "perceived reality." Any life system that was created in form — which occurred at the moment of the Big Bang* — has inherent in it all dimensions and levels that exist both within form and beyond. How a person relates to an individual, object or event depends on his present ability to enfold and envelop its many levels. The scope within which one exists, the reality of one's existence, is truly beyond description. If one understands that the evolutionary force that moves all life systems forward is endless — beyond time — then one must also consider that it is the continuous discovery of these vast levels inherent in all life systems that creates evolutionary momentum. Since that dynamic is beyond time, it is endless, as well.

REALITY: BASIC SENSORY SYSTEM PERCEPTION
DEFINED BY NATURE

We define basic sensory system perception as being that which the vast majority of individuals on Earth experience. The acts of seeing, hearing, touching, tasting and smelling fall within what we acknowledge as a basic, fundamental range of sensory development that is dominant on the Earth

---

* The Big Bang: The gigantic explosion in which the universe, as we know it, began. According to scientists, it occurred between 12 and 20 billion years ago. The Big Bang brought about two major dynamics: individuation and the fusion of soul to form.

level. What is referred to as an "expansion experience" is, in fact, an act or experience that is beyond the normal range in which an individual's sensory system operates. Expansion experiences are not perceived outside or beyond an individual's electrical system, central nervous system and sensory system. These three systems are interrelated, and an accurate perception of an expansion experience requires that the three systems operate in concert. Therefore, it is quite possible for something to occur in an individual's life that registers in the person's electrical system and central nervous system but then short-circuits, is altered or is blocked simply because the person's present sensory system does not have the ability to process, due to its present range of operation.

People say that "these kinds of strange things never happen to me." This is inaccurate. "Strange" things, experiences and moments beyond the present state of their sensory systems are continuously happening around them and to them. Those people are simply not at the point where their sensory systems are capable of clear, useful processing. They waste time by directing their will and focus toward "making things happen." That is useless since things are happening all the time around them. Instead they should relax and continue through an organic developmental process that is already in effect and that will gradually allow them to accurately perceive more of what is happening around them. In some cases, events or experiences are vaguely perceived or processed in outrageous, useless ways because their sensory system is expanding but still not operating in a range where events can be usefully processed.

SOUL
DEFINED BY NATURE

It is most difficult to define soul since—at its point of central essence—the soul is beyond form. Consequently, it is beyond words. However, it is not beyond any specific life form. As we have said, an individual is not separate or distant from his or her soul. Souls, as individuated life forces, were created and fused with form at the moment of the Big Bang. Beyond form, *souls are also beyond the notion of creation. So we refer to the moment of the Big Bang regarding the soul, since this gives you a description of soul that will be most meaningful to you.*

The Big Bang was the nature-designed order, organization and life force used to differentiate soul into countless sparks of individuated light energy. The power of the Big Bang was created by intent. And that intent originated from the massive collective soul reality beyond form.

It is reasonable to look at the Big Bang as the soul's gateway to the immense band of form. To perceive the soul and how it functions exclusively from the perspective of human form on Earth is akin to seeing that planet from the perspective of one grain of sand. The soul's options of function and expression in form are endless. What we see occurring more frequently now on Earth is the shift from the individual soul unknowingly functioning in an array of options, all chosen only because they are compatible with the immediate purpose of the soul, to the individual beginning to function with discrimination and intent in more expanded ways. Using words in their more limited, parochial definitions, we can say that we see the beginning of a shift from soul function in which an individuated personality remains unaware of many of its options to soul function in which the personality begins to take on conscious awareness of all its options.

VERIFICATION

When something fantastic happens to us, we get catapulted out of our framework of logic. Often, the fantastic event includes verification. It is as if a "hand" reaches out of the fantastic event and touches our mundane life in a small but special way that will catch our attention and serve to say, "You are not crazy. This is really happening." For example, one morning something fantastic happens to you that has really challenged your sense of logic. You wonder if it actually happened or if somehow you conjured the whole thing up in your mind. That afternoon, as usual, you walk to the mailbox at the end of your driveway. You take the same

Verification: A fantastic event
touches our mundane life.

path you take every day. But this day
you notice a wildflower in full bloom
growing where you *know* no flower
was growing the day before. And this
is a plant that you have never before
noticed growing wild in your area.
There is absolutely no question in
your mind that the flower is new on
the scene—and it is gorgeous. At the same time, you know that
this flower is saying to you that the fantastic event that occurred
to you that morning really did happen. That's verification.

One of the characteristics of verification is that it is extremely
personal in nature. It is designed to communicate only with those
involved with the fantastic event. Consequently, when you try to
describe verification to others, they tend to look at you as if you
have truly lost your mind. What generally happens is that they
will come up with theories that will satisfy them and reposition
your verification (and the fantastic experience it verified) into
their framework of logic. In short, they try to shoot it down. In
the example above, *you* are the only person who knows for certain
no flower was growing in that spot the day before because you are
the only one who routinely goes for the mail.

THE WHITE BROTHERHOOD

The Mt. Shasta Mission was brought to us courtesy of the White
Brotherhood, a huge organization that is constantly connected to
us in general and to many of us individually. Usually they are only
able to work with us on an intuitive level, and our link with them
is often unconscious on our part. Much has been written about
this group, but I think a lot of it is trash. Some people have felt or
said that they were the sole "channeller" of the White Brotherhood, and this simply isn't true.

The White Brotherhood is a large group of highly evolved souls dedicated to assisting the evolutionary process of moving universal reality, principles, laws and patterns forward through all planes and levels of form. They hold the major patterning and rhythms now being utilized for the shift we are all going through from the Piscean to the Aquarian Era. When we link with them, they support and assist us by assuring that any work we do maintains its forward motion and its connection to the new Aquarian principles.

They have existed from the very beginning of time and history. I first heard about them during my stay at the Findhorn community in 1977, and St. Germain, who had a close relationship with several Findhorn members, including Peter Caddy, was referred to often and described as being a master teacher from the White Brotherhood. I ignored the Brotherhood and its existence for years, assuming that they knew how to do their job, whatever that was, very well without me and that my focus was primarily on working with nature, not on human-oriented evolution. After all, this is the age of specialization.

Now I see the Brotherhood operating in a partnership role with us on this planet. Based on the scope and timing we set for our forward movement, they help us design and infuse purpose and direction into the frameworks of social order through which we on Earth move in order to learn, experience, organize and develop. In essence, they create the many schools through which we grow and evolve. We call these schools religions, governmental structures, educational movements, medicine, philosophy, science…all those massive social frameworks with which we associate and within which we experience and function. This ensures that as we move forward, we will never step into emptiness. There will always be a framework for us to move into to give us what we need in order to continue learning, experiencing, growing and evolving.

Let me say something about the name "White Brotherhood." People have written to me questioning—and sometimes complaining about—that name. They want to make sure this isn't some white supremacist/sexist organization. In these strange and tubulent times, this is a reasonable concern. The name "White Brotherhood" has been used for this group for centuries. We did not coin the name here at Perelandra. It was coined by those folks on the Earth level who first began to work consciously with this group, and it is not a name the Brotherhood chose for itself. It is a name these early folks chose for it. The words "white brotherhood" maintained the intent and integrity of the group, so it has always been acceptable to them. "White" is used to signify the reflection of *all* the rays of the light spectrum. "Brotherhood" is used to signify not only the family of all people but also the family of all life.

◆━◆●◆━◆

Ever since I knew I was going to write *The Mount Shasta Mission,* which has been a number of years now, I always knew what the first sentence of the book was going to be. I truly loved that first sentence, and quite frankly, it made me want to write the book. Well, once I got into the writing, I realized that it wasn't the first sentence. In fact, it didn't fit anywhere in the book. But now, I've grown quite attached to it. So, being the never-say-die person that I am, I'm going to tell you what my first sentence has been all these years any-way. Perhaps, as it helped me want to write this book, it will help you want to keep reading the book.

This is a story that begins with a dream
and a naked man…

Chapter 2

We Begin

THE DREAM

BACK IN 1984, I HAD ONE of those long, vivid, technicolor dreams-that-seem-more-than-a-dream. You know the kind. This one left me feeling exhausted when I woke up. In it, I was seated in a room with Peter Caddy and I was telling him about the unusual change my life had taken. In my dream, I started by saying to him, "I'm working in the Pentagon of the White Brotherhood." And I went on from there.

> Since October 25, 1982, I've been spending half my day at Perelandra [my home and research center in Virginia] and the other half on another dimension in another reality with a group of men from the White Brotherhood led by Dwight David Eisenhower, who are working on the transition of our planet's govern-ment/military framework from operating with the Piscean dynamic to operating with the new Aquarian principles and dynamic.

Okay. There are not many people I can say those first two sentences to without their slowly getting up, backing out of the room and quickly calling the nearest psychiatric hospital for immediate admission of one strange and deranged woman. But Peter Caddy was one of those few people I could safely say this to. So in the dream, I told him about this small group of men I had come to know over the previous two years, what they are doing and a bit about my life on this level. I don't have a transcript of everything I said to Peter in that dream, but I'll give you the gist of it.

First, let me explain something. When talking about this part of my life, I use the word "Cottage" a lot. "Cottage" refers to the large English home these men live and work in. When I first saw their home, it looked like a quaint English cottage from the front. (From the side and back, one can see that the Cottage is huge.) Since then I have called this home and office "the Cottage," the team "the Cottage team" and the level "the Cottage level."

The Cottage that I go to each day is situated in England—the "England equivalent" of a country located on a planet that exists on a sister dimension within another reality. Since it is a sister dimension it operates within five-senses form, just like us. Its currency is British, like ours here. Its customs and social structures are very like our England. The general population speaks with what we would recognize as an English accent. David, the name Dwight Eisenhower goes by now, and the other members of the team do not feel they are citizens of this country or any other country, for that matter. Instead they are guests of this England. Their work is global (regarding our Earth) and multilevel—in the broader universal perspective. But David has a personal history that began with his association with our England that drew him to locate the Cottage in its present setting.

As I've said, the level the Cottage and the "England equivalent" are on is a dimension of another reality within the band of form that is identical to our own in how it lives out the principles of form. It is a planet that is as large and as complex as Earth, but it is not our Earth. I once asked David why he chose to continue his existence in five-senses form. He said, "I believe there is truth in form, and I am determined to discover it." After his death in 1969, and after his subsequent healing process, he chose to set up the Cottage office within this level, once again aligning himself to five-senses form as we experience it on Earth. All who work and live at the Cottage have the same commitment to functioning within this form.

There is an entire population living on the Cottage level. Most of them, like us on Earth, are born into and die out of the level. But there are people, like those at the Cottage, who live beyond time and age, and simply materialize into the level as adults for a specific, and sometimes lengthy, amount of time. David once explained to me that the differences I felt between how people live life on Earth and how they live it on the Cottage level are due to one basic fact: Human life on the Cottage level has been going on quite a bit longer than it has on Earth and, therefore, the population is more mature. The Cottage-level people have lived through more lifetimes in five-senses form than we on Earth have. Consequently, they have already addressed many of the problems that are currently challenging us on our level.

The Cottage world comfortably recognizes people who associate with it by materializing in from other levels for a specific period of time—an afternoon, a day, a week or decades. At the Cottage itself, there is a fairly constant flow of these visitors, and their presence doesn't disrupt traffic or cause people to riot. In fact, the visitors are pretty much ignored. If anything like this happened openly on our level, we'd either create a religion around these people or declare them space aliens and lock them up before they poisoned our water supply or something. Those kinds of interference by the general population can just wreck a visitor's schedule and they'd never get anything done. So these people tend to avoid our level.

Let me give you an example of how the Cottage level openly accommodates people like David and his team. Those who are born into and die out of this level relate to money in much the same way you and I do on our Earth level. They work to earn it. It's a specific and finite method of exchange. Each country, like our planet's countries, has its own currency. (There is no European Union with a common currency on the Cottage level.) However, people like the Cottage team relate to money differently. They have access to an infinite flow, and they exchange it for goods and services based on what they need. When I asked them how one gets into the infinite money dynamic (because I knew people would ask me about this), they explained that it had to do with a person's sense of self-worth, and that this is a different inner journey for everyone. Once an individual truly understood his self-worth, he automatically shifts into the infinite money dynamic.

The bank in the nearby village accommodates both money dynamics—finite and infinite—and there are separate teller windows in the bank's lobby to deal with the different accounts. The men at the Cottage have simple checking accounts from which they can draw any funds needed. They don't have complex accounts for maximizing earnings because their money doesn't have to earn more money. And I don't think the bank gave them blenders when they opened their accounts. They keep a record of what checks they have written, but that's just to keep themselves informed about how they are moving money. They don't bother subtracting amounts, and the monthly statement they get from the bank is to make sure the bank records of all their transactions are in order.

The men feel strongly that they are guests of this country and choose to participate in the relevant governing structures. For example, the Cottage team pays local and national taxes. They each have a valid driver's license and pay into the national medical system, even though they will not personally need this sort of medical assistance. They do not vote, however, because they say it is important that the people for whom the social and government systems were created—the born/die people—determine their own direction.

Although all the men at the Cottage are peers, they function in specific positions that create what appears to me to be a finely tuned team. Until I came to the Cottage in 1982, they went by their real names: David, John, Eric and Stephen. Once I came, we went a little nuts with nicknames and John became Tex, Eric became Butch, and Stephen became Mickey. David remained David. And somehow, I remained Machaelle. Out of habit, I always refer to them as David, Tex, Butch and Mickey.

As might be imagined, the level of interaction among these men is phenomenal. They each possess an extraordinarily high intellect. They express themselves clearly, precisely and calmly—although heated exchanges for the advancement of differing ideas and opinions are not unheard of. As I began my Cottage life and rhythm in 1982, I felt out of place in this well-oiled, close, male community. But immediately, they reached out in extraordinary ways to incorporate me fully into the group. For example, during meetings they often work with large maps. My nature work there rarely has anything to do with maps. One day, after a meeting that included a lot of maps, I protested. I said I wanted a map too. They asked me what map I wanted. I told them the first thing that popped into my mind: Jersey City. At the next meeting, when I started to add my two nature cents, they stopped me and pulled out a large map of Jersey City. Then they told me to proceed. Whenever maps are used in a meeting, they make it a point to pin up my map, as well. When we have visitors at these meetings, David has to tell them not to pay attention to the Jersey City map while I'm talking.

As you can see, they grappled with how I function and think, and then made sure I had the environment that enhances my process. (My office at the Cottage is beautiful—perfect, actually.) It was clear early on that I operate differently than the Cottage men. They are masters of intelligence, intent and intuition. I think and operate more creatively, intuitively and spontaneously.

They approach something by carefully moving from A to B to C
to D, and so on to Q. I tend to start at A and make a fast leap to Q.
I may be correct in my position on Q—something they've come
to accept—but, in the long run, I see that their methodical movement creates greater strength and stability and fewer mistakes.
The two ways we operate weave together well and we function
together easily.

How did I get mixed up with this group? And how do I get to and
from the Cottage?

Since 1976, I had been working with establishing a conscious,
co-creative partnership with the intelligence inherent in nature.
As a result of this partnership, I was researching different ways
we humans can work directly with nature to enhance our environment, our health and our lives. The Cottage team needed
someone who could work consciously with nature intelligence in
order to add nature's input to their projects. They contacted me
one day in 1982, and asked if I might be interested. I said something like, "Oh, sure. Whatever." (It was either say that or faint.)
Here I was, this thirty-six-year-old woman living quietly in rural
Virginia, minding my own business and spending my days happily
working with nature to better understand life and how it worked.
I figured once this team saw me, they'd realize they had made a
mistake, that I wasn't at all qualified to work with them. Maybe
they'd give me some consolation prize for my time and trouble
(like a Troy-Built rototiller for my garden work), and send me on
my way. Instead, they liked what I was doing, said I was just the
person they needed and convinced me that *maybe* they hadn't
made a mistake after all. I've been a member of the Cottage and
the team ever since (that's twenty-three years at this writing),
and I'm still waiting for them to figure out their mistake. If they
ever do, the consolation prize is going to have to be something
more than a rototiller.

This brings me to what I am doing to get to and from the Cottage, and this is where it gets a little dicey. But I'll try to be as brief and as clear as possible. I use a process called the Split Molecular Process (SMP). In order to participate fully and consciously on the Perelandra level and on the Cottage level, my soul operates out of two separate, but related, physical bodies. Both bodies are from my same soul system. From the perspective of Machaelle, I would refer to Katie (the original "owner" of my Cottage body) as another lifetime. She was actually born into the Cottage level, and she died at age thirty-six in a bombing raid during a war on that level. In order for me to accomplish my goal to participate fully and consciously in life on these two levels, I needed two compatible bodies. Both had to be female, and they had to have similar physical characteristics.

Those who have attempted to understand the SMP have tried to liken it to what they call "walk-ins." These are two completely different phenomena. A legitimate walk-in situation occurs when the soul from one body assumes a working relationship with a second, unrelated body. I have to say that I have not met a legitimate walk-in, but I've met a number of people who claim they are walk-ins. After listening to them a bit, they sound more like people who did not like their life, for whatever reason, and tried to assume the role of a new life and "new soul" in order to escape.

To pull off the shift between the two sister dimensions (i.e., Perelandra and Cottage), I had to have one body "stationed" at Perelandra, and the other body "stationed" at the Cottage level. Since 1982, I have spent half my day fully conscious and functioning through my Machaelle body at Perelandra and the other half of the day fully conscious and functioning in the Katie body. I have to maintain this daily schedule so that my soul can energize both bodies and so each body will maintain its strength and health.

On a few special occasions, when it has been necessary for my work (such as at specific times during the Mt. Shasta Mission), I have been fully conscious and functioning in both bodies simultaneously. It's a bit tricky to maintain focus in each body, so I have to have a compelling reason to have both bodies up and operating at the same time.

The story of my Cottage life is long, but, in this book, I will tell you the part of my Cottage story that applies to the Mt. Shasta Mission. Now, here's where I annoy you. If you're interested in knowing more about it, I wrote a book, *Dancing in the Shadows of the Moon,* that details how I got to the Cottage and what I'm doing there. It's a 565-page book, which should give you a bit of a clue as to why I don't repeat all the information for this book. You'd get a hernia just from lifting it.

About the Cottage Work: Their work is global as well as multilevel to include government/military transitions that are occurring on other dimensions within other realities. They tell me that they combine the words "government" and "military" because these two dynamics are connected—the military is an implementation arm of the government. Therefore, they cannot be worked with as separate dynamics.

The Cottage team addresses the government/military changes that must occur when we want new ways of doing things, as well as new systems that reflect these changes. Once we reach new understanding, how do we change structure and form to accommodate that understanding? The White Brotherhood assists us with these changes, and the Cottage team assists us specifically with the government/military changes.

Because of the nature of the Cottage activity, their work does not have publicity surrounding it. The team often works with individuals (either on their conscious or unconscious levels) who are in positions to affect policy and institute change.

The men tell me that we on Earth have gone through an intense period of consciousness raising, starting in 1945 with the dropping of the atomic bomb. Once the bomb was dropped, conventional war, as was developed and practiced throughout the 2,000-year Piscean Era, became obsolete, and the new war that included nuclear weapons became unacceptable. Because of this, governments could and should no longer rely on war to gain for them what it had in the past. So they needed to learn to deal with one another in new ways. Enough of us now understand this, and our government/military structures must change to reflect the consciousness of the people.

This is where the Cottage team steps in.

———— ◆◆◆ ————

In my dream, I went into this much detail with Peter Caddy as I explained what I was doing at the Cottage. When I awoke, I was truly exhausted. I remember thinking, "Boy, I hope I never have to explain the Cottage to anyone."

Chapter 3

Battle Energy Release

THE PROCESS

I HAVE TOLD YOU A BIT about the Cottage level and the Cottage team's work. I suspect now is a good time for me to tell you something more about Perelandra and my work.

Since 1973, Perelandra has been my home, and since 1976 it has been my nature research center. Perelandra consists of 45 acres of open fields and woods in the foothills of the Blue Ridge Mountains in Virginia. My research and development has been going on since 1976, when I dedicated myself to learning about nature in new ways from nature itself. I began working with nature intelligence in a conscious, coordinated and educational effort that has resulted in what I call "co-creative science." Traditional science—commonly known as "contemporary science"—is man's study of reality and how it works. Co-creative science is the study of reality and how it works by man and nature (nature intelligence) working together in partnership.

When I began this unusual journey with nature, I said, "I want to learn everything I can about nature and its intelligence, and I want to do this in the context of a garden." Perelandra's laboratory is its 100-foot-diameter garden. It is here that I work with nature to get the information I need to create an inclusive garden environment based on the laws of nature. We do not use organic or chemical pesticides, herbicides, insecticides or chemical fertilizers. Perelandra's laboratory operates according to nature's principles of balance, and it is the information on how to achieve that balance that I get from my nature partner. As a result of our work together over the past thirty years, we have developed new approaches, guidelines and procedures anyone may use to establish a balanced environment for such diverse areas as a garden, farm, forest, a ranch, the White House grounds, a national park, an apartment, a suburban home and yard, a college dorm, a college program, a business, an airport and the human body.

Each area of research was opened to me by nature, and, at the time, I really didn't understand some of the doors that opened. What did an apparel business or architectural plans have to do with a vegetable garden or ranch? How was the human body a garden? It didn't make sense until I finally asked nature to define "garden" for me. The *Merriam-Webster Dictionary* defines a garden as "a plot of ground where herbs, fruits, flowers, or vegetables are cultivated." As I was constantly discovering, nature had a different take on a garden.

From nature's perspective, a garden is any environment that is initiated by humans, given its purpose and direction by humans and maintained with the help of humans. For nature to consider something to be a garden, we must see humans actively involved in all three of these areas. It is the human who calls for a garden to exist. Once the call is made, nature responds accordingly to support that defined call because a garden exists through the use of form.

Humans tend to look at gardens as an expression of nature. Nature looks at gardens as an expression of humans. They are initiated, defined and maintained by humans. When humans dominate all aspects and elements of the life of the garden, we consider this environment to be human dominant. We consider an environment to be "nature friendly" when humans understand that the elements used to create gardens are form and operate best under the laws of nature and when humans have the best intentions of trying to cooperate with what they understand these laws to be. When humans understand that nature is a full partner in the design and operation of that environment—and act on this knowledge—we consider the environment to be moving actively toward a balance between involution (nature) and evolution (human).

As a result, this last environment supports and adds to the overall health and balance of all it comprises and the larger whole. It also functions within the prevailing laws of nature (the laws of form) that govern all form on the planet and in its universe. In short, when a garden operates in balance between involution and evolution, it is in step with the overall operating dynamics of the whole. The various parts that comprise a garden operate optimally, and the garden as a whole operates optimally.

Nature does not consider the cultivation of a plot of land as the criteria for a garden. Nature considers a garden to exist wherever humans define, initiate and interact with form to create a specialized environment. This is the underlying intent of a garden and the reason behind the development of specialized environments such as vegetable gardens. Nature applies the word "garden" to any environment that meets these criteria. It does not have to be growing in soil. It only needs to be an environment that is defined, initiated and appropriately maintained by humans.

This is what nature means when it uses the word "garden." The laws and principles that nature applies in the co-creative vegetable garden are equally applicable to any garden, whether it is growing in soil or otherwise. In order to understand that the principles and processes described in the two Perelandra Garden Workbooks apply to any "garden," one must understand how nature defines a garden. The principles and processes apply across the board because all gardens are operating under the same laws of nature—only the specific form elements that make up each garden have changed.

When I said that I wanted to learn about nature from nature and I wanted to do this in the context of a garden, I had no idea what I was really requesting or what I was getting into.

In the summer of 1983, I had been working with a fertilizer process in which nature gave me the precise information for fertilizing individual plants, garden areas, rows and sections. Oddly enough, this work led to a new and amazing development: the Perelandra Battle Energy Release Process.

Soon after we moved to Perelandra in 1973, I had a visit from the previous owner and learned from him that our land had been used by Confederate soldiers during the Civil War as a rest and staging area prior to the men marching to the Battle of Manassas. Most of the land around us had been touched one way or another by the Civil War, so I didn't think too much about this information about Perelandra's land.

Then, on April 12, 1983, I raised a number of questions with the men at the Cottage about the effect a battle might have on nature at the battle site. Does nature withdraw from a battlefield? Does the battlefield heal? They told me I'd have to be the one to find out the answers from nature. So I tossed the questions in my ever-growing mental to-do file.

After I put that season's garden to bed in the fall, I was still wondering about the relationship between a battle and the soil upon which a battle is fought. For example, did this impact affect the amount of nutrients plants growing in that soil required for strength? I had recently set up a schedule for having special sessions for the purpose of getting information relating to my work, and I always left the subject of the sessions open so that I would not limit the information I received. The following is a transcript of one of those sessions that I had in the winter of 1983, and much to my surprise it addressed my battle/soil questions in ways I could never have imagined.

The Relationship Between Nature and War

You have been correct in that there is a connection between nature and military history. There is a healing role that must be addressed where military action touches nature.

Remember the concept of horizontal healing: like healing like, form healing form. When war is waged, it is not simply a matter of moving form (e.g., weapons), of creating strategy of form against form (e.g., battle strategy), man against man, equipment against equipment. When war is waged, corresponding energy is moved on all levels. The many sounds of war (we use "sounds" figuratively and literally) are echoed throughout the universe on all its levels. Up to this time, the movements of man through the instruments of war have been appropriate. It has been one structure in which man can grow, change and move forward. It has not been the only structure available to man, but surely it has been the most widely used.

Nature serves as a buffer for man on Earth in regard to the universal energies that naturally flow to Earth. Were it not for nature, those energies would hit man directly, shattering him. Universal energies, by nature, are more homogeneous than the energies of Earth. This, of course, relates to the fact that Earth is of five-senses form: Its energies are in their most differentiated state. Consequently, it is essential that nature serve as the intermediary, as it were, between the souls who reside on Earth in a state of individuation and the larger, more encompassing, homogeneous energies of the universe that are available to them.

We do not indulge in a value judgment of war. As a foundation, as a framework, we do not see war as wrong; we see it simply as a framework. However, war—as a framework for progression, change and growth—is no longer effective or appropriate. The developments in warfare in recent years have unbalanced the relationship of negative creating positive. They now result in negative creating negative.

When regarding nature in light of war, one must look at several levels, aspects, elements, functions and roles that nature has played. Since we have mentioned the role of nature as the buffer between universal energies and man, we will go on and talk about a role that nature plays of which man is not aware: the buffer between man and universal energies regarding man's impact on the universe—war being a particularly prime example of the need for this buffer.

War on Earth is, as a framework, not alien to change and growth processes in the universe. Wars on other levels have been created in similar ways. However, because of the differentiated form that war takes on Earth, it is, in its impact on the universe, extremely powerful in its most dense, most intense way. Consequently, it has been important that nature serve as a buffer between Earth and the universe so that the universe's balance would not be unnecessarily tipped due to the intensity of the Earth's individuated warfare.

We speak here of the specific power that is created when one takes the whole (e.g., a war or battle) and clearly separates it into all its parts, coordinates those parts and moves them as one unit (of its many different parts) in one direction for one cause. World War II is an example of this principle on its broadest level: It was not just one country against another; it was countries against countries—and the whole was larger than ever before. There were more individuated parts than ever before, and the Allies were successfully (albeit not easily) brought together as a unit and moved forward for one purpose.

The impact of World War II beyond Earth was great. Without nature's buffer, the universe would have indeed tipped. By this, we mean universal balance would have shifted to such a degree that its sense of natural timing and rhythm would have been thrown off, and it would have needed a period of time to regain its balance. Nature absorbed the intense energy released by the battles of World War II and, in turn, released it out to the universe as a less intense and more easily absorbed energy form. Not only was the universal balance not tipped, but the knowledge, information and growth experiences occurring within the framework you know as World War II were picked up and used simultaneously in various situations throughout the universe.

One could look at what we have been saying as the vertical role between man, war, nature and, ultimately, the universe. In general, man has not understood the impact of war on the energy around him. All action, all intent, moves energy. This is a law man is only beginning to understand. Consequently, he has gone through thousands of years of battles without understanding its implications.

When war is waged, a release of intense, basic emotions occurs. It is an eruption of emotion. Man cannot sustain his life within that kind of intensity, for when the battle is over, the intensity of the battle remains. We are dealing with the very same principle you deal with in the Energy Cleansing Process*: how emotions remain within a room after grief, or after an argument between spouses. Multiply that by five hundred thousand, and you can begin to imagine the intensity we are dealing with in war. In order for man to survive, to continue living, to move out of the framework of battle and continue moving forward, he must be buffered from this intensity.

As you know, nature absorbs energies but, on the whole, will not transmute them. Consequently, this enormous body of intense energy created in battles throughout the history of man is being held by nature. It has always been meant to be a temporary assignment, but as one well knows, "temporary" (in terms of time) on one level can mean quite a different thing on another level. Man has the ability to transmute, to change, energy from one level to another. However, the process that we will develop for you to use for transmuting these war energies places you as the representative of man back into the field of battle to connect with nature and to release battle energies that have been held for the sake of man. You will then release these energies from nature, call for them to be transmuted, release them from Earth's biosphere, and allow them to take their balanced, healthful position within the context of the universe. Once that is done, this specific battle will become useful to, and useable by, the universal whole.

By confronting these battle energies that have been held by nature, you are not acting in the role of the absorber. In fact, you are not acting in the

---

* See Appendix A.

role of the transmuter. Instead, you are acting in the role of the conductor, the orchestrator with nature. You will facilitate the release of these energies. You will facilitate the transmutation process and the release of these energies into their rightful place in the universe. This work will go on outside you. You will neither move the energies through your body nor serve as the absorber. That has already been done by nature. Consequently, you will be fully protected. Your understanding of the dynamic of energy will allow you to facilitate the processes that must go on without, shall we say, getting in the way of the process. The new Battle Energy Release Process is a technical process within the laws of nature.

Once these battle energies have been released from an area of battle, it will then be appropriate to facilitate the rebalancing and healing process within nature in the battlefield area using flower essences. We recommend that you complete the Battle Energy Release Process, then test with nature concerning the area to receive insight on the essences needed to complete nature's healing process.

Of course, simply left alone nature would eventually achieve balance; but by facilitating this process, you once again step into the role of man taking responsibility for his own actions and working co-creatively with nature for the healing of Earth. Not only will these actions actually facilitate the healing process within the realm of nature, but they will also symbolically sound a note of man taking responsibility for the destruction that he has created within nature. So instead of it taking years for the rebalancing of nature within the area, you will leave the battle area having cleared the energy that has been held within nature all these years and released (in the form of flower essences) to nature precisely what it needs for its own rebalancing—and that is a good day's work.

A few days after this first session, I opened a second session and got the following guidelines for the new Battle Energy Release Process. To do this work, nature also instructed me on how to set up my first four-point coning. This type of coning has in it an enhanced balance between nature and humans that gives it exceptional strength, clarity and protection. This was a watershed moment for me for two reasons: working with four-point conings and developing the Battle Energy Release Process.

BATTLE ENERGY RELEASE PROCESS

1.   *Go to the battlefield or land area you intend to clear.*

2.   *Open a four-point coning. That is, call to you:*
       a. the overlighting deva of that specific battlefield or land area
       b. Pan
       c. the appropriate members of the White Brotherhood that are connected with this work, including Universal Light
       d. your higher self

   The calling together of these intelligences creates a larger vortex of energy called a coning. Spend a moment acknowledging and sensing the presence of each member of your coning. This will stabilize and ground your coning.

3.   *Present yourself to the overlighting deva of the battlefield or land area by stating that you are a representative of mankind who has come to nature in the spirit of love and co-creativity to take custody of these specific battle energies held by nature and to facilitate the release process.*

4.   *The Release: Ask nature to release all battle energies with gentleness and ease.*

   Watch or feel the release process. It may be completed in a few minutes or need a longer time period, such as a half hour. The energy will be released from all surrounding natural form and rest as an "energy cloud" right above the battlefield or land.

5. *When the process is complete, request that the released energy now move to its next higher level within the universe. Do not attempt to determine where that might be.*

6. *Test for any needed essences and place a bowl of this solution* [drops of essences in water] *in the center of the garden.*

7. *Spend a moment feeling/receiving the changes in the battlefield or area that have been made. Note your sensations, intuitive insights and what you see in your mind's eye. This serves to ground the completed release process fully.*

8. *To close the Battle Energy Release Process, release the coning by recalling or focusing your attention on its members individually and requesting that they each now release from the coning.*

NOTE: These are the steps of the Battle Energy Release Process as they were given to me expressly for the initial development of the process and my early work with it. Over the years, I worked with nature to expand the process steps so that they may be used by anyone. If you wish to work with this process, *do not use the steps listed above.* Instead, use the updated process that is available in the *Perelandra Garden Workbook.* The *Workbook* will give you the instructions for everything you'll need in order to do the process: kinesiology testing, how to test for balancers and stabilizers, how to open and close the coning...It's important for something like the Battle Energy Release Process that you do it correctly and safely.

I now had the steps I needed for the Battle Energy Release Process, but I needed to wait for the go-ahead from nature to do this new process at Perelandra. I had long since learned that nature had its own timing that, when adhered to, made things go more easily and smoothly. So, I waited.

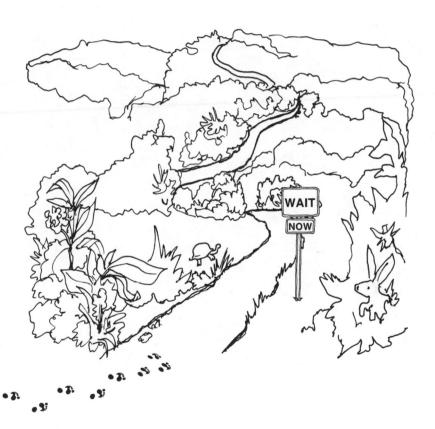

Chapter 4

Gettysburg Battlefield

Aт THE COTTAGE, I TALKED about the Battle Energy Release Process and let the men read the session I had done, as well. So they were aware of this new direction in my work. We had even talked about the possibility of my doing the Battle Energy Release Process for a battlefield someday—a battlefield of their choice, not mine.

On October 19, 1983, I visited a friend of mine, B.D. Salvesen. (I call her "Salvesen."[Sal´-ve-sen]) She had been my friend and chiropractor for years and had done all the chiropractic work I needed in the early days of my going to the Cottage. (I explain Salvesen's work in *Dancing in the Shadows of the Moon.*) Consequently, she was familiar with my life at the Cottage and many of my Cottage adventures. This October day we were "shootin' the breeze," as they say, and she asked me about something she had heard from a mutual friend that I was doing with battlefields. Right about then, she stopped our conversation and said she thought David was trying to get in touch with me. I focused on the Cottage, and sure enough, he had been waiting for us to finish talking before "ringing through." By this time I was quite used to getting "calls" from the Cottage while I was at Perelandra. What was different about this was getting a call with someone else present and that someone was picking up on the incoming call before I did.

David wanted to join in the battlefield discussion. In fact, he got right to the point. He said he wanted Salvesen to go to the

Gettysburg Battlefield* with me to do the Battle Energy Release
Process there. He also wanted to be linked with us once we were
there so that he could work directly with us. Actually, he planned
to function as our tour guide. He suggested we do it sometime in
February or March when the ungodly cold weather would assure
us there would not be many other people around.

Salvesen and I looked at each other, then agreed to go to
Gettysburg sometime in February or March. I figured I had nothing planned for that day (whenever that day was) and Salvesen is
always up for an adventure, so this fit right into her idea of something interesting to do. We decided to hold off setting the date
for the trip to see how both our schedules shaped up over the next
four months.

After I ended the call from David, I received another surprise.
Salvesen is a big time—I mean *big time*—Civil War buff. Who
knew? I certainly didn't. Out of all the surprising things that had
just happened, this was probably the most surprising. She started
spouting all sorts of time lines, facts and events about the Gettysburg Battle—information that I never expected to hear coming
out of her mouth. To keep the record straight: I knew absolutely
nothing about the Gettysburg Battle or the battlefield. Nilch.
Niente. Nada.

I have to admit that I grumbled a bit about the choice of the
Gettysburg Battlefield. Why couldn't we go to the Manassas
Battlefield, which was a thirty-five minute drive from Perelandra?
No, we had to schlep to the Gettysburg Battlefield, which was a
two-hour drive. To me a battlefield was a battlefield.

EXIT !?!
ANY OLE
BATTLEFIELD
NEXT LEFT

---

* The Gettysburg Battlefield is located in Gettysburg, Pennsylvania (U.S.A.). It
is the site of the greatest battle of the American Civil War between the Union
and Confederate Armies and became the turning point of that war. It lasted
three days—July 1 to July 3, 1863.

Chapter 5

The Dream

On January 16, 1984, I had that long, exhausting dream that I described in Chapter 2. Had I presented the dream in its sequential position in this book, it would have occurred here. However, you needed information about the Cottage right up front and I felt the dream told it best. So to give it its rightful position, I'll start the dream again:

> I was seated in a room with Peter Caddy, and I was telling him about the unusual change my life had taken. In my dream, I started by saying to him, "I'm working in the Pentagon of the White Brotherhood." And I went on from there…

At dinner that evening at the Cottage, I told everyone about the dream. David asked me to describe my relationship with Peter. I said that I had seen him very little when I was at Findhorn in 1977. He was away from the community most of my four months there, traveling around the world talking about Findhorn. It wasn't until after I returned to Perelandra that we met in the midst of yet more of his travels and had several lengthy conversations together. Over the years, he had visited Perelandra several times, even stayed for a couple of days, and we had given a workshop together. I felt we had formed a solid connection and a good friendship.

That was about it. David didn't say much. He just asked those few questions and listened to what I was saying. I was used to lengthy, question-filled conversations with him by that time—I

called them "debriefings"—so I didn't think anything odd about
this one. I put the dream and our conversation away and got on
with my evening.

Chapter 6

The Date Is Set

ON FEBRUARY 5, I CALLED Salvesen, and together we came up with March 7 (1984) as the day for going to Gettysburg. There was no magic about our choosing March 7. We knew it would still be cold and March 7 fell on a Wednesday. We didn't think there would be a crowd at the Gettysburg Battlefield that cold day in the middle of the week.

Chapter 7

The Battle Energy Release Process at Perelandra

On February 25, 1984, I *finally* received the word from nature I had been waiting four months for: Do the Battle Energy Release Process at Perelandra and do it now. March 7 was fast approaching and I had been concerned. I wanted to work out any glitches in the process before the trip, and I wanted to have an idea of what it felt like to do this process before having to work it for a large battlefield.

I worked with the entire Perelandra land, which, at the time, was twenty-one acres. As it turned out, it was a simple process that moved easily. But I was surprised at the intensity of the release of the battle-related energies. It was as if steam jets had been opened all over Perelandra, and white energy shot out and up from the fields and trees for about twenty minutes, forming a white cloud about thirty feet thick just above the tree line of our woods. When I called for the energy to move to its next higher level, I watched the cloud move away from Perelandra and felt it being received into the universe.

As the energy released, I had a physical reaction—a clear and dramatic increase of what felt like electricity in my body. I checked to see if the battle energy was somehow going through my body. Nature said no, I was simply responding to all the activity going on around me, and I was fine.

When I finished step 5, I checked for any essences needed to stabilize Perelandra now that these energies had been released.

When I do this kind of testing, I use kinesiology, a simple form of muscle testing as my tool. For the first Battle Energy Release Process, I focused on each bottle of essence, one at a time, and asked, "As a result of this work, does Perelandra need _____ essence?" I then did a kinesiology test. If the result was positive, Perelandra needed that essence for stabilization. If it tested negative, the essence was not needed. At the time, I was using the Bach Flower Remedies and two sets of essences produced by the Flower Essences Society. I had not yet begun developing any of the Perelandra Essences. For this first Battle Energy Release Process, I got a positive test response for Crab Apple, Comfrey, Walnut and Rescue Remedy. (The definitions for all essences referred to in this book are listed in Appendix B.)

I mixed the solution (adding to a glass bowl of water one drop from each essence that tested positive) and put the bowl in the middle of the garden. I then asked Pan to release the solution from the bowl to Perelandra. When I turned around to leave the garden center, I found a gold satin ribbon lying in the grass path where I had just walked less than five minutes earlier—a gift from nature. The process had worked.

Before leaving, Pan told me to check the garden soil. At that point, not more than ten minutes had passed since the release of the battle energy. By this time, I had worked in the garden for six years and I knew the quality and makeup of its soil very well. Its base is clay—good ole Virginia red clay. The kind you can roll up in a ball and bounce off a wall. But after doing the process, the soil I held in my hands had completely changed. It was black and perfectly loamy in texture. I checked the soil in other areas of the garden and found it, too, had changed to a dark loamy texture. Now I knew the process had worked and I had an idea of how battle energy can affect soil.

I remember going inside my garden cabin and sitting quietly for quite a while thinking about what had just happened and what it might mean. I had already been told that Confederate soldiers rested on the Perelandra land as they prepared to go to battle at Manassas. But they had not fought a battle on my land. Now I had to consider that the feelings, thoughts, fears, concerns and other emotions that soldiers experience prior to a battle are also absorbed by nature, including its soil.

When I got the fertilizer readout from nature for the garden that year, there were dramatic changes in what was needed. It felt to me that the plants had been drawing their nutrients through a screen or a barrier. This year the barrier was no longer there. With direct access, it seemed as if the soil's nutrients were more available to the plants and fewer fertilizers were needed.

At the Cottage that night, I told the men about what had happened with the process. They were not surprised at how much energy was released. After all, they certainly knew more about what's involved in battle than I.

Chapter 8

Frustration

MARCH 1, 1984: I HAD BEEN trying for days to get Salvesen on the phone to make sure she was still going to Gettysburg with me. She has a tendency not to return calls. Frustration was setting in fast. I told David I was thinking about going there on my own, but he wasn't at all keen on the idea. He urged me to keep trying to get Salvesen.

MARCH 2, 1984: I finally got Salvesen the next day—on the first try! The Gettysburg trip was set for March 7 as planned. The ball was now rolling.

Chapter 9

The Battle Energy Release Process and Battlefields

THIRD SESSION

Understand that I am a proud, bleeding-heart liberal, a believer in non-violence and a student of those who have advanced the cause of non-violence, such as Gandhi and Martin Luther King, Jr. Walking onto a battlefield and getting up close and personal with the energy released there was not exactly something I ever yearned to do. But then I never yearned to work with the team from the Pentagon of the White Brotherhood either. I just felt so misplaced in all of this.

It was now March, and I had less than a week before going to Gettysburg. At this point, all I knew was that I would be doing the Battle Energy Release Process as originally set up and as I had done at Perelandra. I had several concerns. (I'm understating here.) First, I had only worked the process once at Perelandra. Second, I was a bit concerned about dealing with an actual battlefield. By this time, Salvesen had impressed on me the magnitude of the Gettysburg Battle, and I wondered if I might just blow up from the intensity. And third, the few friends I had talked to about the trip to Gettysburg were telling me that I'd never get the job done because the battlefield is huge. It would take me years. To this third concern, David suggested I not listen to them. He would be directing Salvesen and me around the battlefield, and he knew what he was doing.

77

On March 2, I had a third session on the Battle Energy Release
Process and battlefields that eased my mind a bit.

THE BATTLE ENERGY RELEASE PROCESS, BATTLEFIELDS AND HISTORY

*The Battle Energy Release Process you will conduct is not a surprise to
nature (in terms of your entering an area and activating this process).
Nature is alerted, anxious and eager to cooperate with you in releasing
these battle energies. It has been essential that a representative of man work
in co-creative partnership with nature in releasing the battle energies. This
is an involution/evolution function—nature and man working together in
harmony and balance for the purpose of shifting imbalances within the
realm of nature into balance.*

*Nature is fully capable of releasing these battle energies, but nature does
not have within it the tool to transmute human energy from one level to
another: It can only absorb and release. Consequently, these energies could
have been released at any time, but there has been a higher timing involved.
Mankind had to change and grow to where he could then turn around and
take responsibility for the impact he has had in nature (as well as other
areas) due to his own actions.*

*. . . The energies that are being released on battlefields are not isolated
from the change from the Piscean Era to the Aquarian Era. Timing has
been essential in the development of the Battle Energy Release Process, so
as you move into the battlefields themselves, you will find that nature will
not be surprised by your presence. It has been waiting for man to return
and take custody of that which it has been holding for so long for the benefit of mankind.*

*We warn you that as you move into the battlefield areas, you will expe-
rience a greater amount of energy. This is one reason the battlefields will
have to be approached not as one unit, but as a collection of many different
smaller battles all coming together to create a single larger one. If you
attempted to release the entire battlefield area with all of its parts as one*

whole, you would truly run the risk of being overwhelmed. That is not a necessary experience for you to have, so we urge you to approach any battlefield as a collection of smaller battles all carried out within one well-defined geographical area.

The battle energies released from nature that appear white have not been transmuted by nature, but by history—historical experience, the review and understanding of war; the healing (there have been generations of healing) that has occurred within the families whose husbands and sons experienced that war; and the healing that has occurred as those who experienced the battles firsthand moved from lifetime to lifetime, dealing with their role and their deaths, in that war (they themselves serving in the transmutation process). So as you see, this is not just a collection of battle energies held by nature and untouched since the battle. These energies have been transmuted because of the continuing evolution of those who were a part of the battle and the continuing evolution of the families who were either attached to those surrounding the battle or affected by the battle itself.

If in the future you choose to enter areas of more recent wars where the energies held by nature have not been transmuted by those touched by that war (we think specifically of Vietnam), you will have to alter the process you are using in order to accommodate the untransmuted energies.

Recently you have considered the notion of nothing you experience ever remaining forever on the back burner: how, somewhere down the road, you will have to face everything—all emotions, pain, experience—and fully and completely ground those experiences within you, understand their purpose and transmute them. The transmuted battle-related energies fit within this area of thought, this notion of nothing remaining forever on a back burner. What you are experiencing now by viewing the white, transmuted battle energies is one result of looking at everything on the back burners—bringing it forward, dealing with it, grounding it and transmuting it. That process within an individual soul does not remain isolated within the soul. As each man who died at the Battle of Gettysburg grounded his experience, that battle energy on the field was transmuted.

This only serves to give you another example of the power that man's actions have, the power man has within himself and the broad implications of his actions. If man can act in such a way that he can create a huge, massive body of traumatic energy that needs to be held within the realm of nature so that man himself will not self-destruct from its rawness and intensity, then he also has the power to transmute it. It works both ways. Man on Earth has the tendency to see only how destructive he can be; he does not have self-confidence about how constructive he can be.

The question arises: If man has had the ability and has actually transmuted this energy that has been held within nature, then why have these areas remained ecologically unbalanced? The issue here is not primarily the negative energy, although the initial impact on nature was this intense negativity. It is the massive cloud of raw emotional energy released in war and absorbed by nature that initially threw off the natural ecological balance. However, the energy of the Battle of Gettysburg has been transmuted, and what remains and continues to throw off the ecological balance is not negativity. The simple fact is that a large body of manmade energy is being held in custody by nature. In essence, nature has been willing and eager to perform a service for man at a cost to its own balance and rhythms. While these areas have maintained this service, the ecological balance has never been able to be retained or rediscovered. Once the areas release this body of battle energy, there will be a strong and evident move toward reestablishing an ecological balance on the battlefield.

Regarding nuns praying over battlefields [in response to a question that I had raised at the Cottage earlier that day], *the nuns have laid groundwork upon which you are building....They are, in essence, women who intuitively understand that something within man needs to happen in these areas in order to balance the horror of war. They have responded with prayer, and their response has not gone unheeded or been ineffectual. If one could see the energy of their prayer, one might visualize it moving from them into the massive energy being held by nature, and that in itself has had a healing effect. However, the effort by the nuns has not served to release this energy from the realm of nature because they have not understood the role of nature in this. Consequently, they have not been able to respond with a process that would release the energies from nature.*

At this time, we would like to move on to a related matter: to expand on the notion of how an individual soul can affect the impact of history by looking fully and completely at his role within history.

The concept of history has several levels. One level can best be described as simply what happened: A leading to B leading to C creating D. When looked at sequentially, it is quite easy to see how a single act in history can affect future acts, movements and changes. However, these things of the future and these acts of the past are not static; their impact is constantly changing. First of all, historians look back at events and judge and reevaluate them—that alone changes the impact of history. You may have a specific event that for a number of years carries a particular impact on history. Then suddenly, this event is viewed differently and reevaluated. From that point on, its impact will indeed change; it may change again and again, depending on how many times it is viewed differently and reevaluated. Each time it changes, its impact on the present and its impact on the future also changes.

What man does not fully recognize is the impact of the souls who were involved in a particular event as they themselves evolve, reevaluate, change and look at things they have put on the back burner. As they go through this process, they activate a transmutation process within the event itself.

One might say that history itself goes through an evolutionary process. It is a fluid, moving phenomenon. No one can say within his own life, "Well, I have done that, so now it's over and I never need look at it again." If his personal role in a specific event is incomplete and ungrounded, he will have to look at it again—and again and again. Each time, if he so chooses, he can change his evaluation of the event and his role in it, and thus change the impact of the energy around the event itself.

Another point is that emotions are inherent in every historical event. When individual participants of an historical event place things from that event onto their personal back burners, it is usually in the area of emotions. We would have to say that the principal area preventing, or interfering with, the forward evolution of history comes from the level of the emotions that participants have placed on back burners. As man evolves within himself, he will have opportunity to recall those emotions.

Now, he often places emotions on the back burner so that he can move forward at the time. One can say that the phenomenon of placing emotional reaction to an historical event on the back burner is very similar indeed to the phenomenon of nature absorbing the emotional energy released during war. If nature did not do this, man would not have the space to evolve and grow in order to get to the point of being able to come back and take full custody of what nature has been holding. Quite often, the emotions experienced during the outplay of historical events are so intense and raw that in order to continue, man must place these emotions on a back burner. But they were never meant to stay there—just as nature was never meant to hold battle energies forever—and must be brought back up when he is ready for those emotions to ground fully through him, to be transmuted and released. When that happens, the body of emotion inherent within the historical event itself will also shift. As each man takes custody of his own emotions within an historical event, the general body of the event will shift.

We do not view placing events on the back burner as an escape, but as survival. There are some experiences within each man's life that must be placed on the back burner until he has the full opportunity and wherewithal to ground those experiences fully through himself, transmuting whatever energies need to be transmuted and completing his role on the impact of an historical event (any past event or experience within a person's life, within any lifetime).

The consideration of history as a fluid, evolutionary process is another example of how everything that exists on Earth is an active participant in this change from the Piscean Era to the Aquarian Era. Everything moves, shifts and evolves. Just as separating truth from insanity within the arena of war alters the body of information regarding war that is available to this universe and beyond, so, too, does the fluid, evolutionary process of history change that body of information available to this universe and beyond. These changes are not just for the benefit of Earth; all of these changes are for the benefit of the whole—this universe and that which is beyond.

Chapter 10

On to Gettysburg

MARCH 7, 1984

SALVESEN AND I ARRIVED at Gettysburg by noon. When we entered the town, we found "Eisenhower" signs all over the place. His retirement home, which is now the Eisenhower National Historic Site, is located right next to the battlefield. Hence the reason for the signs.

I pulled my pickup truck into the Visitor Center parking lot. It was empty, except for us. We definitely weren't going to have any problems with crowds. I didn't plan this next thing, I swear. But when I turned the truck motor off, I looked up and right in front of us was a sign, "Eisenhower Tour Starts Here." I said to Salvesen, "This must be where we start." And right next to the sign was a wooden map holder mounted on a post. I went over and found just one map in the holder. When I looked around, I saw that the rest of the holders around the parking lot were empty.

I got back into the truck and gave the map to Salvesen. David had given us each specific jobs. Salvesen was to work with him as he directed us around the battlefield, and I was to concentrate on working with nature and doing the Battle Energy Release Process. Salvesen and I were both wondering how she was going to "hear" David, but as soon as I opened the coning we were to have activated for the day, which included all the members I would need for the Battle Energy Release Process work, David and Salvesen, the two of them became connected and started plotting out our route.

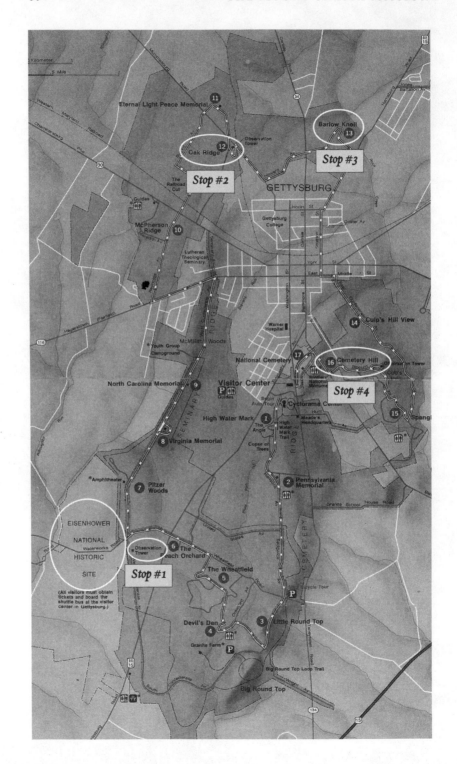

I can't think of a better person in the world to do this kind of work with than Salvesen. She's game for just about anything. She's fearless and she loves adventures. She has a great sense of humor and she loves chocolate. As it turned out, we both needed all of this to get through the afternoon.

Our first glitch occurred as I pulled out of the parking lot. Salvesen told me to turn right. We drove around for a bit, making right and left turns according to what David was saying, and ended up close to where we had started. Had we turned left out of the parking lot, we would have been at our first spot in about two minutes. Because Salvesen got the first turn wrong, David just looped us around and got us back to where he wanted us. By the time we got there, he and Salvesen had worked out their communication kinks.

STOP #1: THE EISENHOWER OBSERVATION TOWER

As soon as we stopped, Salvesen declared David to be brilliant. He was going to have me do the work from the observation towers situated around the battlefield. This way I would be able to work with huge areas of land just by standing on the tower platforms. So much for all the comments I had gotten for weeks about this battlefield being too big for me to do the work.

The Eisenhower Observation Tower* was tall—very tall. I had a backpack with six boxes of essences in glass bottles, spoons, paper towels and a notebook. It had a little weight to it. I stood at the tower base, looked up and I remember thinking, "Ah crap." (Well, actually I thought something a little more crass, but I'm cleaning it up for public consumption. Use your imagination.) It was like climbing the stairs of a four-story building. But when

---

* The Eisenhower Observation Tower no longer stands. It has been replaced by a similar, unnamed tower that stands about a half mile further down the road.

Salvesen and I got to the platform, we were treated with an amazing view. It would have been absolutely perfect if the temperature had been higher than 30 degrees and the wind had died down to a reasonable breeze. I was relieved, but not surprised, to find no one else on the tower platform.

David asked me, as a favor to him, to start by doing the Battle Energy Release Process for the Eisenhower Farm. When I looked out from the back side of the tower, opposite the battlefield, I could see his farm. He explained that this would fulfill a promise he made many years ago when he first bought the property to do everything in his power to restore the land to its original state of fertile soil. I felt it would give me a good warm-up before tackling the battlefield. I said I'd be glad to do that work and set up to do the process. I went through the steps as I had done at Perelandra, and after the release of battle energy, I tested the property to find out what essence stabilizers were needed. I put two drops of Comfrey essence (the only flower essence that tested positive) in a spoon and held it out in front of me. Because I wasn't going to be able to leave glass bowls of essence solution around the battlefield, nature had set up for Pan to shift the energy from the drops in the spoon, expand that energy as needed for the area and infuse it into its soil—in this case, the Eisenhower Farm. The process for the farm moved smoothly and, including the battle energy release itself, took only a total of about ten minutes.

With this, I got down to battlefield business. David told Salvesen I was to work with Big Round Top first. She had to point me in the right direction, since I had no idea where Big Round Top was located. It was all the way on the other side of the battlefield to our right. I focused the coning on this area and did the process. The Big Round Top area tested for Comfrey and Blue Aster essences to stabilize the work.

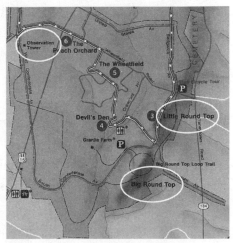

As per David's instructions, Salvesen then pointed me toward Little Round Top, which was an area also on the other side of the battlefield but more directly in front of us. Just as I was about to start the process, we heard footsteps. Someone was climbing the tower. I figured I had time to do the work before this determined and brave person reached the platform. I set up, did the process and tested the essences. This second area needed to be stabilized with Comfrey, Delphinium and Blue Aster essences. I put the drops into a spoon and, just as I held the spoon out for Pan to shift the drops, the stair climber joined us on the platform. I couldn't back away from the work at this point, so when he arrived, he saw two women, one was holding a spoon out in front of her and the other was humming the theme from the television program *The Twilight Zone.* The guy didn't say a word. He walked over to the platform railing, looked out for maybe three seconds, then went back down the steps. By this time I had finished the essence shift, and both Salvesen and I were trying not to laugh too hard…until he got out of ear shot.

STOP #2: OAK RIDGE

David told Salvesen we were finished at the Eisenhower Tower. We descended, got back into the truck and went to the next location. We ended up at Oak Ridge and another observation tower. To my relief, this one was not as tall, but it was closed. That didn't bother Salvesen. Without hesitation, she climbed over the closed gate at the base and headed up. I followed behind with the backpack. We got halfway up the tower, and guess who pulled up in a car right next to the tower? The Eisenhower Tower guy! He took one look at us. We looked at him. And he just continued driving on down the road.

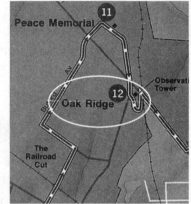

From the Oak Ridge Tower, I did the process three times. For the first one, I faced north and included a school. That area needed Comfrey for stabilization after the process. For the second one, I faced northwest and included the Peace Memorial and a house with salmon shutters that had caught our eye when we drove by. There wasn't anything "special or guided" about this house catching our attention. It just stood out. How often do you see a house with salmon shutters? For the second stabilization, I again released Comfrey essence to Pan. For the third process, I faced southeast and included a church tower. That area needed Comfrey also.

STOP #3: BARLOW KNOLL

Before getting arrested, we climbed back down the tower and over the gate, then followed David's instructions to the third stop:

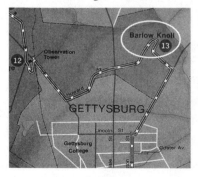

Barlow Knoll. There was no tower. But there was a small and obviously old cemetery. As soon as I looked at it I said to Salvesen, "We're going into the cemetery." There was a car parked on the road next to the cemetery, and a young woman was sitting in it eating her lunch. Now, there were many other more scenic spots around the battlefield, and I wondered what in the world would make somebody choose this cold, windy spot. When we entered the cemetery, I told Salvesen to walk around and look like she was interested in old tombstones while I stood to one side and found out what I was to do there. I had a feeling it was going to be different. I was told to go ahead and do the Battle Energy Release Process for the cemetery, which I did. Once again, Comfrey was needed for stabilization. Then I was told to call for the release of any souls still in the cemetery. I hadn't done this before, so I decided to take a stab at it and just said the obvious, "I call for the release of any souls still present in this cemetery." It worked. I could see and feel a lifting of energy from all around the cemetery. It was strong and distinct enough that it caught Salvesen's attention as well.

When everything was clear, she pointed at one particular gravestone and said that there was a problem there. I walked over to a small gravestone that was cemented in a line with about twenty other gravestones. Only the cement connecting this one stone was cracked through, and the gravestone had separated from the line of other stones. (Fig. 1) It belonged to someone named

Fig. 1: The gravestone at the Barlow Knoll cemetery.

Johnston who had died in 1882. I stood in front of the stone waiting for some clue as to what I was to do. Within a few seconds, I saw a gold ropelike band of light rise from the stone. It shot out at an angle and connected right to the young woman who was still sitting in her car eating her sandwich. I sensed that somehow Johnston and the woman were linked, and I was being asked to cut the gold band. I checked my hunch and found it was correct. I used my two fingers as scissors and successfully cut the band straight through. As soon as I finished the cut, a soul rose from that stone and the woman started her car and drove away.

Fig. 2: The Warren family crypt.

With that, David said we had done good work and could head on home. Salvesen and I left the cemetery and pulled the truck into another empty parking lot that faced Evergreen Cemetery (Stop #4), a large, more formal cemetery than the one at Barlow Knoll. Actually, we were there to catch our breath and eat a bunch of chocolate I had brought along before heading home. So, there we were, sitting in the truck eating chocolate and not bothering anyone, when Salvesen said, "Is there a reason why that door over there keeps getting bigger?" I looked and didn't see anything, not even a door. She pointed it out again, and I realized that the big tree in front of the truck was blocking my view. Before I could declare her delusional, she was out of the truck and heading toward the cemetery. I grabbed my backpack and followed. To get into the cemetery, we had to climb over a fence, something that didn't phase Salvesen in the least. As we walked toward the door she was pointing to, I still didn't see any changes occurring.

The door was part of an underground crypt (which we quickly dubbed "the bunker") that belonged to a Dr. James Warren and his family. (*Fig. 2*) Salvesen told me to test the crypt door for any needed essences. I didn't have a clue what this was all about, so I followed Salvesen's lead and did an essence test. The door needed Pink Nicotiana. I shifted the drop of essence from the spoon to Pan. Then Salvesen asked me to test her, and she, too, needed Pink Nicotiana. She turned away from the crypt and pointed to an observation tower near the cemetery and told me to do a Battle Energy Release for the area leading from the crypt up to the tower. I did this, and after the release the area needed Yarrow and Pink Yarrow. Then I had to test Dr. Warren — and then Salvesen again. Each needed Yarrow and Pink Yarrow. Finally, she told me to do a Battle Energy Release on the observation tower itself. It tested positive for Red Clover.

Right at the point when I began to think she was messing with me and just seeing how many tests I would do before protesting, Salvesen was contacted by none other than Dr. James Warren himself, honored resident of the bunker. He asked to accompany her to her office, where he could observe several techniques she worked with that he needed in order to assist others who had died during the Gettysburg Battle. He had been a physician then, working at a "MASH unit" that had been set up near where the cemetery's observation tower was now located. It would probably be another one of those understatements to say that Salvesen and I were a little surprised by all of this. But she invited him back, and we even suggested he might like to ride along in the truck with us. Which he did. Luckily, we couldn't see him. I think we would have needed a lot more chocolate had that been so. But we could feel his presence. We held the door open for him and made sure he was comfortable before heading out of Gettysburg.

It took a total of two and a half hours to do all the battlefield work. When we left Gettysburg, we had a feeling that this was only the first stage of the work and that I might need to return to complete the job. As we drove south and as we passed the High Water Mark and the Copse of Trees, Salvesen wondered aloud why that one spot had been missed in our work. She explained that this area was the climax of the Gettysburg Battle and that it was a particularly fierce battle leaving bullet shells six inches deep on the ground. I didn't say anything. I figured nature and David knew what they were doing.

En route, we suggested to Dr. Warren, who seemed perfectly happy to be wedged between Salvesen and me in the front seat of a pickup truck, that we stop at McDonald's and give him a real modern-day experience. We didn't sense that he was particularly excited about this, so we didn't stop. Besides, it might have been a little too much experience for him. By 5:30 P.M., Salvesen and Dr. Warren had been dropped off at her home, and I was back at Perelandra.

I spent the evening at the Cottage with the men, laughing and talking about my Gettysburg adventures. They were very pleased about what was accomplished. David was personally pleased that his hookup with Salvesen had worked so well—except for that first misdirection between him and Salvesen. Other than that, his directions to her were clear and unmistakable.

DR. WARREN'S UPDATE

Meeting with Dr. Warren at the battlefield was a factor-x, an unscheduled and unexpected event. I guess he and Salvesen were the right people crossing paths at the right time. He recognized an opportunity and reached out to her, and she accepted.

Salvesen took him to her office the day after we returned from Gettysburg. On April 24, I talked with her and asked how she was doing with the good doctor. She said that originally she had felt he might be there to assist her, but now she knew he was there to learn from her so that he could help those men from the Gettysburg Battle who were still in need of release. He was especially interested in her cranial work. She felt him intensely observing what she was doing every time she did anything with a client's head, so she decided to help him by describing aloud what she was doing. Her clients thought she was talking to them and wondered why she had suddenly become chatty. She expected that he would be going back to Gettysburg to continue his work if and when I returned to do another phase there. I assumed that meant he would be hitching a ride back with me in the truck, but neither she nor I knew how that was going to work.

On May 12, I spoke with Salvesen again. She said that Dr. Warren had left her office on his own about a week earlier. In her mind's eye, she saw him back at the battlefield administering to one soldier after another. After he adjusted each man's cranial plates, the soldier disappeared from the picture. The good doctor truly understood faithfulness to job.

Chapter 11

What Happened

A FEW DAYS AFTER RETURNING from Gettysburg, I again sensed that there was more to do at the battlefield. I verified this with nature and agreed to do phase two of the work—whatever that was. The Cottage men were pleased with my decision.

I also had another session as a follow-up to Gettysburg. You'll note that in this session, concepts were being repeated to me. The issue was not only that these concepts were new to me, but also that I was having difficulty understanding and fully accepting the true impact of the Battle Energy Release Process at Gettysburg. It just seemed too big for me to wrap my mind around, and the session was addressing my hesitance.

FOLLOW-UP TO THE GETTYSBURG BATTLEFIELD WORK

Each battlefield, each battle, each war, is a microcosm reflecting the position of the universe. So often people think war has been an ugly blot on the history of Earth, that it has reflected the ugliness of man on Earth. Well, we do not see it in those judgmental terms. All the wars that have occurred on Earth throughout history have reflected a universal mindset, not a mindset unique to Earth alone. This is another reason how and why the evolution of specific areas of Earth affect the entire universe and beyond. If the effect can flow from the planet Earth out through the universe and beyond, then one must consider that the effect also flows the other way—from beyond the universe to Earth. It is a two-way flow, involving evolution and effect.

The work accomplished at Gettysburg has sounded a clear, strong note throughout the universe and beyond that indeed, the mindset of souls, of all that exists, is changing in terms of problem-solving, teamwork and shifting from violence to non-violence. That which has been rippling throughout the universe was clearly grounded within the arena of five-senses form through the use of the Battle Energy Release Process. What we now have is a transition process that is rippling throughout the universe and is fully moving within planet Earth, as well. If one could look at this rippling as if it were a continuum, one would see the rippling throughout many areas of the line, but it never fully grounded in a constructive, viable, workable manner on Earth until Wednesday [March 7]. Now that entire line, that entire continuum, is rippling and moving in a state of transition. It is completely in a state of motion: Nothing is lagging or holding back.

The work that David and the Cottage team have done within the area of the military has set that continuum in motion in areas other than five-senses form. The continuum had to be set in motion in five-senses form prior to David's releasing to the Earth level the framework and structures that he and his team are creating and building. They would not have been fully and completely received had not the Earth end of the continuum been set in motion.

Consider that the arena of the military (by this, we mean government/military problem-solving) creates a tuning fork that sounds a note throughout the entire universe and beyond. When you strike the tuning fork, the whole fork must vibrate in order for the note to sound fully. If you place your hand on one end of the tuning fork, and restrict the vibration of the note at that one end, the entire tuning fork is affected. The note, the sound, the clarity, is affected and eventually there will be no sound at all. Essentially, what happened Wednesday was that the hand was released from the tuning fork at one end, and consequently the note sounded clearly throughout the universe. The government/military tuning fork is now fully and completely sounding its note.

You are questioning how in the world the releasing of battlefield energies can accomplish what we are saying about the tuning fork, how going *back and releasing the held energy completes a sound of transition within the universe. Remember that a battle is a microcosm of the universal mindset that is acted out in the arena of five-senses form, and it is not that Earth has acted out universal wars or battles. One must try not to superimpose the five-senses form reality of a battle onto other arenas and areas of the universe. What we are suggesting is that man on Earth, in tune with and in touch with the evolution of the universe, taps into the prevailing mindset and interprets that into the arena of five-senses form. Up to now, the primary interpretation has been battle, war. Although man is not acting out some universal war that is clashing well beyond his own sense of vision, he is showing clearly in a form-like manner the implications of the universal mindset were it to be translated into five-senses form.*

Now, a change takes preparation, and the preparation for the change from Piscean to Aquarian in the arena of war has gone on for some time. There have been many questions arising in people's minds. There has been the realization that since the dropping of the atomic bomb in 1945, war on Earth has been inappropriate. This became the catalyst for an intense period of preparation within the mindset of all souls (on Earth and beyond) to move from the old way of doing things to the new. Preparation is not the thing that strikes the tuning fork; it is what gets man to the point where he can strike the tuning fork. Unless one understands that distinction, one cannot grasp how what occurred Wednesday became the thing that sounded the note from the arena of five-senses form throughout the universe.

The change from the old to the new, from the Piscean to the Aquarian, begins in the heart. It is a shift in attitude, in how one perceives something. Man has had to go through years of challenge, thought and struggle in preparation for that shift in attitude, and attitudes have begun to change. But just as a battle is a microcosm of universal thought acted out in the arena of form, it can also serve as a microcosm of a massive change in attitude come together and acted out within its arena (such as a battlefield) — again within the framework of form. The Battle of Gettysburg has represented this universal microcosm of one particular set of attitudes. Wednesday you returned to the very arena where that microcosm was

acted out, entered it, and through the physical structure of the Battle
Energy Release Process, "flipped the coin"* of the Gettysburg Battle. By
using a structure that encompassed all the various changes in attitude, you
were able to strike that tuning fork, thus completing the vibration of the
fork throughout the universe.

Let's break this thought down: The preparation on Earth up to this
point has required that man change his attitude about different realities
and events that have occurred around him. For example, his vision about
war has expanded so that if one were to break down the components of war
and look at just one component—say, death—it would be easy to see how
man has changed his attitudes. The narrow vision from which he has
worked has been that a man dies and that's that. There is nothing more,
nothing further. He dies, rots and goes to earth. Over the years, a large
group of humans on Earth have shifted their attitude and understanding of
what death is. With that one shift in attitude alone, one can reenter a battlefield area and view it from a different perspective.

Death is just one component of war. There have been many components
that have changed, that have gone through a preparation period. What you
did when you reentered the Gettysburg Battlefield was to take the various
components that have changed, create a framework called the "Battle
Energy Release Process" using those new attitudes, and therewith release
the remnants of the old. You created a new framework and released the
remnants of the old that happened to be held within the nature kingdoms.

Again, we would like to point out that neither this change in attitude
about death nor this collection of attitudes surrounding war is unique to
Earth—they are universal. Just as man on Earth is not isolated from the
universe, we can also say that this collection of attitudinal changes is a
result of man's dance with the universal flow, interpreting that which exists

---

* Flipping the coins: A battle is divided into its many different strategies. The
Cottage team calls each strategy a coin. They identify the higher intent and
purpose of that strategy and link it into the higher intent and purpose of the
battle itself. When they have accomplished this, the men consider that this
strategy, this coin, has been flipped from the Piscean dynamic and that it now
reflects the new Aquarian dynamic and principles.

within the arena of five-senses form. Had there not been a universal transition in progress, and had not man on Earth prepared himself to join in
this transition, it would have been impossible for you to effect an efficient
framework to accomplish what you did Wednesday. You would have, in
essence, superimposed a framework onto the situation and struck an alien
note. The Gettysburg Battle was fully connected to the universe, so a manmade structure outside that connection simply could not have accomplished
any kind of energy move. Again, it would have been an alien structure.
Wednesday you tapped into the universe, translated it into structure and
enacted it within the framework of form, thus completing the whole picture. The universal macrocosm, acted out within the framework of war,
has now changed.

The key to more fully understanding Gettysburg is to break down the
framework of the Battle Energy Release Process and see how it relates to
what was released and enacted at Gettysburg. How one traditionally looks
at the Gettysburg Battle is narrow-visioned indeed compared to what actually occurred there those many years ago. (You keep seeing in your mind's
eye a small expanding dot becoming a large circle; that's a good symbol for
what we're describing.)

Gettysburg, in a narrowed, more limiting vision, is the coming together
of men in a destructive yet decisive act for the purpose of one side winning
over the other, thus dictating the direction and future of the country. The
mindset of the time was that it was a terrible battle with a great deal of
death and destruction. That once it was over, the winning side had moved
the country in a particular direction, and that was that. They went about
with the continued movement of the country, their lives and themselves.
You reentered the arena of the battle 121 years later knowing full well that
it wasn't over. That, indeed, the destiny of the country had been affected,
but that on the higher scale, neither side won or lost.

What occurred was an act that affected the direction of the country.
There was, in fact, death and destruction, but when you reentered the area,
your understanding of that was far greater than that of those who have
looked at it in a traditional way. The war wasn't over. Death wasn't its end.

More movement and change were still needed. You see Gettysburg with different eyes—eyes on a more expanded level and reflecting the period of preparation man has gone through to change his perspective about the reality around him. So you came to Gettysburg knowing about energy, knowing that death isn't an end and that there is a relationship between man and nature. You perceived the effect of war, not only on man but on nature as well. You entered with new attitudes and new understandings; that in itself has a healing effect.

Remember that war is a collection of universal thought patterns come together within the structure of five-senses form and acted out in a microcosmic way. At Gettysburg, you took that collection of thought patterns (which had changed since the battle), created new structure, and through the framework of the Battle Energy Release Process, flipped the coin (several coins, we might say), thus releasing the final energy of the old that was being held within the nature kingdoms. Gettysburg was fought within the framework of one understanding. You reflected within yourself the many changes within that framework that have occurred within man on Earth and within the universe. You reflected those changes through the form of the process you performed throughout the battlefields and thus flipped the coins, the result of which was the final release of energy that had been held by nature since the battles.

We understand that all men who live on Earth do not consciously reflect these changes in attitude. This transition within each individual has its own timing. But what you did was to sound a note and fully ground that collection of shifts in attitude so that those on Earth will have an easier time touching into the various ongoing transitions. The vibration of the changes will be more recognizable to them because you have grounded the vibration of those changes within the arena of five-senses form.

The principle of horizontal healing [like healing like] plays a strong role in what occurred Wednesday and in what we are saying. The energies of the transition were grounded into a framework of five-senses form (the Battle Energy Release Process). Because that intent, attitude, shift and change were translated and grounded into form, their effect on what was released in battle was far greater and far more efficient than anything else that could have occurred. This process demonstrates the principle of horizontal healing (*five-senses form healing five-senses form*) and is a fine example of how new attitudes can be translated into a five-senses form structure and used to heal, change and shift the results of old attitudes.

The tuning fork, which you have so clearly visualized throughout this session, is now fully ringing and fully vibrating. The result is that the transition process itself will move forward more easily and efficiently. You will see an increased activity surrounding that transition on Earth, reflecting that change and the ease of the transition throughout the universe. There will be a broader movement of energy around the tuning fork. Whereas up to now much of the transition has gone on at one end of the tuning fork (the end that was vibrating more freely), that vibration will now move around the tuning fork to the other end as well. You will see those changes reflected on Earth more clearly. You will also see more activity as the result of the Cottage work involving the flipping of the coins (changing the universal understanding of history), and it will be reflected on Earth more clearly. As the need for grounding the structures that David and his team are creating arises, that process will be easier.

This brings us back full circle to the word "love." What greater love is there than empathy, compassion and understanding. The impetus to all the changes that have occurred, are occurring, and will occur regarding the concept of war, of battle, lies within the areas of empathy, compassion and understanding—to use one word, love. As empathy, compassion and understanding expand within man, the way he views what is around him shifts and changes. At the risk of sounding trite and using that well-worn concept, we would say that the basis of what occurred Wednesday rests within the area of love.

The preparation for what occurred lies within the area of man's growth in understanding love. The changes in man's attitudes toward history, death, decision-making, nature, his connection to the universe, the universe's connection to him, the dynamic of man's and nature's reality—all those attitudinal changes center around his shift in empathy, compassion *and understanding; his growth in love; and his ability to open himself to something greater, wider and broader.*

When spirit within both man and nature reflects through five-senses form unencumbered and fully, its impact on the whole is extremely powerful. This fact seems to be understood by just about all who exist except those on Earth. They seem to feel they have no impact whatsoever, although the reverse is true. When spirit flows completely, full and freely through five-senses form, that mere fact, that act in itself, creates power. One must know oneself fully in order to reflect through five-senses form.

The Battle Energy Release Process allowed the spirit of the new to move fully and completely into the Gettysburg Battlefield, and it sounded a note that was powerful indeed throughout the entire universe and beyond. One cannot underestimate what happened at Gettysburg in relationship to the whole. The process is complete on one level; that is, this tuning fork within the arena of government and military is now ringing throughout the universe fully and freely.

There is, as you know, more to happen at Gettysburg. In phase two you will plant comfrey plants at the battlefield that will hold Wednesday's process while those people who still have karmic attachments to special areas in the battlefield return within a year's time to complete their personal processes. You and David will deal with the results of that individual karmic influx within the battlefield area at approximately this time next year. You will have then taken Gettysburg to another level.

If one were to see Wednesday's result as a fully vibrating tuning fork, one would also have to see that what struck the tuning fork to make it vibrate fully were attitudinal changes brought about by empathy, compassion and understanding—that is, love. When the tuning fork began to vibrate fully and completely, the universe was infused with an enormous rush of energy of empathy, compassion and understanding. It is no wonder that what may have appeared to you to be a small act (when compared to the universe) had such an impact on the whole.

Sensing that I was now on a roll with understanding the Gettysburg Battlefield work, I opened a coning the following day to get nature's perspective on what had occurred.

BATTLE ENERGY RELEASE PROCESS FROM THE VANTAGE POINT OF NATURE

The role of nature in battlefield areas such as Gettysburg has been to hold vast manmade energy while man has consciously and unconsciously worked to transform that dynamic into something less traumatic until the change has reached the point where man may return to an area such as Gettysburg and reclaim and release the energy. To hold this energy is a voluntary act on nature's part, in its service to all of mankind. But there has been a cost to both nature and man.

When nature holds such a vast body of energy as at a battlefield, its own nature balance is tipped. When nature places its balance to one side, its entire physical makeup reflects this shift in intent. Nature voluntarily has shifted its intent from existing within the laws of spirit flowing fully and perfectly through five-senses form to existing off that balance. When this occurred in Gettysburg, for example, nature's entire physical makeup changed there. It was an all-encompassing ecological shift of every cell and molecule. Everything within the Gettysburg Battlefield shifted its makeup, function and purpose to a position that was slightly at odds with the surrounding environment not touched by the battle. It created an environment of stress, an environment of slight abrasion. We say "slight" because had nature reflected a change on all levels in proportion to what it had absorbed, the environment would have been destroyed. The intensity of what was reflected was less than the intensity of what was absorbed.

Imagine the entire environment of Gettysburg to be a set of gears. Each gear went slightly out of alignment in relation to the other gears, and this created a slightly abrasive situation with an immediate physical change in the environment. The soil shifted, the health of the trees changed, the basic overall health of the environment went from a position of strength to a position of vulnerability, very much like a human body under stress. As the years progressed and nature in the area continued to function off its former balance, its physical form continued to deteriorate. The makeup of Gettysburg shifted as the town grew, more people came and technology changed, and the environment did not enfold these changes into a unified balanced ecology. Very much like the domino effect, an increasingly more complicated and complex imbalance occurred, one imbalance building on another imbalance and so on. The co-creative relationship between man and nature could not exist easily....

The Gettysburg Battlefield instantaneously changed in response to the Battle Energy Release Process. The most dramatic and important change was the shift in the flow of nature energy back to its former nature balance. It is as if the dominos dropping had been falling to the right. That was the direction of the battle imbalance, shall we say. What the Battle Energy Release Process did was go back to the first domino, set it up and tip it to the left, in the direction of a balanced evolutionary flow. This is a dramatic change, and although there were many instantaneous shifts within each cell of nature in that area, there was not a complete restoration to full balance. It had taken a long time for the battlefield area of Gettysburg to establish its complex, difficult position of imbalance. Now that the energy is moving in the proper direction, the former nature balance will more quickly be restored. But certain aspects there will need more time.

There is always the possibility for physical change to occur instantaneously, according to the attitude of the people involved. The Battle Energy Release Process is timely now because people are beginning to change their attitudes toward the environment and war. Your work in the battlefield areas will be received, albeit on an unconscious level, by a less alien society. The changes in man's general attitude toward ecology over the past ten to fifteen years have not gone unnoticed. As the people in the Gettysburg area continue to grow, the environment that has shifted into the direction of balance will move through its changes more quickly.

Chapter 12

Peter Caddy

ALBERT TOWNSEND, A FRIEND of mine, called on May 20 to tell me that Peter Caddy was in town. He had met with Peter that afternoon, and Peter had asked him to invite me to some potluck dinner and talk he was giving on Tuesday evening. Well, to me this was the invitation from hell. In his world, Peter was a star, and he was treated like a star. Wherever he went, adoring fans would cluster around him—especially women. It wasn't a pretty sight. In my head, I was screaming, "No! No!" but I told Albert I'd think about it. What made me even consider the invitation was that Peter had specifically asked Albert to call me. That was unusual because Peter knew not to expect me at these kinds of gatherings.

At the Cottage, I told the men that Peter was in town and trying to get me to travel into the suburbs for one of his public evenings. They urged me not to put myself out right now unless I really wanted to see him.

The next day, Albert called again. Peter was urging Albert to convince me to come see him (Peter). Albert told me that Peter had a couple of hours free the next day before his dinner and talk, and we could speak privately then. Peter had never pressed before, so I said yes. That's when I decided to tell him about the Cottage: I would tell him everything I told him in that dream I had had five months prior.

I arrived at the home in the Maryland suburbs where Peter was staying the next afternoon at 2 o'clock. To my surprise, Albert's wife, Laura, was also there at Peter's invitation. I had already talked to Laura a little about the Cottage and my life there, so I felt her presence wasn't going to pose a problem.

When we settled in the living room, I looked at Peter and said calmly, "I'm working in the Pentagon of the White Brotherhood." Immediately, Peter jumped up and said, "Wait a minute. I'll be right back." He rushed out of the room, opened a door that I assumed led down to the basement and called to whomever was down there to come up right away.

When Peter returned, he was joined by a man. Peter quickly introduced Bob, told him to have a seat and asked me to start again from the beginning. So I said again, "I'm working in the Pentagon of the White Brotherhood." At that point, Bob shot Peter a look and Peter urged me to go on.

When I finished describing the Cottage, the men working there and my understanding of what they were doing with governments and militaries around the world, Peter explained why he asked Bob to join us. At lunch that day, Bob was talking to Peter about a problem with his job. Bob worked at…(drum roll)…the Pentagon. And he was a member of the Pentagon's meditation group. This may come as a surprise to some, but in 1984, there was a meditation room in the Pentagon building where civilian and military staff who worked there met regularly to meditate for peace and to infuse Aquarian consciousness into the Pentagon and its activities. (I don't know if the room or the group still exists today.) The meditation group was not a secret, but they were a quiet bunch and their activity was not generally known. I certainly didn't know about it. It turned out that Bob had a project he was working on both with the meditation group and in his job. But his boss was threatening to move Bob to another office. The move would remove him from his present project, and he would not be in a position to effect and assist some peace effort that was going on. Neither Peter nor Bob gave me details, and I wasn't asking. Bob felt that without being in his present position, the effort would fall.

At lunch, he asked Peter for ideas on how to get beyond these seemingly insurmountable walls. Peter said he had no idea, but he felt the answer would come to them. In I walked. And there we all sat, a little amazed at what was happening.

Peter asked if I could get in contact with David and ask him for his thoughts on the matter. Since I had been working with the Cottage for over two years, it was easy for me to get in touch with David and I was well-practiced at it. But I had never done it in such a public situation. My main concern was whether or not I could hear David while people were staring at me. It was not something I was used to, and it was their focused presence in the room that I had questions about. Would it create an interference and cause me not to hear accurately? I decided I'd just have to give it a shot and see what I could come up with. I connected with David and told him the situation. He suggested that he meet with Bob right after my talk with Peter. I would be operating as their middleman. (I'd tell David what Bob was saying and then I'd tell Bob David's response.) To my relief, I could hear David clearly.

I continued telling Peter about the Cottage and gave him the rest of the information that I had given him in my dream. When we finished, I stretched out on the floor to get comfortable, and by distancing and lowering myself a little from the others, I thought I might avoid some of the energy their focused presence was creating in the room. In short, I was doing everything I could think of to give myself a better chance at hearing David.

The conversation between David and Bob went well. I could hear David clearly, which was important since the two were talking about a situation that was in an area in which I had no knowledge. I had to pass along precisely what each was saying because I couldn't risk inserting my uninformed interpretation. First of all, David was well aware of the work Bob was doing and spoke with clear knowledge of Bob's situation. David gave him advice about priorities and presentation. The only other thing I remember from their hour-long conversation was David telling Bob that he needed to discover the power of his own integrity and learn to stand his ground in his job. If he tried to appease or compromise in an effort to keep his present job, he was going to create problems for himself. And with that, the conversation was over.

While I was still hooked up with David, Peter asked me to ask him if he got the report Peter sent him back in the 1950s. Without hesitation David said, "Yes. I have it right here." Clearly Peter had not expected that answer. He was beyond surprised. I remember thinking that Peter was literally close to falling off the couch and that I had never seen such a strong reaction from him. David then said that he wanted to meet with Peter about the report. Peter told him he had a free day on September 24, when he would be returning to the area and offered this as a meeting date. David asked for a preliminary meeting to be held sooner, if at all possible. Peter's only other free time, between May 22 and September 23 was the next day, May 23. He had three hours in the afternoon, starting at 3 o'clock. David asked him to pencil us in and told me I had to be there to act as middleman again.

After I disconnected from David, I asked Peter what that report was about. He told me that back in the 1950s, he and several others did some "planetary work with space brothers." At the conclusion of their work, Peter wrote a report, *An Introduction to the Nature and Purpose of Unidentified Flying Objects,* and sent copies to twenty-six prominent scientists, world leaders and spiritual leaders that were on a list Peter's wife, Eileen, was been given in guidance. The list included Winston Churchill; the Deputy Director of Intelligence at the Air Ministry, who was responsible for the study of UFOs, Air Chief Marshall Lord Dowding; and His Royal Highness Prince Philip. Peter was to verify that each person on the list had received their report. Getting the report to these people was not simple because they each had layers of staff around them who could divert the report before it got to the right person, and Peter had wonderful stories about the unusual, outrageous, even magical things that occurred that enabled him to get those papers to each person. He had been able to verify that twenty-five of the people had indeed received their copy of the report. However, he had never been able to verify one report—the one sent to President Dwight David Eisenhower.

After giving me a thumbnail description of the report, Peter asked some more questions about the Cottage and my life there. He didn't blink an eye at what I was saying. In fact, it all made sense to him—including my involvement with their work. I told him I was glad it made sense to one of us.

That evening at the Cottage, I asked David what the meeting would be about tomorrow, but he would only tell me it had to do with Peter's report.

Chapter 13

Peter Caddy

MAY 23, 1984

I HAD THE SECOND OF TWO restless nights in a row, something that was uncharacteristic for me. During breakfast at the
Cottage, I talked to the men about my fears and apprehensions
around my new role as middleman for the Cottage and especially
about my concern for accuracy. They assured me I was doing fine.
I realized that the only way through these apprehensions was to
keep moving forward.

I arrived back in the suburbs where Peter was staying right at
3 o'clock, just as a serious thunderstorm started. He met me at the
door and took me upstairs to a small attic room where we had privacy. The storm continued throughout the entire meeting with
David, and since Peter and I were in an attic room, we had to
speak over the sounds of thunder and pelting rain. When I connected with David, he was with Hyperithon, a close friend of his
who is the head of the White Brotherhood science and technology division. They were joined by Butch, a member of David's
Cottage team, who was there to take notes. On our end, it was
Peter, me and the thunderstorm.

David got right down to business. He was planning a mission,
and this meeting was to see if Peter wanted to do more multilevel
work that would build on what he did in the 1950s and the report
he had written. In a nutshell, David wanted to activate the new
Aquarian leylines for the global government/military arena. The
mission would involve a large group of spacecraft and their crews,

plus a major landing attempt at Mt. Shasta in California. It would be a massive, coordinated and en masse action shifting the activation from the full Piscean government/military leyline grid to the full Aquarian government/military leyline grid.

David continued. Peter's job would be to locate a suitable site on Mt. Shasta that would serve as ground zero from where the shift would be triggered. This would be relatively easy for him to accomplish since he was now living in Mt. Shasta, California, and knew the mountain well. Peter was also to get the right people to that site to function as witnesses. My job would be to work with nature to prepare the site for this mission and to act as liaison between the Cottage and those chosen to witness the mission at Mt. Shasta. David's job was to put together the whole shebang.

After he finished giving us an overview of the mission, David asked if Peter and I would like to participate. Peter agreed immediately, both to the plan and the goal. I don't think it occurred to him to say no. I was a bit overwhelmed by it all—I had not been prepared for this beforehand—but I agreed to it anyway. Overwhelming or not, it sounded important. (That's another understatement.)

David told Peter to make sure he penciled us in for that open date on September 24, when we would all meet again. Then he told me I needed to go to Mt. Shasta and begin my preliminary nature work at the site Peter found before the September 24 meeting. Peter and I both said fine, and that was it.

The business completed, David, Peter and I continued talking. It was the most normal-feeling conversation for me to be a part of, only we were talking about some beyond-normal things and one of the participants happened to be dead—or so they say. David spent a fair amount of time telling Peter about how I was getting to the Cottage and about the Split Molecular Process I was using to accomplish it. The two of them talked about simultaneous lifetime experiences, as well. Finally, David and Peter expressed that they were each looking forward to working with one another, I agreed to meet with David at the Cottage that evening, and we ended the meeting.

When Peter and I were alone again, he said he was pleased that his earlier "space brother work was not for naught." He had no problem accepting any of what David said. I, however, couldn't believe this was happening.

Then Peter addressed my life at the Cottage again. He said he had heard of people shifting from one body to another, but he had never met anyone who was doing it consciously. He also said that during their space brother work in the 1950s, one of their group experienced his own simultaneous lifetime as one of the space brothers who was commanding one of the mother ships, and it had been a difficult experience for this man to take in. I had never met the man, but I had heard quite a lot about him and respected him greatly, and it was encouraging to me that he, too, had diffi-culty wrapping his mind around this type of experience. The simultaneous-lifetime business was something I had dealt with in the early months of my Cottage life. Although it had nothing directly to do with the Split Molecular Process that I was using to shift back and forth between the two levels (Perelandra and Cot-tage), it was an experience that helped open the Cottage to me and I had to address it during those early days. (Just in case you're asking the question right now, let me answer: No, I am not also one of the men at the Cottage. Sorry. I'm my own somewhat ex-panded person. Once again, I refer you to the book *Dancing in the Shadows of the Moon.*) Our conversation went on with Peter asking a lot of questions about the nuts and bolts of what I was doing to get to and from the Cottage.

It was time for me to leave and for Peter to get ready for yet another evening with his adoring fans. He gave me his address and phone number at Mt. Shasta, and told me he would let me know as soon as he found the mission site on the mountain. It was a large mountain, and it might take him some time to locate the right spot. When we parted, I joked that since neither of us had anything else planned that summer, why not work in a major global mission. In that understated English way of his, he said this kind of thing keeps life from becoming boring.

◆●◆●◆

By the time I left, the thunderstorm was over. I got into my truck and started the long trip back to Perelandra in rush hour traffic. I must admit that I felt I was in a fog. I simply could not believe this was happening—that I would go to California, to Mt. Shasta this summer to prepare for…what? Some spacecraft landing? This was nuts. This was exactly the kind of thing that drove me crazy. I hated the term "space brothers." I always thought that people who talked about this stuff were goofy, and I had successfully kept them at arm's length—until now. Furthermore, I couldn't believe that on the basis of my middleman translation between Peter and David, Peter was going to get a bunch of people to come to a mountain in California to witness something. I felt out of my league and over my head. My god, what if I had made a mistake, gotten confused about what David was saying and said the wrong thing to Peter? It was one thing to alter my own actions and life based on my ability to perceive communication accurately from one level to another. Now I was impacting others' lives. The idea made me uncomfortable. The whole notion of space brothers, spacecraft and mother ships was, quite frankly, nuts. And at that moment, I felt very, very nuts.

That was when I got stuck in a major traffic jam on the Washington Beltway.

I turned on the radio to see if I could find a traffic report. And sure enough I did. Traffic was backed up for miles on both loops of the Beltway because some guy was jogging down the median strip—naked. (Bet you were wondering where the naked man came in.)

I had two choices at this point: Either sit in traffic and think about David's meeting or think about the naked man. I chose the naked man. I wondered what in the world would make a man jog down the median strip of a major highway at rush hour minus all his clothing. Granted it was a pleasantly warm day, but I didn't think this warranted a public trot in the buff. And such an interesting choice of locations. He must be crazy.

But what about all these people in cars who were barely moving because everyone was slowing down to look at a naked man. No matter how he appeared, whether he was well-toned or a complete physical disaster, it didn't seem to warrant a major traffic jam during rush hour just so people could gawk. After all, it was only a naked man. The gawkers had to be crazy, too.

All of a sudden, the naked man was walking beside my truck. He wasn't really there, but he was there in my mind's eye. He was looking right at me, and he was saying, "Don't worry, Chickadee. You're not the one who's nuts. No one really understands sanity anyway." Well, I couldn't help it. I smiled. This situation I was in

the middle of, this monster traffic jam caused by a naked man and a bunch of gawkers, made David's meeting sound reasonable. I didn't think it could happen, but now that meeting seemed sane. I saw that sitting in my truck thinking about David, Peter, Mt. Shasta, spacecraft, leylines and mother ships was the only sanity in the midst of everything else going on around me at that moment. And that's when peace settled over me—over my mind, my thoughts and my very being.

By the way, I never actually saw the naked man. By the time I got to his location, he had either exited the median strip and the Beltway or had been carted off.

———————— ◦━◦◦ ————————

I returned to the Cottage that evening. The men were sky-high. (Pardon the implied pun.) When I met with David, he told me this thing was coming together just the way they had hoped and that they had officially named it the Mt. Shasta Mission. I told him I was already getting ideas about what I was to do at Mt. Shasta, and it looked like I would be testing to discover the environmental impact such a landing might have on the site.

Later that evening, I had a minor relapse and informed the men that they were all crazy. That's when I told them about my adventure with the naked man.

Chapter 14

Gettysburg Battlefield

PHASE TWO

THE NEXT DAY THE ACTIVITY around the Cottage picked up dramatically. Phone calls were made, meetings were scheduled, planning discussed—all for the Mt. Shasta Mission.

I wanted to duck the hubbub, so I went to Perelandra a little early. I decided that, on this day after finding out about the mission, I needed to put my hands in soil and not think about anything but the Perelandra garden.

March, April and May are my busiest gardening months. Each garden task and all the planting are done according to intricate timing that is reflected in the schedule that I get from nature. It creates an amazing weave of activity that results in a strong, vibrant garden. Thinking back now, I remember that I didn't get my first garden assistant until around 1991, so I can't explain how I managed to keep to that schedule without missing a beat during the Gettysburg/Mt. Shasta Mission time. But somehow I did.

Of course, that day in May as I tried to forget everything I had learned the previous day, I couldn't stop thinking about the meeting with Peter and the mission. I realized that the garden was now a multilevel laboratory for working out the processes needed for the mission. And I had a feeling that I would be using the Battle Energy Release Process and the other techniques that I had worked with at Gettysburg, as well.

For the next few days, I also thought about my fears and hesitations about my new role in this mission. Once again, I did not feel up to the task. The Cottage men told me these feelings were normal and that the apprehensions would lessen as I got more in-volved with the mission work. They also felt that a healthy dose of nerves at critical times keeps a person honest and on their toes. In short, they seemed to feel that I was up to the task.

On May 29, I needed to schedule a return trip to Gettysburg for phase two of the battlefield work, and I needed to find out what I was to do. I already knew that this was not going to be a repeat of the Battle Energy Release Process and that planting comfrey was involved. I set up a coning with nature and had the following session.

GETTYSBURG BATTLEFIELD
PHASE TWO

As you already know, you will need to plant comfrey within the boundaries of the Gettysburg Battlefield. There are three phases to the completion of the work there. Phase one, completed by you, David and Salvesen in March, was the initial clearing, release and rebalancing of the battlefield area. This set the stage for phases two and three. The battlefield has now begun its movement back to its nature balance and, if you so choose, you could consider the Battle Energy Release work complete. However, because of the significant role Gettysburg played in the destiny of the United States—and the rest of the world, when one takes into account the impact post—Gettysburg United States has had on it—there are two additional stages to complete if all of the ramifications surrounding Gettysburg are to be dealt with. In light of the Mt. Shasta Mission, these last two stages are now essential.

As you already know, between the completion of phase two this year and spring of next, certain souls will be drawn back to Gettysburg to experience an internal shift and release regarding their personal karmic connection to that battle. Besides freeing themselves, this will also free the battle itself from the karmic bonds it holds with participants of the battle. This will allow the energy of that battle to move fully onto the levels of its higher intent and restore it fully to the level of its higher purpose. It is this restoration that will be key to the Mt. Shasta Mission. The energy of the higher purpose contained and played out upon the Gettysburg Battlefield will have a direct bearing on the Mt. Shasta Mission. (Just how, we suggest you leave for later.)

Phase two, the planting of comfrey, is to facilitate the internal shift of the souls who will be drawn to the battlefield. Comfrey essence assists the healing of higher soul damage that may be the result of this lifetime or another lifetime. The "call" has not gone out yet to these souls and will not go out until the comfrey is planted. Your concern that any delay on your part in getting the comfrey to Gettysburg might be hindering what is to occur there with these souls has been misplaced. The timing for your return is quite fine. We fully recognize your desire to complete phase two, and we are cooperating with you.

When you arrive at Gettysburg, David will tell you where the comfrey is to be placed. Open the coning (as you have today), and include in it the Overlighting Deva of the Gettysburg Battlefield. The combined insight of this deva, along with the intent of the phase two framework held within the White Brotherhood, will feed into David, and he will intuitively know where to direct you. This teamwork (you, David, nature and the White Brotherhood) is also setting the tone for the Mt. Shasta Mission. So although there may be a number of ways to approach phase two, this particular way has been set up for a specific purpose and will be referred back to in the future.

As for phase three, we can only tell you at this point that you will need to return to the battlefield in the spring of 1985. By this time, the Battle of Gettysburg will be released from all karmic ties and can be fully raised to the level of higher purpose. The co-creative and cooperative nature of that phase-three shift will hold great importance. We suggest that next spring you open this coning and receive full insight into phase three. You will be directing that phase's shift.

❧

I shifted a copy of this session to David so that he would know what nature was saying. I was surprised to learn that the Gettysburg Battlefield work itself was going to link with the Mt. Shasta Mission. As I said, I thought I would only be using what I learned at Gettysburg for the mission.

Salvesen couldn't return to Gettysburg with me, so I called Laura Townsend, the woman who was present at my first meeting with Peter Caddy. She said she would be delighted to accompany me and suggested we go that Friday, June 1.

I drove up to and into Gettysburg knowing exactly where I needed to go and how to get there. I was no longer a stranger, and headed right to the Eisenhower Tower because my gut feeling was that this was where I was to begin. Things were a little different now. It was a beautiful, warm, sunny June day, not a cold, windy March day, and there were busloads of kids all over the place, many scampering up and down the Eisenhower Tower. Laura and I climbed the tower. We did not scamper.

At the platform, I opened the coning, connected with David and told him (silently, so as not to frighten the tourists) where I was and that I was going to check the battlefield to make sure the first work held. I then connected with the Deva of the Gettysburg Battlefield and tested that, in light of the Battle Energy Release Process work, the battlefield only needed Zinnia essence. Other than this, the work was holding well. I put the needed essence drops in a spoon and held it out as nonchalantly and inconspicuously as possible. I discovered something important: If you appear only slightly mad, people will give you wide berth and ignore you.

I asked David where to plant the comfrey. He said I was to go to the Copse of Trees and plant the comfrey in a triangle configuration nearby—not *in* the Copse,

Fig. 3: Copse of Trees.

but *near* it. With my marching orders in hand, Laura and I headed back down the tower and over to the planting site.

The Copse of Trees is a circle of trees, approximately 100 to 150 feet in diameter. *(Fig. 3)* The Copse is part of the High Water Mark where Pickett's Charge was halted on July 3, 1863, and it was the climax of the battle at Gettysburg. Also it was then the #1 stop on the tour map.* The bus and tourist activity at the Eisenhower Tower was nothing in comparison to what was going on at the Copse of Trees. I quickly saw that it was a good thing I didn't have to plant the comfrey *in* the Copse because it was surrounded by a tall, lethal-looking pointed iron fence. I felt certain that David had remembered the fence, and I also felt certain that he made a point (pardon the pun) of telling me not to plant inside the Copse because he could visualize me climbing over the fence and impaling myself. This turn of events would be counterproductive to my goal that day.

So Laura and I strolled around the Copse area among the crowd looking for a good place to plant comfrey. It is illegal to plant things anywhere on the Gettysburg Battlefield. (God, I do

---

* Since 1984, the tour map has been revised and the High Water Mark and Copse of Trees are now the #15 stop on the map.

hope the statute of limitations has expired on this offense.) I had the three plants, a hand trowel, a gallon bag of potting soil and a gallon bottle of liquid seaweed and water mix (fertilizer) in a picnic basket, along with a towel and lemonade that Laura had brought so that it would appear we were looking for a picnic spot—something that was not illegal. We found an area among some rocks and honeysuckle where the grounds keepers obviously could not mow. To continue our illusion, we spread the towel on the ground, sat down and drank lemonade. All the while, I was stabbing the ground around me with the trowel to find three spots in a triangle alignment where I wouldn't hit rock after one inch. This wasn't going to be easy.

I finally found my three spots, quickly planted the comfrey and liberally watered them with the seaweed/water mix. I got up and stood back to look at the finished results. Thankfully, the plants looked like they belonged. Just to make it official, I told nature the plants were in. Then, per nature's instruction, I put out a silent call to all who needed to return to the Gettysburg Battlefield for healing. Because the Copse of Trees was the #1 stop on the tour map, I knew most visitors would make it to that spot. For those who were there because of phase two, nature would shift comfrey energy from the plants to their systems, thus making sure they had the support they needed for easy and comfortable release and healing.

And that completed phase two. Immediately I felt a tremendous sense of relief. I had no idea how much phase two had been weighing on me. Now I felt light, even giddy. It surprised me a bit that Laura felt the same and that the phase two process had affected her, as well.

When I finally got to the Cottage that evening, David told me that Hyperithon had called to confirm that phase two at Gettysburg was complete and in motion, and to give me his heartiest congratulations. I know the words "in motion" begged for a question or two, but frankly, I was too tired to ask or to care. My part of the job was successfully completed. I went to bed.

The next day I just relaxed and putzed around the Perelandra garden. I enjoyed myself so much, I took a second day off.

Chapter 15

The Summer of '84

As the days wore on, I turned my attention to settling the garden in for the summer. I also turned my attention to the processes and procedures nature was telling me I would need for the work I was to do on the mountain in California once Peter Caddy located the mission site.

Had this been it for the summer, I would have had a gentle, quiet, typical groundbreaking time in my garden with nature. But, of course things got more…well, let's just say interesting.

I made two trips back to Gettysburg with people who were keen on seeing the battlefield with me in light of my work there. Both times I checked the comfrey plants to make sure they hadn't died.

In mid-June, I worked with nature on a new development: the Post-Death Process. This is a process where we connect with the electrical system of an animal or person who has just died, and assist their death and post-death healing process by testing for and administering flower essences to them. Nature shifts the essences into the deceased's electrical system. The impetus for the development occurred when I worked with a dog that had just been hit by a car close to Perelandra.

About a week later, I had a lengthy meeting at the Cottage with Hyperithon about the process, how it could be set up to assist humans, and what my doing the process might mean for me. He told me that I would not be inundated with a never-ending line of people seeking help after death, and anyway, only those who are open to using essences would seek my assistance. Also, I needed to do the process within the first seventy-two hours after a person's death. Both things shortened the line tremendously. Hyperithon explained that by administering essences in that first seventy-two hours, the person's initial post-death healing is greatly accelerated. (See Appendix C for the Post-Death Process.)

At the end of June, a friend from the Netherlands flew in for a two-week visit. A visit I was looking forward to turned into an exhausting and frustrating time for me—and I suspect the same was true for her, as well. She had come to hear about the Cottage. (The Cottage team and I had decided back in 1982 that, as long as I was comfortable, it was fine to tell friends about what I was doing.) Once she arrived, she wanted to hear about the Cottage, then she didn't, then she did, then she didn't, then she did, then she got angry because we weren't talking about *her* life, then she didn't want to talk about her life and got angry because I wasn't telling her more about the Cottage…I didn't need this. But that was a time in my life when I was prone to accommodating people's silliness because I thought it was the polite thing to do. One of the wonderful things about aging is that we old codgers get a different perspective on life and tend not to put up with that kind of crap. Had this occurred today, I'd be taking my houseguest to a pleasant local motel and telling her to call me when she figures out what the hell she wants. To both our relief, she returned to the Netherlands on July 7.

On July 16, Salvesen visited me at Perelandra for a special procedure I was to do for her. She was to receive a transmitter that would give her a direct hookup with Hyperithon, and I needed to assist with that process. Hyperithon had offered her a transistor, and she felt drawn to accept. It was as simple as that. To assist, I needed to be physically present at both the Cottage and with

Salvesen in my cabin at Perelandra. When I arrived at the Cottage, Hyperithon was there to meet me, and when we were ready on both levels, he handed me a small, gold transistor that was about one-quarter the size of a dime. He placed it in my left hand (at the Cottage) and told me to position my right thumb (at the cabin) about an inch or two above Salvesen's forehead. With Hyperithon's direction, I shifted the transistor from my left Cottage hand to my right cabin thumb, then moved it as an energy package across the inch of air space and, finally, into her forehead. I felt the transistor energy pass through me and smoothly shift into her forehead. When it was over, I was no longer holding the transistor at the Cottage.

Hyperithon now needed to activate the transistor. For this, he held my left Cottage hand and moved energy through me, into my cabin thumb (still an inch above her head) and, from there, moved it directly into the transistor in her forehead. Once again I could feel the energy move through me, and as it activated the disk, Salvesen's eyelids fluttered. The entire procedure took thirty-five seconds.

Once the job was complete, I gave Salvesen the "phone number" for "dialing up" Hyperithon, and she tested the transistor to make sure it worked. I already knew about the phone number and the transistor because Hyperithon had placed one in my forehead several years earlier. Salvesen told me that as soon as the transistor was shifted into her forehead, a pressure she had experienced in that area for almost a year was released.

By July 29, I had been experiencing head and neck pain for several days. Since I began going to the Cottage two years before that, it wasn't unusual for me to have some kind of pain or glitch as a result of physically acclimating to this new life and the two bodies. Normally, when the pain popped up, I would visit Salvesen in her office and she would adjust my body according to its newest need.

On July 29, the pain in my head was worsening and I couldn't get an appointment with Salvesen for two weeks. I knew I wasn't going to have the patience to live with the pain for two weeks, so I opened a coning and said, "I need help. Can someone help me?" It was as easy as that.

From the coning, Hyperithon began talking me through my first multilevel medical session. For this, I had to split so that I was physically present both at the Cottage and at Perelandra. He explained that to work on me at Perelandra, both bodies needed to be activated so that they could be addressed simultaneously. I needed for David to sit by my side at the Cottage because, Hyperithon explained, David's presence would stabilize both bodies during the session. After I lay down and David positioned himself, Hyperithon told me that he was connecting me to the White Brotherhood "medics," and that all I had to do was give them the go-ahead to work on me, lie still and let them do their job. This was simple enough, so I said, "Do it."

They began by gently holding my head for awhile—at least, that's what I felt they were doing because I could not see the medics. It was a comforting experience, and I could feel myself relaxing. Then they began the "real" work. I felt things happening in my head, in my diaphragm, under my sternum, the pelvis, the diaphragm again, the head—the right femur rotated in, and the pelvis shifted down toward the floor for a second time. Each time they rotated the right femur, I felt emotion rise and I would cry. At one point, I sensed the medics wanted me to give them permission to continue, so I did. That's when they worked on my head one more time.

When my body parts stopped "moving around," we talked—for the first time since the session had begun. They said that this was a medical procedure I could use from that point on and that it could be done with or without Salvesen's presence. I told them that I wanted to pursue this thing, and they gave me details on how to set up the coning and the sessions. They recommended that I work with them frequently and urged me not to hesitate contacting them if I felt pain anywhere. With that, they suggested I close the session (which they then told me how to do) and go for a short walk both at the Cottage and Perelandra.

As I walked, I could feel distinct differences, especially in my Perelandra body. I no longer had neck pain, there was no pressure or pain in my head, my hip sockets were operating differently, and I had a deeper lumbar arch that made me feel more stable, more balanced. It also felt like the walking was "greasing" me structurally and pumping the cerebrospinal fluid (CSF) more strongly.

Four days later, I had a medical session with Salvesen present so that she could see what I was now doing. I set up at the Cottage and in Salvesen's office, and was told to have David seated at my head at the Cottage and Salvesen seated at my head at the Perelandra end. When I settled in, Salvesen tested both bodies (something she had been doing with me over the previous two years) and found that my Perelandra body was fine, but my Cottage body's pelvis was out. She did not adjust it. We'd see what this team could do.

Then, I told the "medics" to begin. My entire right side felt like it was being gently tilted, then lowered. This was relaxing—especially the lowering part. They did that three times. Then they did the same thing twice to the left side. As they worked on my head, Salvesen cupped her hands around each side of my head, holding them two inches away. She said she could feel energy passing from one side of my head to the other side. Next, the medics did a lot of work on the diaphragm area.

Salvesen saw two "supports" forming, one from the left leg to the right shoulder and the other from the right leg to the left shoulder. They created an X, with the supports crossing at my diaphragm. When the medics finished their work, I felt a heightened stabilizing effect from the X. Salvesen was instructed to test me for essences, and I tested for three to be taken at the Cottage level only. The Perelandra body was clear and the Cottage pelvis was now aligned. Salvesen was asked if she understood the relationship between the X stabilization, the point at the diaphragm where the supports cross and the head balancing. She said she could feel that relationship, but she didn't understand it intellectually. They assured her that she would understand after observing further sessions as they continued to work on my X.

At the Cottage that evening, Hyperithon joined us for dinner and we discussed the medical sessions I was having. He told me the White Brotherhood medical unit (headed by a physician named Lorpuris) had not been able to work directly with individuals on the Perelandra level because they had difficulty stabilizing the sessions to the degree needed for their work. Having a medical team functioning from one level with a person on another level was not easy. On top of this, I added an additional challenge. They had never before worked with two physical bodies operated simultaneously by one *conscious* soul. Under these circumstances, my two bodies were intricately woven and the balance of either body depended on the balance achieved by the two bodies functioning well as one unit. Hyperithon told me that our success with my medical sessions with Lorpuris hinged on the four-point coning we had created for this medical work. It was this coning that included nature that gave them the stability they needed.

Over the next couple of weeks, Salvesen observed three more medical sessions. After this, I continued the sessions on my own. By September, I had opened sixteen more sessions. Over the next six years, I worked with nature, Lorpuris and my medical team on a regular basis to test and refine this medical process so that we could make it available for anyone to use. In 1991, I introduced the program and published *MAP: The Co-Creative White Brotherhood Medical Assistance Program*. Over 150,000 people have successfully added MAP to their health regimen, it has been listed in a number of alternative health encyclopedias, and some physicians are even beginning to recommend it to their patients.

Back to the summer of '84: In August most of my work in the garden was Mt. Shasta related. I was especially concerned about soil testing because, all of a sudden, I wasn't getting clear test results. On August 11, I had a session with nature to find out what was going on.

Your concern is the preparation of the Mt. Shasta site and how to accomplish this in a co-creative manner. The key here is not simply adjusting the Mt. Shasta ecosystem to bring it into balance. You are also seeking to prepare the ecosystem to support a specific event—the Mt. Shasta Mission. This intent is key and must remain clear in your mind in order to get the accurate information needed for the site preparation. Nature has the information for what you will be doing ready to be tapped into. But two aspects must come together before this information can be unlocked for your use as well as ours as we proceed into the co-creative adventure that lies ahead.

Our suggestions: Go to the mission site. Fully define the site—allow it to integrate into your sensory system and knowledge bank. Then, acting as a connector, open a four-point coning that includes the relevant devic levels, Pan and Hyperithon. Allow Hyperithon to shift in imagery and energy through you the actual vehicle they wish to land at the site. Allow the image and energy to marry with the site, and hold that marriage of the two realities for us while we register what will be needed to prepare the site for a successful mission landing.

We suspect that some preparation work can occur during this fall's visit. But you will most likely have to return to the site just prior to the event in order to finish the work. It would not do the Mt. Shasta mountain ecosystem any good to have to hold an extraordinary, but smaller, ecosystem (that of the site) within its larger whole. You are not seeking to impact or adjust the evolutionary process of the mountain. You are seeking (1) to guarantee that this evolutionary process isn't disturbed while using the mountain site for an extraordinary event, and (2) to learn what this type of event demands from nature in order to be fully stabilized and grounded. In the process, we all learn. However, should current conditions change, we may reverse ourselves and separate the mission site from the mountain in order for it to establish its own rhythm and timing earlier than presently expected. We will inform you of this should it be needed.

We suggest you put the soil tests away for now. You are "jumping the gun" by trying to break down the work for the mission this early. The confusion in today's test results is due to the many options available to you and us (nature) for accomplishing the needed goals. We need more precise input from you—i.e., the marrying of the two realities at the site. Once you return from California, work with the soil tests again. The confusion will be cleared up.

We suggest you take the full soil balancing kit and the full array of flower essences to Mt. Shasta in September just so you'll be prepared for any work that might occur then. The important thing for all concerned in September is that you identify the site and marry the vehicle to the site so that we can get the precise information of what will be needed at that location for the mission.

On August 16, Peter Caddy called me with good news: He had located the Mt. Shasta Mission site. He also verified that it was the site with two "sensitives" who were friends of his. I didn't think their input was going to matter since I knew the Cottage team and nature would be giving the final okay, but I didn't say this to Peter. He said that getting in touch with the potential witnesses was proving effortless, and that everyone he had spoken to was excited about the mission. David had asked me to tell Peter that St. Germain (another member of the White Brotherhood whom Peter had known and worked with for years) was now involved with the mission. Peter responded, "I'll say he is!" He had already gotten information about St. Germain and the mission, and St. Germain was the one who had given Peter the list of names he was to invite to Mt. Shasta as witnesses.

Peter called back a few days later, and we settled on the dates for my California trip—September 10 through September 16.

On August 27, I received surprising news from nature: I was to develop a set of essences—the Perelandra Rose Essences—from the rose bushes growing around the outer perimeter of the Perelandra garden. To my relief, I didn't have to worry about developing the Rose Essences until the following spring when I was to start production. There are fifty-four rose bushes growing in the outer ring, and I have to admit I wondered how many were going to be used for the Rose Essences. In the back of my mind, I was hoping it would not be all fifty-four.

I had been pretty concerned about my role in the Mt. Shasta Mission from the moment I heard about it with Peter. By the end of August, I had calmed down quite a bit as I became more deeply engrossed in the work I would be doing with nature—just as the Cottage men had predicted. However, I was still nervous. It was one thing to be working with nature with new processes in the garden and have a broccoli plant drop dead because of a mistake on my part. It was quite another thing to work with nature in the Mt. Shasta Mission and have a mistake cost us global peace or some such thing. Let's face it, the stakes were a lot higher.

Around this time, I had a vivid dream. I was trying to help a spacecraft land into our physical level, but I was having difficulty. The craft was stuck and just "sitting" in the night sky. It finally landed when I worked with nature and supplied the craft with four times more phosphorus than was available in the land where it was sitting. I experienced tremendous physical stress in my chest while working with this craft. When I woke up, my sternum felt like it had been "exercised," as if the power to get the craft into the physical level came primarily from my sternum. I had felt power surge from that spot during the dream, and I awoke with the residue of the surge and a constriction in my chest.

At breakfast, I told the men flat out that I was not sure if I could take it if the mission did not succeed as a result of my role in it. I felt I was their weak link. I was concerned that I wouldn't be able to step around my fears and that this in itself might adversely affect the mission. As I spoke about these things, I realized I could identify the pressure I had been experiencing in my chest the past few days—and the scream I felt building up inside me the past few weeks. I had held the pressure from my feelings inside, not wanting to burden the rest of the team. I was feeling too young, too inexperienced and tiny.

Even with all that I was saying, none of the men seemed concerned about me. In fact, they were downright calm. Again they reminded me that what I was experiencing was natural and that they would be worried if I didn't have those feelings. David said he was confident that the mission would succeed and reminded me that they had the benefit of a broader perspective about the mission that I didn't have. He strongly suggested that I unload the pressure I was feeling and talk with them about it—often. They were the ones who could understand what I was going through because they were the only ones out of everyone I knew who understood the scope of the mission and why I would be so concerned.

In retrospect, I think I was still expecting them to figure out that I wasn't up to the task, fire me (nicely), give me my consolation prize and get the real professional in. Especially in this early stage of the Mt. Shasta Mission, I felt overwhelmed by the other team members' expertise and experience. In comparison, my qualifications seemed to be lacking. What I didn't understand was the value of my previous eight years of work with nature and my proven ability to function consciously among and between different reality levels.

In early September, I prepared for my trip to California. Hyperithon came to the Cottage for a series of mission meetings and to go over how he and I would work together on the mountain. Along with the Cottage team, we wrote the list of members for the Mt. Shasta Mission four-point coning:

1. Devic Point: Deva of the Mt. Shasta Mission,
   Deva of Mt. Shasta (mountain), Deva of Perelandra
2. Nature Spirit Point: Pan
3. White Brotherhood Point: David, Hyperithon, Lorpuris
4. Earth level human point: myself/my higher self

I knew I would be using this coning for all my mission work, including what I would be doing during this coming trip. I had my pre-trip medical session with Lorpuris and was declared ready for the trip. And I had a final preparation session with nature. I can't say it helped my nerves.

We, like a number of others, are waiting for the results of your work with us at Mt. Shasta. What you fail to realize is that we are not leading or guiding you through this. Rather you, through your work with Hyperithon, are giving us the direction that must be taken for the coming together and successful completion of the mission next year. So, the next move is not ours. It is yours.

As you've speculated, we would like you to work within the new Mt. Shasta Mission four-point coning. There will be no issue of "holding" us in the coning while you do your work. The activated coning will remain "in place" until you close it down after the work. If there is to be specific input from us, you will either receive it directly through your intuition or via the suggestion of any of the others present in the coning on any of the levels. So you see, you will not have to enter the Mt. Shasta work with concerns regarding your connection with us.

After the initial work has been completed and its results have been registered with all concerned, we suggest that there be a meeting prior to your leaving California that includes you, David, Hyperithon, Lorpuris, us in nature and any others David feels would be important to the proceeding. Set this meeting up within the Mt. Shasta Mission coning. The purpose of the meeting is to establish whether there is any follow-up work you should do while you are still there. This can only be determined after the initial results are reviewed by everyone. We also suggest that time be given during that meeting for nature to express its views and suggestions. There might even be the need for a question-and-answer session between the various levels and nature. Again, this is to establish and verify that all the necessary information has been received from the trip. It is not to move into different areas of planning. For this trip, you are our liaison through whom we can gain clear access to new and necessary information.

With this said, we will close. Know that many are with you as you leave Perelandra and go to Mt. Shasta. We truly look forward to being a part of what will happen this week.

Chapter 16

Let the Games Begin

My FLIGHT TO REDDING, California, was uneventful. Peter Caddy and his new wife, Karen, picked me up at the airport and drove me to their home in Mt. Shasta, an hour and a half north of the airport. (Okay, here's were you may need a little help: Mt. Shasta, the mountain, is in the town of Mt. Shasta, California. And all of this is not to be confused with Mt. Shasta, the mission.)

I had dinner with the community of people who lived and worked with the Caddys, and after dinner, they asked me to join them while they dedicated something called a medicine wheel. Afterwards, Peter and two other community members asked me questions about the Cottage, which was when I learned that Peter had filled them in on some of the details of the Cottage and its work. But it was obvious that he had not talked about the mission.

I went to bed in the Caddys' guest bedroom in their basement around 11:30 that evening. I showered, got into bed and shifted to the Cottage. It was especially critical for my two-body system that I continue spending the required number of hours at the Cottage while I was in California. I hooked up a medical session with Lorpuris for calibrating my bodies to the time-zone change, thus eliminating jet lag, and he made sure the two bodies were well synchronized.

As soon as I closed the coning, something strange happened. Without any forethought on my part, I curled up in a *tight* fetal position—that is, my body that was in bed at Mt. Shasta—and I began to shiver uncontrollably. I was also hit with intense feelings of insecurity, and my mind was racing all over the place. It was impossible to go to sleep, so I reopened the medical session. Lor-puris checked my two bodies again and said everything was okay from his end.

Well, I still couldn't get to sleep. As soon as I started to drift off, it was like I hit some internal trampoline and would bounce right back up to a state of alertness. Plus I was still *very cold* and continued shivering. I took another hot shower, but as soon as I got back into the bed, I started shivering uncontrollably again. By morning, I think I had managed to get maybe two hours of restless sleep, and I was annoyed. We were scheduled to go to the mountain that day, and I was going to have to do my work there after almost no sleep. On top of it all, no one at the Cottage could figure out what had happened that night. I could tell they were concerned.

As soon as Peter saw me the next morning, he cheerfully asked how I had slept. I decided not to say the usual, "Oh, fine," and told him what happened. Without missing a beat, Peter said that they had had trouble with that room before. Over a hundred years ago, there was a massacre of Native Americans in the area, and Peter had been told by one of his psychic friends that the guest bedroom was located where a mass grave connected with that massacre had been. He had three local medicine men work on getting the souls out of the grave and moved on, but it didn't solve the problem.

Now last night made sense to me—especially the cold chills and strange emotions. I wanted to pummel Peter for not giving me a heads up about that room. And I knew I would have to deal with the situation that night if I was to get any sleep.

That afternoon, Peter, Karen and Edith Laming, a friend of Peter's and another one of his "sensitives," headed off to the mountain. Peter had planned for Edith to join us, mainly because Edith said she had gotten guidance that she was to join us.

On September 11, I saw Mt. Shasta for the first time. It was
and is beautiful. It is not especially tall, not like the Alps, but it's
majestic, all the same. I thought about how this mountain that I
had previously never seen nor known anything about was now
my office.

We got to the mountain and Edith went off on her own. Peter
and Karen surprised me by saying they had *two* sites to show me. I
had been under the impression that they were going to take me to
the site. Peter and Edith had picked out the first spot together—a
huge, open, flat area complete with a stone "altar" that someone
had erected at one end—that was not very far up the mountain,
called Sand Flat. Peter liked this site because it was easy to get to
(in fact, you could drive to it) and because he was concerned
about the older witnesses. I guess on paper this site was perfect—
for a rock concert—but everything about it rang wrong with me
for the mission. Among other things, I didn't think it had the privacy that was needed. But what did I know? I was just the mission
nature person, and site selection didn't fall within my job description. I opened the Mt. Shasta Mission coning and tested if this
was the site. "No." I asked the question several different ways to
make sure I was getting an accurate response, but I still got a big,
fat, emphatic no. So I told Peter this wasn't the site. Immediately
Karen said she knew where the site was and led us to the one she
had picked out that was near the first rejected spot. I got a negative test response there, too.

Before I could panic (something I was seriously close to doing
at that moment), Karen said, "Follow me." And off she and I went
on a trail that led further up the mountain, leaving Peter to find
Edith. Eventually Karen turned off the trail, and we began a more
strenuous climb up the side of the mountain, over big rocks and
fallen trees. I will always be amazed and impressed with Karen
during this hike. I don't know why, but she chose to wear high
heeled sandals that were held on her feet with skinny straps. I, on

Fig. 4: Mt. Shasta Mission site.

the other hand, was wearing hiking boots. But she didn't let those high heels stop her at all. She was in front of me the whole time and I figured if this woman could trek up the mountain in those silly shoes, I could follow her without complaining.

At one point, I looked up the mountain and saw something… a small bump or hill jutting out from the side of the mountain. In unison and out loud, Karen and I said, "There it is!" and we continued up to the spot that she estimated was at least 8,200 feet up the mountain. We climbed over an enormous fallen tree that was laying at the edge of the spot, and once again in unison we said, "It's full of trees and rocks!"

I couldn't imagine how this could be a site for anything except one camper with a small tent. Because it jutted out from the mountain, it was relatively flat. Large fallen trees that were about three to four feet in diameter fenced in the site in a near-perfect circle around the perimeter of the hill. But there was a forest of enormous live trees and large rocks in the site itself. *(Fig. 4)* Despite this, I strongly felt we had found the site. I reopened the Mt. Shasta Mission coning, asked the question of the hour, and the site tested positive. This was it. But how in the world were they going to land a spacecraft in this mess?

Then it hit me. They needed the rocks, the minerals to stabilize the craft and landing. And nature was telling me it was going to shift the trees and rocks from five-senses form to an energy level beyond form, which would allow the craft to land through the trees and settle into the site as if it had been cleared. Brilliant.

THE FIRST NATURE WORK
AT THE MISSION SITE

We didn't know where Peter and Edith were at this point and I didn't want to wait for them, so I got down to business. First, I walked the circumference of the site around the "log fence" and took time to take in as much of the detail at the site as I could. I looked, I smelled the air, I touched things and I listened. I focused on the coning again, and asked once more, "Is this the site to be used for the Mt. Shasta Mission?" Yes.

From the backpack I had hauled up, I got out six boxes of essences, two boxes of soil balancers, paper and pen, and began working. I had already put together with Pan an outline of how I was to proceed with the testing, but I quickly saw that I needed to allow for flexibility in that outline. In short, nature and I were winging it a bit.

1.   My first question: Did the site need an energy cleansing to prepare for today's work? *No.*

2.   Did I need to clear the site with essences? *Yes.*
       Pan let me know that two tests, each with different focuses, were needed:

       Test A – To prepare for the day's work: Clematis, Comfrey, Zinnia, Larkspur, Yerba Santa.

       Test B – To clear out a "glamour" problem that was attached to the mountain: Orange Marigold, Larkspur, Blue Aster, Elm, Holly .

       Working with Pan, I shifted a drop of each needed essence for Test A to the site. Then I did Test B and shifted those essences with Pan to the site. I was told always to administer whatever was needed for one testing focus before I went on to the next question or test.

3.   Pan let me know that the mountain was ready for the day's mission work. I lay down on the ground and shifted to the Cottage so that I could be present at both locations. I was joined at the Cottage by David, Hyperithon, Lorpuris and Butch. Then Pan told me to expand the Mt. Shasta Mission

coning to include Universal Light, a consciousness I had been working with for over a year and who was already included in the Mt. Shasta Mission itself. With this addition, the Mt. Shasta Mission coning was now set.

Karen was standing off to one side watching me. For some reason, her presence didn't disturb me at all. I felt comfortable, which surprised me a bit because, up to that point, I had only gone through my Cottage process in front of Salvesen and Peter.

4. I was told to test Karen and myself for essences.
   Karen: Yerba Santa. I also got the intuitive hit that her adrenal glands were weak.
   Me: Zinnia, Comfrey.
   We each took the essences that we needed.

5. I tested the site using the vials of soil nutrients I had put together at Perelandra for this work: calcium, silicon, boron, sodium, aluminum, potassium, chlorine, iron, nitrogen, carbon, magnesium, phosphorus, potash, molybdenum, copper, sulphur, manganese, zinc, chromium and iodine.

   Site deficiencies: iron, magnesium, calcium, chlorine, boron, sulphur, aluminum, sodium, molybdenum.

   Pan told me not to supply any of these needed balancers to the soil. I was just to get a readout of the soil to establish a baseline prior to the mission work I would be doing with Hyperithon.

6. I shifted my focus to the Cottage. When I indicated I was ready, Hyperithon held my left hand, created in his mind a miniature energy replica of the spacecraft that was to land on the site, and shifted the energy spacecraft through me at the Cottage and into me at the site. He then moved the

spacecraft through me and into the ground, which was pretty easy since I was already lying on the ground. When it settled on the ground, the spacecraft expanded in size. I didn't move for about thirty seconds to make sure the shift was complete. In my mind's eye, I could see what seemed to me a full-sized spacecraft sitting in the site.

7.   I sat up and retested the site for changes.
     Deficiencies: magnesium, potassium, potash, phosphorus, sulphur, aluminum.
     No longer deficient: iron, calcium, molybdenum, chlorine, boron, sodium.
     I re-checked Karen and myself.
     Karen: She had a serious potassium drain and her adrenal glands were still weak. But she did not need any essences.
     Me: I tested clear; nothing was needed.

8.   I waited about fifteen minutes, then I lay down again and Hyperithon reversed the process by removing the craft energy from the mission site through me there, through me at the Cottage and back to him. He told me to tell Karen that she needed to take a potassium supplement that day and to have her physician check her adrenal glands.

I now understood something about what I was doing with nature on the mountain. It had to do with the impact one biosphere has on another biosphere or environment. In this case, it's the impact of a spacecraft on the site environment. From the testing, I saw there was a natural exchange that occurred between the two environments. The readout of what deficiencies were in the site's soil prior to landing the craft gave us a baseline and defined the playing field we were working with. Then Hyperithon introduced the spacecraft, which is its own environment or biosphere. When it settled into the site, the iron, calcium, molybdenum, chlorine, boron and sodium that had previously been deficient were no longer so. These elements had been drawn to the soil from the spacecraft. However, the spacecraft itself drew minerals from the soil as it settled into the site: magnesium, potassium, potash, phosphorus, sulphur, aluminum. So now we had an idea of what kind of exchange would occur between the site and the craft, and what the site still needed in order to physically support the landing of this spacecraft.

You'll notice that potassium was not deficient in the soil prior to the craft landing. However, after it landed, potassium was now not only deficient in the soil but in Karen, as well. Karen said she saw that spacecraft land in her mind's eye, and she said it was physical to her. It was clear she had experienced it in her sensory system. This told nature and the Cottage team that a high level of potassium would be needed by the craft itself for a successful landing and by the people present. (I have no explanation as to why I did not have a potassium drain during the landing as well. But I didn't.)

<hr />

I had finished the work, which had taken about an hour, pulled myself back together into my one body, closed down the coning and was just telling Karen to eat lots of bananas when Peter came walking up to the site. He told us that Edith was angry that I had ignored her guidance and that she had just gotten new guidance to tell Peter to go find us because she had found a new site. And to prove it was the "true" site, two birds had landed on her outstretched arms as a sign. To me, Edith was proving to be a problem, so to keep things from getting out of control, I agreed I would look at her site. Peter led us to a path that was on the other side of the spot where we had been working, and our trek down the mountain was a lot easier than the trek up had been. On the way, I quietly contacted David and told him about the new developments. He told me the site we just tested was the mission site and, to keep peace, reopen the coning and do the soil test for Edith's spot. He felt that once she saw the test results, she would know that (1) we tried her site, and (2) it didn't hold up in the testing. I really wasn't too thrilled about doing more testing, but the diplomatic approach made sense. It made more sense than thumping Edith over the head and burying her at her site. I didn't have a shovel with me.

We met Edith at her site. It was another wide-open space that was conveniently close to a road. After I set up the coning again, switched to the Cottage and got into the first tests, Edith became increasingly agitated. She left us and began *furiously* pacing off a huge five-pointed star in the middle of her site. This old woman was literally stomping around in the field. And she was angry. I felt like I was being slammed with tidal waves of energy and was having difficulty holding my focus. Hyperithon, sounding alarmed, told me to ask Karen to stand quickly between me and Edith (who was still stomping around) so that I could switch out of the Cottage and close down the coning. When Karen stood between us, she commented that she could feel the waves from Edith pelting her in the back.

I was furious at Edith's rudeness. I was also stunned that someone who had been "in the trenches" for many years could act so irresponsibly. I think she was just angry that I was the one working with the mission and not her. She was older, she certainly did not miss any opportunity letting me know she was more experienced, and who the hell was I, this unknown young nothing that even the birds refused to land on? Now I understood why I had needed to do Test B in step 2: "To clear out a glamour problem that is attached to the mountain." As we drove back to the Caddy home, I could not speak to this woman. Diplomacy was the last thing on my mind.

When we got back to the house, I contacted the Cottage to assure David and Hyperithon that I was fine. I told them that I felt good about the testing at the mission site, that it felt clear and accurate. David confirmed that the site I tested was the one they were going to use.

That evening, I retired to my mass grave to deal with a bunch of dead Indians so that I could get some sleep. Having developed the Post-Death Process, I had an idea about how to approach the situation. But this would be different because I was now working with people who had died over a hundred years prior rather than within the three-day window needed for the process. I was going to have to start the ball rolling and see where it would lead me.

I opened a four-point coning for this process and asked if people from the mass grave had tried to contact me the night before. I got a strong yes, so I asked to be connected with these people. Immediately, I felt a clear, tangible connection, and before me stood twelve gentle, grateful people. With them, I ended up having one of the most wonderful experiences of my life.

Pan told me they needed flower essence testing so that they could balance, detach and move on. They stood in a line, and one by one, I worked with them. I'd finish working with one, he/she would fade out of sight, and the next one would stand before me. I did regular surrogate essence testing and had each put a hand on my knee (I could feel the warmth from their touch) to connect their electrical system physically with mine. Then, I tested them for essences using the surrogate kinesiology testing method and placed a drop of each needed essence in each person's mouth. I saw no drops fall to the floor, so I assumed the drops were administered successfully.

Some of them touched my cheek; some had tears in their eyes. Some quietly said what I thought was "thank you." There were adults and children, including a set of young twins. I must say, working with these people was healing for me, as well—especially after my experience with Edith.

When I finished working with the Indians, Pan told me to balance and stabilize the grave-site area. That was easy since I was sitting in the middle of it. Pan explained that this work would "close the door" on the grave so that no other souls would be drawn into the site. The medicine men that Peter had gotten to work on the mass grave before may very well have helped some souls release, but the site itself was acting as a magnet and drawing more souls to it. Balancing and stabilizing the soil would eliminate the magnet effect, thus keeping the grave site clear.

Once completed, Pan explained that what I experienced the night before was the result of these Indians trying their best to contact me. They knew what help they needed and they knew I could provide that help, but they had not meant to cause problems or discomfort when they tried to contact me. The simple explanation is that they didn't know how else to get to me. Because their situation was thwarting their evolutionary development, they had only the most rudimentary skills for connecting between levels. What I experienced from them the night before was the result of giving me their best shot: extreme cold, emotions of insecurity causing me to ball up in a fetal position and mental disruption. Then it was up to me to figure out what was happening. Once I called them to me from within the coning, they were given the stable environment in which to connect with me and I experienced them in the "normal" fashion.

I finally completed the work after two hours. I remember feeling especially relaxed and tranquil when it was over. Dealing with Edith on the mountain was crazy. Dealing with the Indians in the mass grave was sane. I took a shower, returned to the Cottage, had soup with the men while we talked over the day and my adventure with the Indians, and went to bed at both locations. I slept peacefully.

Chapter 17

The September 24 Meeting

I RETURNED TO PERELANDRA on September 16, after spending the week in California testing the soil in Peter's numerous
gardens (at his request) and speaking with the board members of
his community about nature's role in community balance (also at
his request). When I had the scheduled Cottage/nature meeting,
I found out the September 11 work was holding and no one had
anything else for me to do, so I did not have to return to the
mountain. At Perelandra, I refocused my attention on the garden
while the Cottage men did whatever it was they were doing with
the information from my mountain work.

On September 24, Peter came to Perelandra for the next Cottage
meeting. Before we got started, he gave us an update on Bob's
progress at the Pentagon. Everything David had stressed to Bob
in the spring when they met had worked out perfectly. He used
David's advice and stood his ground. Instead of being fired, he
got transferred to a more advantageous position. This was terrific
confirmation of that spring meeting and just what I needed to
boost my confidence for this meeting.

We had in attendance on the Perelandra side of the "table"
Peter, Salvesen (David had asked that Salvesen join us) and me.
On the Cottage side of the table, we had David, Butch, Tex, Hyperithon, Lorpuris and Universal Light. I connected everyone in
the mission coning, and David conducted the meeting.

First, he gave an overview of the purpose and goals of the mission to make sure Peter and Salvesen were clear about what was

planned. He told us that it would be advantageous for all concerned for the leylines that have supported the Piscean military
and government structures and activities throughout history and
around the globe to be deactivated en masse. And it would be
equally advantageous for the new leyline grid supporting the
Aquarian structures and activities to be activated *simultaneously*
and en masse. It would be a massive and unprecedented under-
taking, but if accomplished, it would give each person on Earth
the opportunity for an exceptional level of efficiency and effec-
tiveness when establishing the needed changes.

As I understand it, leyline changes traditionally occur piece-
meal. But this creates "evolutionary lag time" for us, and progress
is more challenging. David felt he had the right team, and it was
time to attempt the en masse changes. He explained that to do
this, thousands of spacecraft would be positioned beyond Earth's
atmosphere in a pattern mirroring the layout of the Piscean gov-
ernment/military leylines. Command central would be at the Mt.
Shasta site, and the shifts would be directed from there.

Another of David's goals, and one that would create an additional major challenge, was to make sure the craft at the site and
the people aboard the craft (the team, crew and invited guests)
were fully in five-senses form and that each of the witnesses Peter
was inviting would be able to see and hear them. The issue about
having the Mt. Shasta Mission in five-senses form was a critical
one to David and the team. He wanted the new evolutionary impulses and government/military information to be fully accessible to everyone on the planet, no matter what sensory range they
had. Everyone was different. So to cover everyone, the mission had
to be in five-senses form.

He then announced that the mission date would be between
July 14 and July 17, 1985, with the target date July 15. They would
be landing at the mountain site at dusk. And he confirmed that

the site's privacy, size and natural stabilizing support that were key to the mission had been approved.

Peter asked if a mother ship would be landing. When David told him yes, Peter said he thought the diameter of the site was too small for a mother ship. (I have to tell you that, at this point, I just let the conversation roll. They were seriously talking about mother ship sizes. How often does this come up in conversation?) David said, "You're thinking of the older ships. Like Japanese cars, the new ones are smaller, more efficient and technically better." (And I'm thinking, "Well, of course. Makes sense. Why would we want an old clunker with a rebuilt motor, retreads and faded vinyl upholstery?")

David then turned to the medical aspect of the mission. My work at the site and Karen's reaction to it confirmed that medical preparation would be needed for all Peter's witnesses and all the invited guests that were coming on the mother ship. Lorpuris would work with the invited guests. Then David asked Salvesen if she would join the team and provide the medical work for the witnesses. To my surprise, rather than just saying yes, she said she would give a definite answer by the end of four weeks, but that she felt it would be yes.

David explained that it was critical that everyone at the Mt. Shasta site be physically stabilized so that their sensory systems functioned well throughout the mission. To this end, Lorpuris and Hyperithon put together a simple process that could be used to prepare the witnesses prior to the mission. It was a process based on what we had done on the mountain.

I.   First, Salvesen would get an initial readout of the witness, establishing their medical baseline: What essences, structural alignments, supplements and cranial adjustments were needed? She would do any needed work, thus aligning and balancing their body.

2.   Then Hyperithon would shift the mission's mother ship as an energy package through me—Cottage body to Perelandra body—and into the system of each witness. (I would need to be present in both places for this process.)

3.   Salvesen would get another readout that would show how each person's body reacted to the ship. With this information, she could shore up and strengthen their weak spots prior to the mission.

4.   Finally, Hyperithon would remove the ship from the witness's system, through me (my two bodies) and then back to himself. Salvesen was to check the person again for any aftereffects of the process.

Peter volunteered to go first. We set up and Salvesen checked him. To start, he had a tight left psoas that was pulling his pelvis out of alignment, a weakened solar plexus, and he needed Cherry Plum essence. His endocrine glands tested strong. He also needed a cranial adjustment—a temporal plate adjustment strengthened with breathing balancing. She did all the work, checked him again and said he was ready. As we had done on the mountain, Hyperithon shifted the ship as energy through my Cottage hand, into my Perelandra hand, and I then shifted it into Peter's system. We waited about fifteen seconds, then Salvesen checked him again. His left psoas was tight again and his pelvis was out on the left—again. He had a potassium, phosphorus and B-vitamin drain. He needed no essences. She gave him what he now needed, then Hyperithon moved the ship out of Peter's body. When Salvesen tested Peter again, he had held and tested clear.

Lorpuris suggested we wait an hour and do the process with Peter once more. He suspected that Peter's body would respond better to the ship after this first experience.

The second landing process did go a little more smoothly for Peter. He had another B-vitamin and phosphorus drain, his thyroid was now weak, and his left pelvis was out again. But it was clear that the more we did the landing process, the more the body learned to identify and successfully sort the experience. We suspected that we would have to do a landing process for all the witnesses three times before they could respond to the ship on the mountain without misaligning, draining or short-circuiting. For this, everyone would have to be at Mt. Shasta several days prior to the mission so that Salvesen and I could work with them. We also decided that Salvesen and I would try to work with any witnesses living on the east coast that winter and spring so that we could make the work load at Mt. Shasta more manageable. (We really needed Salvesen to say yes to the Mt. Shasta Mission.)

David asked Peter about the people he was inviting to the mission. Peter explained he had been getting the "witness list" from St. Germain and felt there would be a total of about twenty to twenty-five witnesses present on the mountain. David warned him about not including any press people because this was not to be some "glitzy publicity show."

David asked if we understood the mission and what we were each to do. Peter restated his understanding of what was to happen on Mt. Shasta, and after making a few minor corrections, David okayed Peter's understanding of the mission. When we ran out of questions, we ended the meeting and I closed down the mission coning.

That's when Peter jumped up and called the first six people on his list. He got everyone right away—which he pronounced a miracle. Salvesen and I listened to the conversation he had with each person. It went something like this (to be read with a warm and cheery British accent):

Hello, _____ . [Name inserted.] Peter Caddy here.
Dwight David Eisenhower is planning a mission to
shift the government/military leylines around the
planet next summer. Are you busy between July 14
and July 17? [Wait while the person checks their calendar.]
No? Good. He will be landing a mother ship at Mt.
Shasta sometime during this period. Would you like
to come and be among the witnesses? [Listen.] Good.
We'll get in touch with you shortly with the details.
Goodbye.

No one seemed to blink an eye at what Peter was saying or at the
imminent appearance of the "dead" Dwight David Eisenhower, as
if they get this kind of phone call every day. All six people said
they would be happy to witness the event, and two even agreed to
meet with Salvesen and me the following Wednesday at Perelandra for their first round of the landing process.

Chapter 18

The First Bodies

SALVESEN AND I MET WITH the first two witnesses, Jack and Ann Winslow, on October 3 at Perelandra. I was a little concerned when they arrived because Jack and Ann were older, in their mid sixties. But I remembered Peter's comments about the people on his list and realized most of them were experienced in this kind of work and, therefore, most would be elderly.

Before getting down to business, we spent half an hour getting to know one another a little. Jack told us he had "an intimate space contact" when he was five years old and had been in contact with space brothers frequently since then. So here I was, face to face with one of those people I had always tried to avoid. But, from all that he was saying, he was a reasonable sounding man who obviously translated information and experience easily between levels. I never did figure out what his work was, but I'm pretty sure it had something to do with space. He also told us he had already had two contacts with David—the first one two years ago and the second one just six months back. He said David's most recent contact was regarding some intelligence work.

Now, I have to tell you that I really didn't know what to do with this conversation. At times he was using a vocabulary I was not at all familiar with, and I didn't know anything about that intelligence work he insisted on describing. So I let his words roll as if this were the most normal conversation a person could have. I nodded my head and, at the right places, calmly said, "Why, yes. Of course." I also didn't ask questions. I had a job to do and grilling Jack wasn't part of it.

I explained David's connection with the Mt. Shasta Mission and the goals and objectives of the mission itself. I also talked about their role as witnesses, as I understood it. I told them about the mother ship landing on the mountain and the need for the witnesses to remain fully aware of what was happening. Then I described the medical work we had done with Peter and explained what we would be doing that day with the two of them.

A few days prior to this meeting, Hyperithon, Lorpuris and I had gone over the landing process that we had used with Peter and refined it a bit. We decided we would try to do the critical shift of the ship without my having to split and be present on both the Cottage and Perelandra levels. We felt that doing this split over and over for all the witnesses would put too much of a strain on me. This time, with Jack and Ann, I would connect with Hyperithon and Lorpuris in the coning, and when the time came for the shift, Hyperithon would move the ship to me using the transistor in my head. (You can get these transistors in the Hyperithon section at your local Electronics and Transistors Store.) I would then shift that energy from the transistor through me, into the person's hand that I would be holding and into their body. If this worked equally as well as the first procedure, it would make life a lot easier for me.

First we worked with Jack. Salvesen did the initial check to establish his baseline: He needed three pelvic adjustments, he had a liver/pituitary weakness, and he needed one essence. After she balanced him, I set up with Hyperithon, who then shifted the ship's energy into my transistor. I moved the ship's energy from me and into Jack. The whole process took about twenty seconds.

I guess Jack wasn't kidding about that long history with space brothers because when the mother ship moved into him, his body strengthened. When we moved the ship into Peter, his body had strongly reacted and Salvesen had to make a fair number of adjustments to restore his alignment. Jack just needed one pelvic adjustment. Everything else held its alignment and balance. No cranial adjustments needed. No essences needed. No supplements. When we removed the ship from Jack, everything held except for that one pelvic adjustment that needed to be done again—and that was it. Obviously, identifying and processing a mother ship was not a traumatizing experience for Jack's body.

Ann was a different story. Prior to the landing Salvesen needed to make four pelvic adjustments for her. Ann also needed one essence. But her cranial plates were aligned. After moving the ship into her body, things got a little dicey. She needed four pelvic adjustments again, her solar plexus and thyroid were weak, and she had a major drain: B-vitamins, phosphorus and potassium. She also needed an essence for the drain. Salvesen determined that for Mt. Shasta, Ann would need to make sure her solar plexus was well covered with some kind of shield (such as a stone or heavy belt buckle) that would reflect energy away from that area. The solar plexus was where the incoming energy at the mountain would hit, and Salvesen felt that no matter how much strengthening Ann could do for her solar plexus between now and the mission, the energy on the mountain was still going to be too much for her. She would also need to drink a lot of comfrey tea during this period before the mission for strengthening her thyroid. When we lifted the ship out of Ann, her pelvis remained aligned, her solar plexus was fine, and she needed no additional adjustments. She also did not experience another B-vitamin drain.

Salvesen later explained that when she was doing the work with these people, she was in an information-gathering mode. She needed to establish a strong neurological foundation with them and she needed to understand clearly where their baseline was—the level of health and structural balance they were coming in with. This way, she would know how to respond to them on the mountain as the ship landed. She also felt they needed a strong pelvic foundation for the mountain or they would "blow out" during the mission. She understood this was going to be a major experience for these people, and she was concerned about who we might have to carry off the mountain.

On the mountain the previous month, Karen had a potassium drain as the ship was shifted into the site. Many of the people Salvesen and I worked with, including Peter and Ann, also experienced a potassium drain along with a B-vitamin drain during their landing procedure. Salvesen said these elements are basic nutrition for the nervous system, and when the nervous system is working overtime, it uses up these elements fast. In this case, the nervous system was working overtime and scrambling to identify, process and sort a mother ship. Hence, the drain.

Neither Peter, Jack nor Ann sensed a shift in their body's energy field when the mother ship was moved in, but all three registered dramatic changes in the body nonetheless. Hyperithon verified that today's procedure was a success, and much to my relief, we could continue using it. We did the landing process just once that day for Jack and Ann. Based on our experience with Peter and seeing how quickly his body learned to adjust to a mother ship, we felt confident that we could do the additional "landings" in California prior to the mission.

The other good news of that day was that Salvesen officially committed to the mission. She told me she had been concerned initially about several changes that were going on at her office and the fact that her daughter's second birthday was right at the time she would have to be at Mt. Shasta. Recently, when I asked what made her commit to the mission, she simply said, "The mission was important." And that was that.

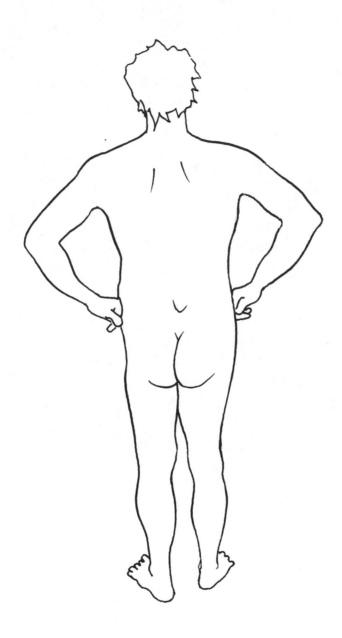

Chapter 19

The Gold Dome

ON THE EVENING OF OCTOBER 15, after I returned to the Cottage for the day, I had a strong gut feeling that I needed to do something with nature that night to protect the mountain site. When I told David what I was feeling, he suggested I check it out right away, and he wanted to sit in while I did this. The only thing I knew to do was open the mission coning and see where it led me. At midnight Perelandra time and 9 P.M. California time, I opened the coning.

Nature wanted me to activate a dome over the site that would function as protection. It was to cover the entire area plus twenty-five feet beyond the site's outside perimeter. I was also to link David, Hyperithon and myself to the dome, and the three of us would remain connected to it until after the mission was completed in July. This way, if anything happened at the site that needed attention, nature would be able to contact any of us directly. Here's what I did:

1. I called for a protection dome to form over the site area, extending twenty-five feet beyond the site's perimeter. Immediately, I saw a high dome of golden light covering that entire area.

2. I tested the dome environment for flower essences: Oak and Comfrey. Pan shifted the essences from my hand (at the Cottage) and infused the drops into the soil at the center of the site.

3.   Pan then told me to do an Energy Cleansing Process for the dome area. I set up for this process and moved the cleansing sheet through the dome, stopping it five feet above the top of the dome. I again tested essences in case anything was needed as a result of the energy cleansing and found that nothing was needed.

4.   I offered my assistance for any maintenance or repair the dome and site might need anytime up to and including the mission. Immediately, I saw a gold beam of light connect the site with the topaz in the center of the Perelandra garden. Then I saw three beams of light move out from the topaz. One beam connected to David (the commander of the Mt. Shasta Mission), one to Hyperithon (the head of the spacecraft division and landing) and one to me (the human working with nature for the mission).

5.   Finally, Pan told me that within three days after the landing, I was to work with nature to release the protection dome and the gold-beam connections between the Perelandra topaz, David, Hyperithon and myself.

The dome process took about an hour to complete. I came out of it convinced that nature had now separated the site from the mountain and set it up especially for the mission. That was a change from the information nature gave me just before my visit to Mt. Shasta. At that point, there was to be no separation of the site from the rest of the mountain until the week before the mission. Now, with the work that had been done on the mountain in September, combined with how the mission was shaping up, nature decided to create the site as a separate, mission-focused biosphere with its own rhythm, timing, balance and stability. And by isolating the site now, we would be minimizing, perhaps even

eliminating, our impact on the rest of the mountain as we prepared for the landing in July.

While working to activate the dome, I felt my co-creative partnership with nature more strongly than ever. I "walked" into this
situation with only a gut feeling and the knowledge that I was to
open the Mt. Shasta Mission coning. From there, nature and I
worked together in an easy-flowing manner. I realized, once again,
how much I love this partnership, and I came out of the experience feeling confident that, with nature, I could do whatever was
needed for the mission.

Chapter 20

Igor Speaks — Again

Iᴛ's ᴛɪᴍᴇ ᴛᴏ ɢɪᴠᴇ ʏᴏᴜ ᴍᴏʀᴇ information about Universal Light. I connected with him back in the winter of 1983, as part of a coning session. Actually, I had a feeling I was to make contact with someone, so I opened a coning session, asked about my suspicions, and Universal Light introduced himself. He suggested we have regular scheduled time together so that he could give me information that would be pertinent to my work. Among other things, these sessions with Universal Light gave me the information on battlefields, nature's role during and after battles and the steps for the Battle Energy Release Process.

I refer to Universal Light as "he." He tends to refer to himself as "we." Actually, he's an it. This is how he described himself to me during our first session together.

You ask who we are. Specifically, we are an intelligence beyond that which you have known. We are basically without individual identity. We communicate to you using the total coning, for we are a force so large and inclusive that simultaneously we can use four separate avenues—the devic, the nature spirit, the White Brotherhood and the earth soul—to come to you. In that way, the information you receive from us is far more balanced than if you tried to bring it through one avenue only. We encompass too great a consciousness to come through one avenue only, but we are neither a collective consciousness nor a collection of souls come together as a group: We are one consciousness. We are massive and great and have existed since the beginning of time. We are beyond the akashic records and enfold not just

Earth but its entire universe. Aware of the balance Earth plays within this universe, we have a greater understanding of Earth's progression from the Piscean Era to the new Aquarian Era—a progression with which we are intimately involved.

One might say that if one could visualize us—our position—one would see us as a gaseous membrane encompassing this entire universe. But since reality is ultimately limitless, one must also see that not only do we encompass this universe, we are the gateway to all the rest of reality that exists. It is as if we are a skin, similar to your own skin. The inside of your skin surrounds your body. The outside of your skin places you in touch with everything else that is around you, everything else that exists. There is a continuous feeding of information in and out through this membrane you call skin. We function in the same way. If you were to picture the transition of a single molecule on Earth, you would see the molecule change, shifting from the Piscean to the Aquarian dynamic. All that was experienced, learned and known in that shift would then be available to all else on Earth. It would then become available to all those around Earth who are keenly interested in and of service to Earth, then to that which is beyond Earth, the solar system and your universe. Ultimately it moves (if one can visualize it) into our level, passes through and becomes totally accessible to, and totally part of, all other reality beyond this universe. Conversely, all knowledge, experience and understanding from all other realities is experienced by us (in that it touches the outside part of our membrane, passes through us and becomes accessible to all that is within this universe).

When you opened the coning, we gave you the image of the universal light, which you took time to look at from every angle. You saw that it is not just light moving in one plane, but as you observed the sides and back of the ball of light you saw its rays moving out in all directions. And that is the image we wish to give you so that you may understand more clearly the scope of our understanding. When we see something on one level or plane, we see that which is happening from every level, every plane. The universal light has vertical and horizontal direction....From all sides of the ball an equal amount of rays move out vertically and horizontally. In essence, *insight is moving in all directions at all times, connecting that which seems to be vertical with all that is horizontal, and vice versa. We give you this imagery so that you may understand our vantage point more clearly. One may talk about us and describe us, but it is not nearly as effective as experiencing us.*

I came out of the session thinking, "Okay. Universal Light is really big—and knowledgeable. And a smidge overwhelming...Maybe more than a smidge." In order for me to wrap my mind around this new, big thing in my life, I needed to make it warm and fuzzy. So I decided to give it personal pronouns (he/him), and I nicknamed him "Igor." Privately I referred to my sessions with him as "Igor sessions." Publically, they're known as Universal Light sessions. But since this story that I'm telling is just between you and me, I'll refer to him as Igor.

On October 17, two days after our work at Perelandra with Jack and Ann Winslow, I received a clear hit to open an Igor session and set it up as a meeting with David present as well.

Universal Light (U.L.): *Well, hello. The preliminary work that has been done regarding the Mt. Shasta Mission has now been completed by all those concerned. That preliminary information has also been received and has registered on our level so that we're very aware of the dynamics of the mission, its balance, its direction and its projections. Until this time, what we had to say about the mission was minimal because we had to wait until this preliminary period was complete.*

What we would now like to suggest is a series of meetings with you. We suggest that not only David and you, Machaelle, be present, but also Tex, Hyperithon and Lorpuris be present during these meetings as well. You will function as the translator for us, and

David will function as your session stabilizer and also conduct the meetings in which a free flow of information and ideas can be expressed among us all.

The Mt. Shasta Mission has ramifications that go beyond Earth itself, and it is now time that a broader picture be considered. We foresee the need for three meetings and suggest that they be held fairly close together. There might be a need for a fourth meeting, but that won't be known until the third is completed. We perceive that you, Machaelle, will not have difficulty in holding the various levels of energy during this more intense meeting process.

We recommend that the meetings begin as soon as possible, for we see you are now entering the next planning stage of the mission. There are broader opportunities you might wish to take into consideration, and it would be best to discuss them before you get too far along in this next planning stage. With that said, we simply recommend that the meetings be held as soon as possible.

Are there any questions regarding what we've said or the meetings themselves?

David: Is there any issue in having others present beyond those you've suggested?

U.L.: *We leave additional participants up to your discretion. There is not a number issue here. As we get into the meetings, you might see that some might need to be present for one of the meetings and not for any of the others.*

Machaelle: What am I going to need in order to stabilize myself during these meetings? [Previously for the days I was to have an Igor session, I needed to eat 90 additional grams of protein and double my intake of carbohydrates in order to remain stabilized throughout the session because Igor's presence created a strong drain in those areas.]

U.L.: *Because of your position as translator and David's as your stabilizer during these sessions, only you two need be concerned about the additional protein and carbohydrates needed for the meetings. This coning may tire the others present just slightly, but it will not throw them off balance physically or drain them. It may even energize them. The key issue here, in terms of nutritional support, is that no one other than you and David need be concerned, and your regular protein and carbohydrate intake for our sessions will hold you for these meetings, as well.*

David: I think we should have the first meeting here this coming Wednesday.

U.L.: *Beginning the meetings next week is fine. Please don't misunder-stand—this is not an emergency situation. We feel strongly, how-ever, that you will want this information and you will want to think about these ideas before you proceed any further with the mission planning.*

We have nothing more to add at this point. We will assume, along with you, that we'll begin the meetings next Wednesday. We'll see you then.

With that, I closed the coning and looked at David for a clue as to what was going on. Either he didn't know, or he wasn't talking.

Chapter 21

Igor Meeting #1

OCTOBER 24

O<small>N</small> W<small>EDNESDAY WE ALL</small> gathered at the Cottage. I opened a four-point coning and included David, Hyperithon, Lorpuris and Tex. I functioned as Igor's translator for the others present. The following is a transcript of that meeting.

U.L.: *Good afternoon. This meeting is to be a free flowing exchange of ideas. I hope at any time you will feel free to stop the proceedings with questions or ideas you might have. I would like to begin by giving you our perspective on the Mt. Shasta Mission based on your planning up to this point.*

As all of you know, anything that occurs on Earth, particularly of such magnitude and scope as this mission, will affect the entire universe and beyond. Nothing has been accomplished so clearly within the level of five-senses form as the promise this mission carries. Consequently, we not only wish to support the Mt. Shasta Mission, but we also wish to participate in it. So far, we see the planning and the preliminary work that has gone into the mission point to success. In essence, we're saying that we feel the success of the mission does not depend on anything or anyone beyond that which you have already pulled together. What we would like to propose is an expansion of the mission for the purpose of aligning your particular mission to the greater whole, that is, the reality beyond the universe. What is completed on Mt. Shasta in five-senses form will resonate through the entire scope of reality, and will go a great distance in shifting all that is in the arena of Government, from the Piscean dynamic to the Aquarian dynamic. (In this particular case, we feel that the word "Government" should carry a capital "G.")

We've talked about the effect of the work done at Gettysburg on releasing the constrictions that are interfering with the pure tone of the tuning fork that we refer to as battle, war. In the case of the Mt. Shasta Mission, we fully expect the tuning fork of Government to be set free. (Machaelle, you are presently seeing two tuning forks, one smaller than the other, and that's an accurate insight. To clarify our imagery, hold one end of the smaller tuning fork with two fingers. While still holding it with your fingers, strike the tuning fork with a small mallet. The sound from the fork will be muffled. Now let go of the tuning fork and strike it again. The sound will be strong and clear. A tuning fork may be held by any number of "fingers" such as history, karmic connections, human emotions and society's mindset toward a particular institution or action. When we refer to "releasing a tuning fork," we are referring to the release of any "fingers" that are restricting the pure tone of the fork.)

As the Mt. Shasta Mission is set up now, it will release and allow the tone of the smaller tuning fork that is connected with Earth to be fully sounded. What we would like to do is also release the larger tuning fork—the one that attaches to and extends beyond this universe—well into the realms of all reality. The clarity, sensitivity, balance and teamwork that are going together to make this mission successful are of such a degree that the clarity of the mission's intent can move the ringing tone of the smaller tuning fork into the larger reality, thus releasing and sounding the larger tuning fork.

This one particular mission—with its link with various levels through those who are participating—can have ramifications well beyond your perceived scope of the Mt. Shasta Mission. It is this we wish to address.

Those of you present in this room know that the concept of Government exists within every level of existence. Although the forms may be different, there is a relationship of intent among all these levels of Government. What will shift at Mt. Shasta and around the planet next July is the energy of intent encompassing that which we call Government. Beyond the July 15 shift, David and his Cottage team will be working with the various forms of Government functioning around Earth in order to assist each to move forward and more fully encompass the new Aquarian intent.

Our primary focus, at this point, is the new Government intent. We have not had the opportunity to participate in, and experience the effect of, a shift of intent so clearly grounded and fully expressed in five-senses form within the area of Government. We would very much like to link with the Mt. Shasta Mission for the purpose of using the tone that will be sounded by the smaller tuning fork to connect with and resonate through the larger tuning fork, thus set-ting that tuning fork free as well. Of course, at this point we would like to say (in case there's any question) that our support for this mission is fully with you, whether or not we participate actively. What we are proposing is an expansion of your mission beyond what you have perceived. If you'd like a moment to discuss it among yourselves, please feel free.

David: I'd like to know how you're planning the expansion.

U.L.: *The most important thing is to maintain the integrity of the intent of your mission. You've set an ambitious scope of clarity in which you desire to proceed. In order to maintain that clarity and the power of that clarity, we would have to work with you with the same intent. In essence, although there may be more than one equally successful approach to this mission on Mt. Shasta next July, it would be disastrous if, after choosing your intent, we participate with a different direction. Although they may be equal, the two energy fields they would create would collide, and the Mt. Shasta Mission would experience such an inflow of abrasive energy that the chances for success would be minimal. We say this so that you'll understand that our suggestion is to join with you, not create a different mission of our own.*

Based on your preliminary work, we understand that you intend to enact, through a five-senses ceremony on Mt. Shasta, the shift of power and energy from the Piscean Government Era to the Aquarian Government Era, and that the energy from this shift, once accomplished in five-senses form, will be received by selected crew members of a large assemblage of spacecraft hovering above the Earth and its current Piscean Government leyline system. Those members will then deactivate the current Government leylines. They will form the new grid of leylines in the pattern that will support the Aquarian Government dynamics and then activate the power points and circuits of the new Aquarian Government leyline system. Basically, are we correct in our understanding?

David: Yes. That's correct.

U.L.: *What we wish to do is mirror your group of spacecraft by having another group of intergalactic craft move into position directly above your craft, including your command ship that will be hovering above your mother ship on the mountain. When the energy is received from the mountain by your command ship, we propose that the energy be transmitted not only horizontally into your craft assembled around the planet, but also vertically into our command ship that will be just above yours. Once we receive that energy we will move it horizontally to our craft that are paired with your craft. When you have completed this phase of the mission, the energy we hold will then be transmitted in pattern through the universe and received by another primary ship beyond your universe. It will then be transmitted and transfused directly into the corresponding new Government leyline system that will be set up beyond Earth's universe. This will result in the release of the larger tuning fork and the full sounding of its tone, thus releasing Government beyond Earth from its Piscean dynamic to the new Aquarian dynamic and principles.*

David: Will this expansion diffuse the power of our mission or the energy we're working with in any way?

U.L.: *We would not wish to diffuse that power. This is why we've proposed to pair our spacecraft with your craft, thus duplicating the pattern you're working in. As for the energy, there will be a 100 percent/100 percent split of the energy that is received by your command ship so that no power, clarity or intensity will be lost. With these elements in place, we feel that not only will there not be a diffusion of energy, there will be a strengthening of energy. The energy of the shift will move from your command ship horizontally to your craft and then be seated into the leylines of Earth. At the same time, it will also be received by our command ship and shifted horizontally to our spacecraft who are paired with yours and held there throughout the entire work with Earth's leylines before it will be transmitted vertically to our primary ship (which will be positioned beyond your universe and aligned to the new universal Government leyline system and larger tuning fork). We see an enhanced stability in the mission by holding the energy from the mountain while the old leyline system around Earth is being deactivated and the new system created and activated. The key to our proposal is that our craft exactly mirror your craft so that at no time will any one of our craft work in opposition to, or differentiation from, your craft. Once Earth's new leyline system is fully and completely activated and stabilized, our paired craft will move the held energy vertically to our primary ship beyond the universe and into the new Government leylines that support the universe and beyond. But while the Earth's new leyline system is being activated, our craft will be completely focused on the mountain and your mission.*

David: Will your craft be able to move into position with ours as
they are positioning, or will it be necessary for us to wait
for your craft to get into position?

U.L.: *We can coordinate that with you so that the positioning will be
simultaneous. Our suggestion is that the positioning be simultaneous because the more the parts of this whole move as a unit, the
clearer the movement itself. This is especially true for a mission this
complex and this large. It would not be good to have two separate
disturbances within the atmosphere as these craft position themselves around the world when there only need be one. Our suggestion is that the spacecraft pair up beyond the solar system, move as
pairs into the solar system and position themselves as pairs around
Earth. In that way, the pairing and mirror movement will already
be stabilized as the craft move into the solar system itself.*

*To be clear, we are differentiating between the mother ship that
is going to land on Mt. Shasta and the command ship that is going
to be hovering above the mother ship to receive the shifted energy as
it takes place on Mt. Shasta. We will not have a duplicate mother
ship at Mt. Shasta. We will only start the mirror process with your
command ship. One could say our answer to your mother ship on
Mt. Shasta will be the primary ship outside this universe that will
receive the fully grounded energy initiated at Mt. Shasta and move
that energy into the larger leylines and tuning fork beyond the
universe.*

Hyperithon: What are the drawbacks of your proposal?

U.L.: *We have considered as many potential drawbacks as we could. We
consider the weak link to be the pairing of the craft. We feel we
have answered the issue of atmospheric disturbance by pairing the
craft beyond the solar system and having them move into position as
paired units. The other weak link that we considered was the issue
of diffusing or dispersing the mission energy that will be created on
the mountain, thereby making the grounding of the shift into the*

Earth's leyline system of lesser impact than it would have been had
we not been part of the mission. We feel strongly that by using the
100 percent/100 percent energy split and holding the energy from
the mountain while the work is being done on the Earth leyline system, we have eliminated the possibility of dispersal.

The two problem areas we've just mentioned are the two primary areas we feel need to be considered. As Hyperithon has
pointed out [a reference to a comment he made earlier in
this meeting], there are other issues about the spacecraft themselves, one of which is the different systems and designs used in craft
technology and their working together in partnership and balanced
pairing. We feel strongly that there is going to have to be an extensive coordination effort between representatives of our craft beyond
this universe and representatives of your craft within the universe
so that the spacecraft can be paired in such a way that the craft
themselves create their own balanced energy field. We do recognize
the issue of pairing two different craft (which would resonate two
different energies) to function as one unit within the atmosphere
without creating waves as they move together. We have representatives on standby who have full knowledge of our available craft,
their capabilities and their energy output. One of the reasons why
we suggested these meetings this early on in the mission planning is
so that, if you wish (and so choose) to allow us to link up with you
in the mission, we may get about the business of pairing the craft.

David: From your perspective, do you see any impact on our
mother ship and the actual activity and transference of the
shifted energy on Mt. Shasta itself?

U.L.: There cannot be any impact on what will occur on Mt. Shasta. It is
vitally important to all that what will occur there be experienced
and held solely by the team and the participants that David has
pulled together. We, of course, will be focused and fully supportive
of what is happening on the mountain, but we will not be actively

participating in any way. You must understand that when we talk about the energy that will be used to intone the tuning fork beyond the universe, we are talking about that which is created at Mt. Shasta. It's important that this event be carried out clearly and fully in its original purpose and design so that the energy it creates will contain the full intent of the mission. This is necessary not only for your leyline system, but also the leyline system and the ringing of the larger tuning fork beyond the universe.

Tex: Would this expanded mission with its second tier of craft affect the energy on the mountain site itself beyond what is already anticipated?

U.L.: *We took that into consideration. But you have already addressed the issue yourselves. The protection that Machaelle and nature placed over the site will stabilize the area in such a way that the impact of our being present in the mission will not be felt by those present at the site. There will be a heightened energy in the atmosphere, but we do not perceive, in any way, that this will present a danger to Earth, its atmosphere or the atmosphere beyond. We would suggest that the question be dealt with by representatives from both spacecraft groups and that between now and July—to assure that what we consider safe is, indeed, safe—some test runs within Earth's atmosphere of paired craft be completed. It will be essential that the protection dome that Machaelle has placed over the landing site remain activated and is maintained until the entire mission is over. We recommend that the protection be lifted from the site no sooner than twenty-four hours after the mission has been completed.*

Hyperithon: Can we be assured that the energy created by the double spacecraft will be safe to all concerned, whether on the mountain as part of the mission or not?

U.L.: *The information that we will gather between now and July from the paired craft test runs will be enough to assure us about the safety.*

Tex: Should the existing protection dome be enlarged?

U.L.: *At this particular point, we don't see the need to broaden the protection. But as time grows near, if any of us feel that it should be enlarged, we feel that can easily be accomplished and need not be an issue. The present protection is fine for maintaining the stability of the site until July. If the protection is to be enlarged, the appropriate time to do it would be in July when Machaelle goes to the mountain to do the final preparations of the site for the physical landing and mission.*

Hyperithon (to Machaelle): If the dome needs to be expanded, can that be easily done?

Machaelle: Yes. I don't think it's any different than expanding a simple four-point coning to include everyone sitting here.

Hyperithon: If it needs to be heightened, can this be done?

Machaelle: Yes, if you give me the specifics, I'll have nature expand the protection to your specific requirements.

Lorpuris: I have felt all along that it is important to protect those whom Peter is inviting as witnesses prior to going into the mountain area. Now it might be doubly important with this expanded mission. (To Machaelle) Can that be done?

Machaelle: Yes. I can work with nature to protect them prior to their going to the mountain with the same energy that's protecting the site itself.

David: We're going to need to think about this proposal. Do we now have enough information to make a decision?

Tex: I'm still concerned about the jeopardy issue. I'm not comfortable with the ramifications of this proposal yet.

Hyperithon: It seems to me our main concern is to make sure

that our primary mission is successful. The expanded
mission can't occur without this.

David: Yes, and also that it doesn't damage any of the participants. We need to talk to representatives from the other
craft group.

Hyperithon: I'll have a better idea about stabilizing this pairing
process once we meet.

Tex: That seems to be a key issue.

Hyperithon: You bet.

Machaelle (in a brief moment of near-panic created by a sudden
thought, she feigns calmness and quietly asks): Could
atmospheric disturbance created by the spacecraft affect
or damage Earth in any way?

Hyperithon: With the amount of craft we have coming in—now
double that number—it's quite possible that we could
change Earth's weather patterns if this isn't done correctly,
and that would be dramatic. This is critical and that's
something we want to avoid.

David (to Hyperithon): Can you meet with these fellows tomorrow?

Hyperithon: I can meet with them any time they can get to me.

U.L.: *We anticipated that you would want to meet prior to making your
decision. We have members of our group positioned and ready for a
meeting with whomever you please at any time. Just give us a time.*

Hyperithon: Can we meet on the Cottage level?

U.L.: *Yes. We've provided for that if you wish.*

Hyperithon (to David): Do you want to be present?

David: Yes.

Hyperithon: Can they come into the Cottage?

U.L.: *Yes.*

David: Then we'll have the meeting here. I'd like it as soon as possible. How long do you think that the meeting would take?

Hyperithon: At least half a day.

Tex: Why don't we get those fellows to have a preliminary meeting with our crews, and they can battle out some of these issues before we meet with them?

David: No, I want them to battle out issues in the same room with me there. It'll save time.

U.L.: *The representatives of our crews can easily be within the Cottage level and at the Cottage by noon tomorrow.*

David: Is there any time limit as to their staying on this level?

U.L.: *No. They're more than willing to stay as long as they're needed. Mind you, we have only considered solutions to the problems that were raised today, so we are anxious to get the two groups together to make sure that what we've proposed is indeed stable and effective.*

David: Tomorrow at noon then. (To Lorpuris) Can you be present?

Lorpuris: Yes. I want to be present. There are some medical considerations I want to discuss.

U.L.: *We propose the next full meeting for this Friday. Of course if more time is needed for your decision about expanding the mission, there is no issue with us in moving the meeting to Saturday, or beyond, if necessary.*

David: My preliminary feeling is that we go with the expansion
as long as we can be assured that our primary mission will
not be complicated or endangered.

U.L.: *We fully agree with you on this matter.*

Tex: If we need to discuss a matter with Igor tomorrow, do we
need to have Machaelle present?

U.L.: *That won't be necessary tomorrow. There will be several crew mem-*
bers who are capable of opening communication with us.

David: Good. I'd say then this meeting is a wrap.
(General agreement).

U.L.: *We agree as well.*

With this, I closed the coning. At that point, I deeply, truly, down
to the bottom of my heart and my gut and my toes hoped that I
would not see a bunch of little green people wrapped in aluminum foil running around the Cottage the next day. Picture it.
Little green people sitting in the living room drinking coffee and
discussing spacecraft pairing problems, saying things like, "Oh
Cedric, I don't think we should pair the turquoise Ford Pinto
craft with the Buick craft with the orange racing stripe. It's just
not a good match. It'll look like a flying Howard Johnson's."

I remember this meeting well. How could I forget it? As it went
on, I remember thinking: "Oh crap, I can hardly get a handle on
the size of this mission now, and they're talking about doubling its
size! Thanks a lot…Where *is* the universe and beyond, and what
kind of government systems do they have? Do they pay taxes?…
Did they just say we might blow up the planet? Bummer…All my
life's a tuning fork…"

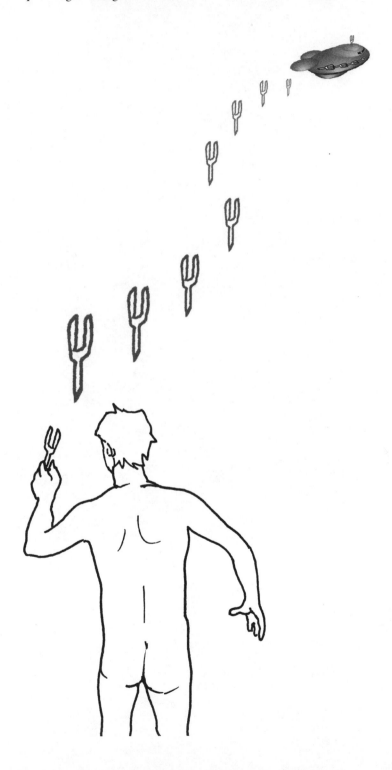

Chapter 22

Igor Meeting #2

OCTOBER 27

The next couple of days after that first Igor meeting, the Cottage was bustling. Meetings, visitors, phone calls, more meetings, more visitors. Generally, I ignored everyone and just left each day for Perelandra, but every once in a while I would slink around the Cottage and "check out the scene," as they say. I didn't see any little green people. Just a bunch of regular looking men and women. Where were the giant bald heads with no lips and one bulging eyeball in the middle of the forehead? Where were the antennae? Who started those rumors about these people? Were they on drugs?

For the second meeting, David included two additional people from the Cottage team: Butch and John. Although John is a member of the team, he is not a full-time resident of the Cottage and visits for a couple of months about three times a year. Butch is a full-time resident. The others present for this second meeting also attended the first one. I opened the coning as usual and connected us with Igor.

U.L.: *Good afternoon. It's good to see all of you. I am reading that it is your intention to expand the Mt. Shasta Mission. Is this correct?*

David: As of this point, we are planning to expand the mission as you've suggested. We've talked with your fellows, together

with ours, and we don't feel that there is any problem or
logistical issue in expanding the mission that can't be sur-
mounted. You must understand that our original mission
is to remain our primary concern. If we understand you
correctly, you agree. Is this correct?

U.L.: *Absolutely. As we've said to you, the primary mission must be
successful in order for the expanded mission to occur.*

*I am assuming that we have all agreed that "primary mission"
means the exchange of energy and the shift of that energy within
the arena of Government (and by "Government," we include its
implementation arm, Military, as well) from the Piscean dynamic
to Aquarian dynamic among the people present at Mt. Shasta, and
"expanded mission" means the receiving of that energy after it has
been grounded into the new leyline system around Earth and the
transmission of that energy outside this universe for the purpose of
freeing and intoning the larger tuning fork regarding Government
and Military. Have we agreed on those terms?*

David: Yes. That would be the reasonable separation of the
mission, in terms of language.

U.L.: *We are sensing, and let's get agreement on this as well, that you
want to reserve the right to cancel the expanded mission at any time
if it is felt that the expanded mission is jeopardizing the primary
mission. Is that correct?*

David: That is correct. We must ensure, as much as possible, that
the primary mission will succeed. There is so much that is
going into the planning that we feel it would be folly to
expand the mission beyond its own capability.

U.L.: *We fully agree with this.*

David: As of now, it's our intention that we do a considerable
amount of work with the spacecraft pairing prior to July.

We have agreement from the fellows that we met with the day before yesterday that for this particular part of the mission, the weakest link is the coordination of the spacecraft and their crews.

U.L.: *We felt the same, but we think you will find that the quality of the crews and the craft will be more than comparable, and certainly the intent for cooperation is there.*

David: Yes. We found that to be strong, of course, and that's not a surprise to us. Is there anyone who has any thoughts that they would like to express regarding our meetings Thursday and Friday?

U.L.: *We have been entertaining questions regarding the added intensity of the energy because of the expanded mission and its effect on the people involved. One of our key concerns is that no one involved experience any problem or receive any damage due to the intensity. Do you feel clear and certain that the proper protection can be maintained for the individuals involved?*

Lorpuris: I would say that right now we're 98 percent sure. We feel the protected environment of the mother ship coming into the protected environment of the landing site will protect those coming in for the mission on the ship. Some questions remain and we need to make sure there is nothing we're overlooking. We'll be doing some work very similar to what Machaelle is doing with Salvesen with those who are coming to Mt. Shasta on the mother ship. We are discussing contingency plans, however, that will be ready for all involved [those coming in on the mother ship and the witnesses who will walk to the site]. We feel it's important that we have three, perhaps four, backup protection systems ready to go into action at any time we see it's necessary. We can perceive the impact of the mission only so far and feel it's important that it be recognized how unique this situation is.

U.L.: *We agree that it is.*

Lorpuris: Therefore, you would understand the need to anticipate as many problems as possible. We're now preparing everybody involved on the Perelandra level for the intensity of the actual landing and finding that their bodies do indeed experience some trauma from the landing. We have not, however, attempted to shift a ship landing through the protection dome that Machaelle has placed over the site. The protection may shift that environment, the impact and the trauma to our favor—we're not sure. We'll be researching this. I think all we need to do is test two or three people, and we can get a pattern from that.

U.L.: *Since the protection dome is going to remain intact until twenty-four hours after the mission is complete, would it not be wise, from this point on, to simulate those landings within the protected environment with the rest of those involved?*

Lorpuris: Yes, it would be, and we intend to do that. There is a lot of flexibility within that protected environment, and we may need to adjust the dome at the last minute in order to infuse it, shift its energy and soften the trauma. Now, we're still assuming that there will be no craft and crew from outside this universe mirroring our mother ship at the Mt. Shasta site itself. Is that still correct?

U.L.: *That is our plan.*

David (to Lorpuris): Well, you'll make sure I get that information if there's any kind of change. Changes can't happen without me knowing.

Lorpuris: Yes, of course.

U.L.: *We agree, as well. It is understood that nothing from our end can happen without you first being consulted.*

David: That's critical. There would be no way to maintain coordination without it.

U.L.: *It is fully accepted and agreed upon that you are the commander of the primary mission and the expanded mission. That position will be respected.*

David: Thank you. That's going to be needed in order to maintain coordination. This is getting to be a massive operation.

Hyperithon: The question arose yesterday at our meeting about the issue of whether something should be designed into the ceremony on Mt. Shasta—something that would acknowledge and perhaps help the movement of the energy from the primary mission to the expanded mission. Have you had any thoughts regarding that?

U.L.: *Yes, we have. The issue here is the conflict between the participants invited by Peter Caddy knowing about the expanded mission and risking the dispersal of the energy of the primary mission, and their not knowing about the expanded mission and maintaining the focus of the primary mission only. That's the conflict, and we feel that the answer to that situation lies in your hands. This is a risk factor that you will need to weigh.*

David (to U.L.): We agree. If we do not acknowledge the expanded mission at the Mt. Shasta site, how does that affect the expanded mission?

U.L.: *As in every case (and this is something I know you gentlemen know well) an acknowledged action carries more power and impact than an unacknowledged action. We are prepared, and we feel strongly that the expanded mission can be successful, even if it remains unacknowledged at Mt. Shasta. We have a number of options that we have considered. One option is to build acknowledgment into the ceremony at Mt. Shasta at some particular and appropriate point. The impact of that would greatly enhance what the expanded mission has to carry forward. Another option would be an acknowledgment of the expanded mission only by those who are coming to the site on the ship. That can occur either at Mt. Shasta, privately among those people, or beyond Mt. Shasta once the actual transference of power to the expanded mission has been accomplished. The key issue here, as we all acknowledge, is the maintenance of the integrity and essence of the primary mission. However, the question still remains: Can something for the expanded mission be built into the ceremony at the Mt. Shasta site without dispersing the energy of the primary mission?*

David: We already have an additional issue that we're incorporating into the primary mission that we haven't discussed with you yet. St. Germain is going to take the opportunity to shift the Aquarian energy that was seated into the leylines thirty years ago to a level that is more discernable and acceptable to the sensory systems of those on Earth. They were unable to achieve this level of grounding thirty years ago. We do have that issue at hand. I'm not sure if you're aware of that.

U.L.: *Yes, we are aware you have accepted this an additional phase of the primary mission.*

David: We're dealing presently with how to accomplish that second shift without dispersing the primary mission goals. As of now, we feel that something can be built into the ceremony on the mountain that will allow St. Germain to accomplish his goals without dispersing ours. I suspect that when we find the answer to this issue, we'll find the answer to the expanded mission as well.

Hyperithon: It seems to me that if we clearly separate the intent of the focus on the mountain—first focusing on the primary mission; then shifting the focus completely to either St. Germain and his goals, or the goals of the expanded mission; and then following up with the third focus—we can maintain the balance we need, especially among Peter's witnesses. It would be very much the same thing that's accomplished in a guided meditation in which everyone's focus is corralled and moved from one point to another.

David: The issue we're considering, which would be different than a guided meditation, is the extraordinary sensory impact on everyone on the mountain: first, being faced with a mother ship and still maintaining focus; and second, being faced with the historical leaders coming by ship. That's going to be a difficult thing for Peter's witnesses—keeping these people corralled and holding the primary focus. You're suggesting we do it not once but three times.

Tex: That may be a reason for priming Peter's witnesses so that they'll be ready and won't be starstruck when they see what's going to happen. I have felt strongly that everybody should be informed about the scope of the mission, especially about the parts of the mission that touch them. It seems to me that giving the information beforehand to those on the mountain will take the Hollywood glitter out of the mission.

David: I agree with you about the glitter, but I'm not sure I agree with your approach. John, you're coming in on this new. What do you think?

John: You mean in terms of the focus issue?

David: Yes. How do you feel about keeping these people focused
solely on the primary mission or giving them more information?

John: I'm inclined to lean toward Tex's direction. First of all, my
understanding is that the people who are being invited by
Peter Caddy to witness are a select bunch.

David: That's true.

John: I am assuming a certain level of mental discipline.

David: That's fair, but not everyone there has experienced what's
going to happen at Mt. Shasta. Do you think they can
maintain their focus on the primary mission and not let
their minds wander to the expanded mission or St.
Germain while the primary mission is going on?

John: Quite frankly, I have the feeling that this is going to be
such an overpowering experience that the sheer power of
it is going to help people maintain their focus on what's
happening in front of them. You feel you're going to lose
people's attention because the sensory systems will be
overloaded. I have the feeling that there's going to be so
much sensory input on such a fantastic level in such a
tightly coordinated ceremony that the people there will go
beyond the point of dispersal and be mesmerized as to
what is going on. It's going to be an extraordinary experience for everyone involved, and I think there is a point
beyond dispersal that's not being considered. And, as you
know, quite often the more you explain what's going on,
the more at ease and receptive people are.

Hyperithon: We've considered the educational aspect in regard to Peter's witnesses and have run into a problem of logistics. We can't get these people together without a considerable amount of effort on everyone's part until just a few days before the mission.

David (to Machaelle): Do you think we can develop a framework that would move the focus of Peter's people through three separate stages of the mission—that is, without jeopardizing any one stage, especially the primary stage?

Machaelle: I can only answer that with my experience.

David: Well, that's what I'm asking for.

Machaelle: The more disciplined someone is, the easier it is for them to hold the focus, but it helps to keep everyone on the same page if someone leads a group—like in a guided meditation. With the right leader, it's easy for a disciplined group to maintain focus and movement. But, you're talking about an active, complex event and not a guided meditation. These people are going to have their eyes open, taking in a mother ship on top of a mountain with a bunch of historical "dead" people staring at them. It's difficult to keep anyone's focus when they're faced with this kind of thing....Well, I'm not really answering your question, I'm raising the issue even more. The only idea that comes to mind right now is that we incorporate on the mountain something similar to what I went through when I opened the coning today. I spent a moment focused on each one of you. This gives my sensory system time to adjust to the impact of the individual dynamics and elements each of you brings to the coning. That might be the key to the situation on the mountain. With each element, give each witness time to adjust before moving on to the next sensory input. It'll slow down the ceremony, but it may be worth it.

Hyperithon: I agree.

Lorpuris: So do I. We've got to give their sensory systems time to adjust. Otherwise the strain would be enormous, and what you would have is people blacking out on you. You don't want that to happen.

David: No. We want them to remain fully aware.

Machaelle (to David): You've suggested that the landing occur at dusk. Am I correct?

David: Yes.

Machaelle: I think that's one thing we've got going for us. The night would limit visual input and give Peter's witnesses a feeling of being in a confined space. I find it's pretty essential that most people feel walls around them when trying to focus.

Hyperithon: They're going to feel walls at the site because of the dome, aren't they?

Lorpuris: Unconsciously they will.

Machaelle: I hadn't thought of the dome.

U.L.: *Can the protection dome be expanded to include the sensation of an enclosed environment so that their sensory systems will register a sense of being in a protected room?*

Machaelle: I don't know. I'll have to ask Pan in a coning. It would certainly be worth a shot.

Hyperithon: I think that's possible.

David: We're already dealing with changing the focus from the primary mission to St. Germain's shift. I think if we can come up with a plan for changing their focus successfully with this, we'll be able to change their focus for the expanded mission successfully.

U.L.: *There is another issue here, which is that Peter's witnesses have a comparatively extensive background into the concept of, what they call, the "New Age," which is part of St. Germain's area. His work won't be unfamiliar to them, but you again run into a problem when you talk about shifting the focus to the expanded mission. Most people, and I would suspect those called to Mt. Shasta, are not used to working on such an expanded level.*

David (to Machaelle): I'd like to ask my question again. Do you think, from your experience and vantage point, that Peter's witnesses can fully focus on the primary mission and then successfully move their focus to two additional stages?

Machaelle: Yes, I think it's possible, but something comes to mind here that might be an acceptable compromise. Certainly the whole process on Mt. Shasta is going to be carefully constructed—the ceremony, the timing and all of that. I'm assuming this.

David: Yes, that's true.

Machaelle: And you have your primary mission scheduled as the first thing—I'm assuming that. That's the way it has always been presented to me. Is that correct?

David: Yes.

Machaelle: The chance of success of the primary mission focus is the best of the three because it's first. If you give people time to adjust their sensory systems to what they're experiencing before them, if you give them enough time to beat their heads against the trees and say, "I don't believe this is happening"—once you give them that adjustment period, you can move them into the primary mission and they'll be ready to hold their focus throughout that stage. Now, you've already accepted St. Germain's work at the site?

David: Yes, we have, but that has always been on the condition that at any time, if we felt the primary mission was jeopardized by his stage, we would back off that. There's been agreement on that.

Machaelle: I would say to go ahead and move the group's focus into the second stage. At that point, you've already finished the primary mission. If you lose something on that shift, you still haven't lost anything on the primary focus. The primary mission is protected and you have nothing to lose.

U.L.: *We have no problems with that approach. It's clean.*

David: We're talking about separating the three focuses, making them separate and distinct from one another. Correct?

U.L.: *That's correct. The issue, as we've understood it, has been maintaining clarity throughout this mission.*

David: That's correct. This would certainly be the cleanest route. The thing we don't want to do here is manipulate anyone. All we want to do is help them to maintain their focus and give everybody there the chance to participate as fully as possible in what is happening before them on the mountain. We're not asking anything of these people except the strength of their focus.

We need time to bat this around. I say we plan to include all three stages on Mt. Shasta. I'm just not clear on how to do that yet. Universal Light, do you have any additional input at this point on this focus issue and the three stages?

U.L.: *Our only input is just a simple reminder: Conscious action is more powerful than unconscious action. Beyond that, we have no specific suggestions at this time. As you well know, David, the more compli-cated a mission, the more complicated and vast the possible logistics in pulling a mission off.*

David: Then I suggest we bounce some ideas off one another, see what we come up with and get back to you on it.

U.L.: *That will be fine. We'll need to understand the framework of the mission you will be using for each of the stages, particularly the expanded one, in order to adjust and coordinate our actions to it.*

David: That's certainly understood. Does anybody else have anything to add?

Tex: Is Universal Light our primary liaison with the expanded mission?

U.L.: *Yes. I will be the liaison for you.*

Tex: I think we need a couple of days to make some decisions before we get back with Universal Light.

David: I agree. I think we need more than a couple of days. (To Hyperithon) I'd like you to start working with the paired spacecraft and crews. I want to know how those exercises progress.

Hyperithon: There's no issue; they're ready to start at any time. We're going to make some preliminary pairings within the next couple of days and start maneuvering as pairs to see just where our difficulties lie in that.

David: Do you know yet how close together the individual craft in a pair will be?

Hyperithon: No. That's going to be one of the first questions we deal with, just technically, to determine what's safe.

David (to Lorpuris): We have some issues to nail down about the safety factor with the mother ship and Peter's people now that we have the dome in place. When can we get information on that?

Lorpuris: Machaelle has scheduled Salvesen and Laura Townsend for the mother ship landing process, but not until the 7th of November. We can then test them within the protected dome environment. I have also been monitoring Machaelle, and I monitored her while she was at the Mt. Shasta site in September. I will see the difference in her when she simulates the ship landing with the protected environment. (To Machaelle) You'll include the focus on that protection and visualize it with the landing?

Machaelle: Right. Okay. Just remind me.

Lorpuris: I'll be happy to do this. (To Hyperithon) We can work with you on the dynamics of the protection dome.

Hyperithon: I know we've got some options there that we can play around with that will stabilize the mission better.

David: I would like to have a preliminary report on those options as soon as possible.

Lorpuris: We need to work with a couple of people on the Perelandra level in order to test the protection as we go along. We can certainly work with Machaelle, but she's already in an extraordinary position with the two bodies. I'm going to want to know the dome's effect on her, but we need, shall we say, some normal people also.

David: We'll work on that. We'll get that set up.

Lorpuris: That's fine.

David: I think we'll need a week before we'll have enough information for another meeting. Is that agreed by everyone?

Tex: You have no arguments here.

Hyperithon: We may need longer.

David: If we need longer, we'll take it.

U.L.: *We agree that more than a few days' time is needed, but we would like to get back together with you and learn what direction you're going in as soon as it's feasible so that we can plan from our end.*

David: We agree. I say we aim for a week, give or take a day or two. Does anyone have any problems with that? (All agree.) Good. Then close down the coning, Machaelle.

There wasn't much I had to do from this meeting except wait. I had to wait for November 7 and the next body tests with Peter's witnesses, and I had to wait to hear if there were any changes to the protective dome over the site. I have to say that this meeting proved to me how quickly we can adjust to "insanity." Throughout the first meeting, I felt like I was hanging onto the edge of my sanity. But for this second meeting, we were talking technical nuts and bolts, and it all sounded reasonable, even normal. The Mt. Shasta Mission was beginning to feel a little comfortable to me.

Chapter 23

Igor Meeting #3

NOVEMBER 15

Everyone who was present at the second meeting was at this third meeting. I opened the coning and hooked us up with Igor.

U.L.: *Good afternoon. We feel that this will be our final meeting regarding the expanded mission. As you might imagine, we are aware of the specific preparations that are underway. From our vantage point, we see no problem or complication in the way the plans are moving, either technically or otherwise. We are particularly interested in the balance and the flow of the Mt. Shasta Mission and have seen nothing that could be considered disruptive or threatening to the success of the primary mission as developed so far. One of our specific awarenesses is the state of balance within the universe. We are particularly adept at perceiving balance and imbalance. If you wish, we would be happy to keep in touch with you through Machaelle regarding our perception of that balance or any imbalance that might occur as the Mt. Shasta Mission continues to develop and formalize.*

David: I have no issue with your keeping a watch over the development of the mission. Would you stay in touch with us through the scheduled sessions Machaelle has with you, or do we need to schedule a special time...or can Machaelle do this intuitively?

U.L.: *We don't need to schedule a special time, and would, of course, utilize the regularly scheduled sessions if necessary. We can also reach you through Machaelle intuitively as we did six weeks ago when we wished to speak to you about expanding the mission. We'll utilize both avenues—the sessions and Machaelle's intuition.*

David: Fine, then we'll leave it at that. I'd appreciate your input. Would this also include the expanded mission's balance?

U.L.: *Yes. The Mt. Shasta Mission has now become one unit that comprises Earth, the Cottage level within the White Brotherhood, the universal level and the levels beyond the universe. It's one complex unit of several levels, so any issue of balance on one level will have to be addressed in light of the balance on each of the other levels.*

David: That sounds fine.

U.L.: *At this time, we would like to point out something else to you. Because this mission has come together as one unit through the cooperation of teams on many different levels, any information regarding the mission on one level—either its preparation or the mission itself—will be automatically available and useful to any of the other levels that are represented in the mission. For example, the work that Machaelle is doing on the Perelandra level with nature in preparation for the landing—that information regarding nature's principles and laws as seen from the perspective of the Mt. Shasta Mission—will automatically become available to any other level represented in the mission. She need do nothing special to make the information available. This will occur, as we have said, automatically. The others can then extrapolate from her work and apply these principles and laws on their level.*

Another important point is that everything that is going into the success of the Mt. Shasta Mission may also be applied to future complex, multilevel missions put together by teams on the same levels represented in the Mt. Shasta Mission. What is achieved with

the Mt. Shasta Mission will be fore
this mission. So you see, the proc
plishing the goals of the Mt. Sl
and-take of information an
and on a number of differ

   And conversely, any infor.
the mission beyond the universe wn
universe, including the Perelandra level. 1.
Earth's universe and the reality that is beyond is
information from beyond the universe can then become.
within Earth's universe and be made available to all people, to.
life, that inhabit the universe. Although you may be initiating new
and expanded understanding of the laws and principles contained
within Earth's universe, you will also bring into this universe—
through the grounded, peaceful framework of the Mt. Shasta
Mission—concepts and laws that are already established and func-
tioning beyond the universe.

   As you can see, the Mt. Shasta Mission is not just a gateway to
Earth, but beyond Earth and beyond the universe as well. If one
could look at the Cottage with its White Brotherhood team as the
central point, one would see it as the hub for the information coming into Earth's universe from beyond and the information coming
into the beyond from Earth's universe. The Cottage level is the balance between the two. It's the initiator for the action on both ends
and the coordinator of the action on both ends. Perhaps it would
be more clearly understood if one saw the Cottage as a switching
station for that which will occur on Earth at Mt. Shasta and that
which will be activated beyond the universe. Because of this unique
position, it is important and imperative that the coordinator of the
mission be situated and seated in the position that we have referred
to as the hub or switching station. One could not fully coordinate
the Mt. Shasta Mission if one were solely "of Earth" or solely "of
beyond the universe." That's why, for example, we on this level

t coordinate this kind of expansive mission: We are not in the
per position for effective, grounded coordination.

: Does anything special have to be done here to make
the information from us accessible to you fellows beyond
the universe and vice versa?

U.L.: *No. Because we are functioning within the unity of the mission,
that information is automatically accessible to you, to Earth and to
the universe. The mission itself sets up a framework of accessibility.
Of course you understand we are not talking about setting up classrooms on these different levels. By "accessibility" we mean the information will simply be available to those who reach out to it on these
different levels. It is simply available to them.*

David: Is it still agreed that our primary focus, our sole focus, as
we pull together the mission, is that which will occur on
the site at Mt. Shasta?

U.L.: *It must be. The success of the mission—on Earth, on the White
Brotherhood level and beyond the universe—depends on that
intense but relatively small, pinpointed action on Mt. Shasta.*

Lorpuris: Just to be sure I understand you, you're saying that any
medical information resulting from the mission from all
levels that were represented in the mission is going to be
automatically accessible to my office and team. And this
includes information from beyond Earth's universe?

U.L.: *Yes. All the information beyond the universe will be accessible to
any person or team working within the mission. And it will be
automatically accessible, which means that you will not have to go
through Machaelle for a translation of that information. Among
the various options open to you, it will be intuitively accessible.
Because of the mission goals, the information will be accessible in
a grounded manner and also available through five-senses form.*

We now want to switch to the subject of Gettysburg, for we all now know that the Gettysburg work is going to tie into the mission. Now as you gentlemen know, that which has occurred on Earth in the form of battle has in energy and intent occurred on all other levels throughout the universe and, we might add, beyond. Although there haven't been great cosmic wars within the universe, there has been intensity equal to that of the intent, emotions and energy that were released in five-senses form through the battle known as Gettysburg. We would like to add to the insight of Gettysburg at this particular point because, from our perspective, this is the last piece of the Mt. Shasta puzzle to come into place.

In the spring, Machaelle will return to Gettysburg. At that time, Gettysburg will be entirely and fully detached from its karmic links. Those souls who still have karmic attachments to Gettysburg will have been called back by that time and will have gone through the release of that connection (and we might add, the healing process that will accompany the release).

At this point we digress for just a minute: Machaelle has received word from friends who have recently visited Gettysburg that the comfrey plants are no longer visible. However the comfrey is fully seated into the environment of the Gettysburg Battlefield and functioning in cooperation with nature. The plant form will return in the spring. The plants are dormant but the roots are alive. Although the form is not visible to the eye right now, the plants' essence is there and fully accessible to nature. There need be no concern over the reports. The comfrey is functioning fully within its triangulated position just behind the Copse of Trees.

In the spring, Machaelle will return to Gettysburg. The precise framework that this third phase will take need not be discussed at this point, and quite frankly, it is too soon to discuss that particular framework. But the results of the third phase will raise the Gettysburg Battle to the level of its higher intent and purpose. This level has always existed and has been a part of the Gettysburg Battle *from its moment of conception through its being played out in battle. The highest intent and purpose was never lost. It was made complicated by a multitude of karmic connections that wove a pattern of intensity and complexity, separating the Battle of Gettysburg from its higher purpose.*

That weaving and that separation is what is being removed this year as each soul is called back to Gettysburg to go through their karmic release. Each soul who comes back releases his karmic link and his part of the weave, so what you will have in the spring is the echo of the battle that occurred and the superimposition of the higher intent of what occurred at Gettysburg. These two will mesh. The battle itself, in energy, will take on a new identity. In order for this identity to be achieved, we needed to erase that middle ground, the karmic links. The higher level and the level of the historic battle will come together to create the new identity; this has been referred to at the Cottage as raising a battle to its higher purpose, its higher intent. When this occurs, all the levels within the universe and beyond that have, in any way, been connected to, and resonated to, the Battle of Gettysburg will shift to their higher identities, as well. An entire tuning fork throughout the universe that is related to the Gettysburg Battle will be released and shifted into its higher purpose.

The full and complete shift of the battle into a new identity with a new vibration is what will be linked with Mt. Shasta. It will infuse the energy that will be grounded into the leyline system around the world and be released into the universe and beyond. It will sound the note of the new direction and new intent of the framework known as Government—Government around the world, beyond the world and beyond the universe. We all know there is order—on Earth, beyond Earth and beyond the universe—that relates to the concept we call "Government." We also know the idea of Government is not unique to Earth. But what reflects on Earth in five-senses form is also reflected beyond

Earth and beyond the universe. And the Government beyond Earth has also resonated with the complication that was played out and represented at the Battle of Gettysburg. When the Battle of Gettysburg is shifted, the note will be sounded and the remainder of the Gettysburg-related levels will also shift to the new level.

A very real consequence of this shift will be with the work that has gone on at the Cottage up to this point. At the moment of the Mt. Shasta shift, when the new leyline system is activated, the work that has gone on at the Cottage—what you call "flipping the coins"—will also be activated and infused with the new intent that the raising of the Battle of Gettysburg will initiate. After this activation, that Cottage work may be successfully used to create, formulate and move Earth within the framework of Government into the new, which, up to this point, without that particular activation, has not been appropriate to use. As you look at the specifics of the already flipped coins after the activation, you will note a new power, clarity and intent that will simply be there, held by the words and the studies. If one looks at the words and the research as a vessel, one will see that at the moment of the Mt. Shasta activation, those words and that research will receive the power that will move this particular Cottage work to a new level. Because the mission itself has included in its framework the various levels that we have referred to within the universe and beyond—because of this and because of the infusion of the shift at Gettysburg within the mission—the work that will continue at the Cottage in reference to creating, formulating and moving Earth within a framework of Government into the new will be accessible to those levels and beyond. In essence, gentlemen, what you have is a multilevel mission that clearly will not end after the landing at Mt. Shasta.

A coning, a framework—whatever you wish to call it—has been created and will function through the preparation and the conclusion of the Mt. Shasta Mission and will continue to function beyond the conclusion of the mission. The information, knowledge *and activity that will be initiated from the Cottage in reference to the movement, balance and shift of Earth into the new—all of this will be received and utilized on the other levels beyond Earth and beyond the universe that were involved in the Mt. Shasta Mission. Conversely, the information, knowledge and activity that will orig-inate from beyond the universe as a result of the mission will become available to those at the Cottage to be considered and appropriately applied to their work, including their work with Government on Earth. Once again, the Cottage will function as a switching station, the midpoint of a flow of information between it and Earth, and a flow of information going throughout the uni-verse and beyond and coming back. We might add at this point that, yes, this same dynamic will occur with any office or person attached to, and working and functioning within, the Mt. Shasta Mission. This movement will include the Brotherhood offices of medicine, science, technology and nature, and any other office or level that is attached to the Mt. Shasta Mission. But because the major thrust of the mission has to do with Government, the major thrust of this information flow will be in the area of Government.*

Are there any questions on anything up to this point?

David: We better keep our focus on the direction of the mission and make sure we pull it off. And we need to be careful about moving the Gettysburg Battle energy into the mis-sion. It seems to me that once the mission has been com-pleted, then we can open another meeting and talk about how we proceed from that point to function with this new information flow. If we concentrate too much now on what's possible, we'll be like the receiver in football who thinks about running before he catches the ball: He invari-ably drops the damned ball. I don't want to drop this ball.

U.L.: *We agree, but we felt you needed to have this information in order to understand the importance of Gettysburg and phase three.*

David: There's no argument there. I agree that phase three at
  Gettysburg this spring is going to be important. But with
  this potential, quite frankly, I can see where we might lose
  sight of the football.

Tex: Do I understand correctly that you are not suggesting that
  we pull back on the current research in this office that
  creates the flipping of the coins?

U.L.: *That's right. We're not suggesting that at all. We're only sug-*
  gesting—rather we're actually confirming your feeling—that it is
  not yet time to put that information together in a new framework.
  That time will not be until after the Mt. Shasta Mission.

Tex: If the mission, for whatever reason, is not completely
  successful, will that interfere with shifting the Gettysburg
  Battle energy into the Cottage work?

U.L.: *No. The Mt. Shasta Mission will occur. The question is in regard*
  to what degree it will be successful. Your aim has always been five-
  senses form. If the mission is not within the band of five-senses
  physical, that will not stop the energizing, the shifting and the
  movement on the mountain. It will simply not be a 100 percent
  five-senses form mission. And the research at the Cottage will still
  be energized.

Tex: I would agree then that after the Mt. Shasta Mission we
  have another meeting to discuss the work here in light of
  the expansion of the information flow and how we're going
  to use it.

David: Certainly it's an exciting notion to think about. But we
  still need to keep our eye on the ball.

John: The question that occurs to me is this: If the Mt. Shasta
  Mission is anything less than five-senses physical form,
  what do we end up with?

U.L.: *There will be a degree of difficulty on all levels regarding the activation and accessibility others will have with the impulses of information moving through the new leylines because of the inaccessibility grounded into the mission should the mission not be fully five-senses physical. If this were not true, then St. Germain would not be interested in aligning the entire Aquarian leyline system, which personally does not have incorporated in it five-senses form, with this mission. He fully understands the importance of grounding these things through the five-senses. This is important not just to Earth, but to all other levels. Does that answer your question?*

John: Yes. And the same constriction you're talking about will be felt within the work that's going on here?

U.L.: *Yes. It will show up primarily as you pull the information together and actually attempt to ground it—that's where it will show up.*

John: I understand.

David: We don't have to do anything about Gettysburg until the spring. Is that correct?

U.L.: *That's correct. Phase two has already been set into motion and is functioning beautifully.*

David: Does anyone wish to add anything or to ask any questions? (No one had questions.)

U.L.: *I would suggest at this point, if there are no other questions, that we go ahead and close this meeting.*

David: I agree. Thank you for your information on this.

You'll notice I did not say anything during this meeting. I just translated Igor and, otherwise, kept my mouth shut. Once the meeting was over, everyone else in the room was pretty excited by the possibilities Igor presented. I, on the other hand, was worried. I wasn't sure what I was going to mess up if I screwed up the third phase of the Gettysburg work. And what was I going to be doing at Gettysburg in the spring? Wasn't it something about activating the very work the Cottage men had been doing all these years? No pressure there. And something about intergalactic, beyond-the-universe communication flow? Western Union, move over. It was clear that opportunity was knocking, and the men at the Cottage were happy about it. Intergalactic office doors were springing open. Very looooong communication lines were being laid. Information would be flying everywhere. You know, I don't mind the fate of the Western world depending on my work …well, I don't mind *much.* But I have some serious problems with the fate of the Cottage, the planet, the universe and beyond depending on it.

I especially remember thinking two things after this third meeting was over: (1) Where was my naked man when I needed him? (2) When were these men going to figure out that I was not their "nature girl," give me my rototiller and kick me out of there? Boy, they were stubborn.

Chapter 24

Pan Speaks

WHEN I THINK BACK TO THE four months after Igor's third Mt. Shasta meeting, I tend to remember this time as quiet and easy going. But when I look at my notes covering that period, I realize it was anything but quiet and easy going. At times, during the first six weeks especially, it was hell. You see, I made a mistake.

I needed help doing the chores around Perelandra while holding down the garden research, keeping up with the Cottage schedule, having MAP medical sessions two to three times weekly and preparing for the Mt. Shasta Mission. I met a couple at Peter Caddy's community during my September trip, and they wanted to come to Perelandra to work. At the community, these people were pleasant, hard working, and we got along well. They came to Perelandra just after the third meeting and stayed in our home. But from the moment they arrived, they were different people from the ones I met in California. It would be an understatement to say that they were needy—and sometimes unbelievably outrageous. (The woman showed up at our Thanksgiving dinner dressed in a negligee. That's right. A flimsy, lacy nightgown. My other dinner guests were a little bewildered, but amused.) They really did not want to be told what to do at Perelandra. They wanted to figure it out on their own and do the jobs "in their own timing," thank you. They agreed to work six hours a day (five days a week), but almost immediately they started working three hours a day and complained about how hard they were working.

The Cottage men told me to hold my ground and let these two people adjust to me. They also told me—often—that my new helpers were goldbrickers and I needed to get rid of them. I kept thinking the Cottage men were being a little tough and all that was needed was time for these two to adjust to Perelandra. But I was a fool. Adjusting wasn't the problem. The first one left Perelandra within six weeks and the second one followed a few weeks later. It was truly unpleasant for all of us while they were there, and they took up a lot of my time and energy, neither of which I could spare.

In January 1985, the work at the Cottage stepped up to a new level. Except for an occasional discussion with the men about the nature work at the mountain, I wasn't involved in their planning. So I turned my attention to nature's information for the 1985 Perelandra garden. In February, I was talking to the men about how the garden work was coming along, and I started describing a gardening book. In half an hour, I had written down a list of chapters, and it was clear to me that this was a book I keenly wanted to write. I decided that I would not start it until August of that year, after the mission, and it would be called the *Perelandra Garden Workbook.* Thus, in the midst of the Mt. Shasta Mission madness, we have the birth of my second book.

On March 17, I had an appointment with four women who wanted to talk to me about something—I wasn't sure what, but they said it was important. They would be driving from Baltimore, Maryland, to Perelandra, so I figured I'd give them some time for their effort. As it turned out, they only stayed about a half hour, and I never did figure out what they wanted from me. As they were leaving, one of them offered me a gift. She said it was a Hopi paho. I had never heard of pahos before and knew nothing about them. Through the lens of ignorance, all I could see in my hands was a feather, obviously a special feather, with a long string tied to one end. The woman explained that the Hopi

Indians are the guardians of peace on our planet, and wherever a Hopi planted a paho, peace was grounded. I accepted the gift and thanked the woman. Then they left Perelandra.

Even though I had no idea what this paho thing was all about, the comment about grounding peace caught my attention, and I felt that somehow it was going to be used for the Mt. Shasta Mission. The fact that I was quarter Navajo and not Hopi must not be an issue in these modern times—perhaps any Indian can bury a paho. I opened the Mt. Shasta Mission coning and asked if I was to take the paho with me to the mountain. The answer was yes, but we wouldn't know if or how it was to be used during the mission. I would be told what to do on the mountain. Terrific. Now I had a mystery in the form of a string tied to a feather.

Also in March, nature told me to begin developing the Perelandra Rose Essences and that the Rose Essences were to play an important role in stabilizing the people and the site during the Mt. Shasta Mission. I began the development by opening a four-point coning for these essences and, once again, followed nature's bouncing ball. First, I balanced and stabilized the entire rose ring (the outer-most ring in the garden) and each of the fifty-four rose bushes growing in the ring. Then, still connected with nature in the coning, I walked around the rose ring and tested each bush individually to find out which ones were to be included in the Rose Essences set. I was relieved to discover that only eight roses out of a possible fifty-four would make up the set. The next day, I set up with nature to get the definitions for these eight new essences. And on the third day, nature gave me the procedure I was to use to make the flower essence tinctures, step by step. I was set to go. Now all I had to do was wait until May for roses to bloom on these eight bushes.

The new Rose Essence information raised a lot of questions about how they were to be used for the mission. Also, the Cottage team and I had more questions about nature's role in the grounding process at the site and for the mission. And by this time, Hyperithon had made several successful landings on the mountain. (He was keeping them out of full five-senses range so as not to scare or excite the folks living around the mountain.) All of this left us with a list of questions that I needed to ask nature about. On March 22, I opened a four-point coning and included, along with David, Hyperithon and my own higher self, the Deva of the Mt. Shasta Mission, the Deva of the Mt. Shasta Mission site, the Deva of Perelandra and Pan. I then told them what I wanted to do.

Machaelle: We need information for the mission from your perspective, and that's why this meeting is being opened. I have a list of questions that I'd like to go over with you and I'd like to get more insight on how I can work with you before, during and after the landing.

I'd like to open with some questions on the protection dome at the site. Are there any problems maintaining this dome at the site through the day after the mission landing? As you know, Universal Light has recommended this timing, but I want to verify it with you. You originally stated when we set up the dome that I could maintain the dome at the site for several days after the mission landing. My sense is to go back to the mountain the day after to personally release the protection and also to return the site back to its rhythm with the mountain. What are your thoughts?

Pan: *The protection dome is firmly in place, and it is (and has been) functioning perfectly since you placed it in the fall. There is no problem with keeping this dome functioning with its full intent through the landing, plus any period of time you so desire after the landing. Your intuition to return to the mountain personally to* release the dome is, from our point of view, advantageous. Although you placed the dome and activated it from the Cottage, it is better for all concerned if you return to the site personally to release the dome. The primary concern at that point will be to shift the site back to the natural rhythm of the mountain, and that shift needs to be made prior to releasing the dome.

You will need to return the site to the mountain from within the dome itself. The reason for this is that the environment that has been created within the dome is, shall we say, mission-focused. There have been changes and shifts that have gone on within the site since the dome was placed that are primarily for the purpose of the success of this mission. Those shifts are going to have to be recognized by you and changed in order to return the site to the mountain. It would be far easier for you to do this within the environment of the dome—that is, the environment of the landing, of the mission itself—than to first remove the dome and try to work within the domeless site that is no longer of the mission. You might say that this site is on loan from the mountain to the mission and that the environment being created there is completely mission-oriented. The foundation for that special environment comes from the balance that was present in the mountain prior to the dome. Once the dome was activated, the site itself was removed from the overall timing and rhythm of the mountain. That is why we say the site is on loan to you from the mountain: It is an environment that is at your service specially for this mission.

There is no issue, as far as we're concerned, regarding the maintenance or upkeep of the dome. It is firmly in place and a reality unto itself. It is functioning and strong. You need not be concerned about its presence or its strength. Now, we might say at this point that the presence of the dome is due to your intent, not ours. We have, from the position of nature, accepted your intent (and we might add, with gratitude) because we understand the purpose of *your intent to be one of care and concern for all — including the people coming to the mountain by foot and by craft and the nature that is involved at the site. Once your intent was accepted, there was no issue as to whether this protection dome would be anything other than strong and fully functional. The environment within the protection dome is the result of a co-creative process between us of nature and the humans represented by you.*

We might add at this point that the landings that have gone on at the site in preparation for this mission have been as helpful to us as to those involved in the landing. Each time there is a landing, even though it be out of the five-senses range, we are able to further fine-tune and adjust the environment within the protection dome for the mission. We would like six more landings to complete our process. If more landings are needed (beyond the six we have requested) for your purpose, there's no issue as far as we're concerned. Just as you were able to receive data regarding the actual landing and the ship when Machaelle went to the mountain in September, we have been able to receive valuable data on how best we may support this mission every time the ship is married to the site. So, as we've said, to complete our process, we would like six more landings — is that agreed?

Hyperithon: That's agreed. We will supply all the landings you need. My question to you is this: Do you need those landings at specific times in a specific rhythm, or is it just that you need six landings no matter when they occur?

Pan: *The timing and rhythm don't matter. Each time a craft lands, we go through a fine-tuning process and we shift resources into the site and the dome as part of a creation of that landing environment.*

Hyperithon: I suspect from our end that we'll need more than six landings.

Pan: *That's fine. Then we'll have what we need plus a little extra. What-*
ever you have over the six, we'll use to check our work.

    We perceive the next question about the protection dome having
to do with whether the protection needs to be broadened in area or
intent. At this point, the dome need not be changed, either in size or
intent. It is set up and functioning in a manner that responds com-
pletely to the site's preparation needs between now and July. The
"mission preparation" intent must be shifted prior to the physical
landing, and that would be the purpose of Machaelle going to the
mountain prior to the landing. She need not do this work just
twenty-four hours before. It can be one, two or three days before—
whatever she feels comfortable with. At that time, because of the
actual physical landing, the ceremony and the work that's to occur,
the site will have to change from the intent of preparation to the
intent of "mission go." No one need concern themselves with that
shift in intent at this time. When Machaelle gets to the mountain
in July, she'll know precisely how that shift is to occur. In essence,
she will be the representative of the mission at the site and will be
the person to shift the dome to "mission go." Now, if she's feeling
uncertain about her position in that role, in terms of representing
the mission itself, she can come to the mountain as liaison for the
mission and connect with David. His understanding of the mission
and his intent will initiate the shift to "mission go."

Machaelle: I would prefer that I work with David because of his
position in the mission. His understanding and knowledge
about this mission is far greater than mine. My focus is primarily on nature, so I'm deliberately not taking in other
information that I'm not involved with.

Pan: *Then we agree with you: You will be connecting with David. Just*
as the mother ship landing was shifted through you to the site from
Hyperithon when you visited the mountain in September, David

can initiate the shift to mission go at the site in July through you. We're talking about the concept of intent here and are treating it as an ingredient within the protection dome. The ingredient we have in the dome at this point is one of mission preparation. In July when you come to the mountain, you will shift into the dome the ingredient of mission go because it will no longer be appropriate for the protection dome to maintain an environment of preparation. Is this concept understood?

Machaelle: Yes.

David (to Machaelle): I'd like to be with you however possible when you go to the site in July anyway. I think it's going to be important.

Machaelle: Good. This leads me to an area that I wasn't sure we'd be able to address today and that has to do with Peter's witnesses. We've talked about different ideas in terms of protecting them and what I'm wondering now is, should their reality as a group become included in the protection dome when I go back to the mountain to shift the protection from mission preparation to mission go?

Pan: *The protection dome is a complex creation of energy. Don't lose sight of that fact because as we deal with the dome you will see a number of energy principles coming into action. I wanted to remind you of that before answering your question. It is a good idea to include the group dynamic created by the collection of witnesses and any others coming to the mountain by foot. We distinguish between group and individual here. For the Mt. Shasta Mission itself, these people are to witness the ceremony as a group. They will be functioning as a group. Therefore, at the mountain site, we will be addressing their needs as a group. You are dealing with their individual needs through the work you and Salvesen are doing with them regarding the shock and trauma their bodies experience when faced with a mother ship. The information you get from that work will allow Salvesen to anticipate their needs as individuals and to prepare them as individuals prior to their coming to the mountain.*

We recommend that you introduce their energy as a group into the dome and do an essence readout for them as a group at the time you shift the dome from preparation to mission go. You will introduce the essence or essences they need into the protection dome at that time. Now, what that will do is two things: One, it will add their group reality into the protection dome itself so that when they enter the dome, they won't feel they have entered an alien environment—they will enter an area already adjusted for their reality as a group. You want them at ease and relaxed, and we see it as essential to their comfort that their group reality be introduced into the dome prior to their coming to the mountain. They will sense the familiarity as soon as they enter the dome, and they will feel comfortable. The second advantage is in regard to the addition of the essences they need as a group. These essences will be present in the dome and available to the group once they physically enter the dome. The essences released will be made available to them automatically, and whatever imbalances they may experience as a group will be balanced. If we understand the intent of the mission for these people, which is to perceive the landing through their five senses, we feel that this will be an essential step toward that goal.

Machaelle: In light of what you're saying about the people and the dome, are you recommending that, from this point on, the simulated landings move through the protected environment and that this combined reality be infused into the individuals—is this what you're suggesting?

Pan: *Absolutely. Universal Light has already suggested this, and we agree. There is no need, from this point on, to simulate a mother ship landing without moving it through the protection dome—except for research and that can be done after the mission. We perceive*

*your question regarding whether or not the dome can be removed
from that simulated landing prior to the mission and recommend
that you not tamper with the removal and replacement of the dome
in order to understand the effect of the dome on the individual. If
you wish to understand that, we suggest you work with people who
were not part of the mission after the landing and simulate the
landing without the protection dome. Our primary point is that
the protection dome not be tampered with now for the sake of
research and that all those going to the mountain be prepared with
landings simulated within the protected environment at the site.*

Machaelle: Since you're changing the dome environment every
time a spacecraft comes in, will that affect the simulation
process Salvesen and I are putting these people through?
Should we wait until after the sixth landing to continue
their preparation?

Pan: *No. The impact of our dome changes to the people will be minimal.
The shifts we're making are in response to the landing of the mother
ship itself, not to the people. If there will be any effect on the people
at all, it will be one of stabilizing them even more than they were
prior to our changes. We suggest that you do the simulations within
the dome anytime you wish. The final shift of the environment,
which will take their presence into account, will occur in July when
you come to the mountain and enter their reality as a group into
the dome environment.*

Machaelle: I'm a little out of my area here, but what about the
people who are coming in by mother ship? Does their
reality need to be entered into the protection as well?

Pan: *When you connect with David for the shift to mission go in July,
you also allow their reality as a group to move from him into
you and into the dome environment. We will then shift and*

accommodate their presence as well by infusing the environment with the essences this group needs. We recommend highly that this shift occur prior to your introducing the group coming in by foot. That will allow the reality of David's group to interact with that of the other group; whatever trauma or imbalance occurs when these two groups actually meet will show up there, and you can test for and introduce essences into the environment that will accommodate that particular, shall we say, shock. The group coming by ship will not have nearly the shock factor to deal with that the group coming in by foot will. The group coming by foot, we understand, will be dealing with, for lack of a better term, a crisis of faith. Most likely they will not be convinced this is going to happen until it actually happens. The group coming in by ship understands it is happening and will not be dealing with this crisis in faith.

Machaelle: I don't need to know the makeup of that group as long as David has it in his mind, do I?

Pan: *No. Just move his information as energy through you. You will function (as you functioned in September) as the conduit.*

Machaelle: Since you've not mentioned this, I take that it's not important one way or another whether Salvesen goes with me to the mountain prior to the landing for the mission-go shift.

Pan: *It's not important. It's your choice. I suggest strongly that you take whomever you feel comfortable with and that whoever goes understands that they are not to press you in any way in terms of timing. Your shifting of the protection dome to mission go is going to be critical and shouldn't be interfered with by anyone who doesn't understand the importance of what's going on.*

I want to explain to you at this point the dynamics of what you are receiving from us for this session. I [Pan] am functioning as the conduit for this meeting, meaning that the information you are getting from me automatically includes information from the Deva of the Mt. Shasta Mission Site, the Deva of the Mt. Shasta Mission and the Deva of Perelandra. In order to facilitate this session, I am speaking to you in one voice, but with the four avenues. I realize that you were both questioning the devic input and also vacillating between whether to use "I" or "we" when translating from me. It is fine to use the singular with the understanding that I speak in the plural.

Machaelle: Ugh…You noticed I've been tripping all over myself a bit here. Thank you for clearing that up. It helps.

Pan: *I thought it would.*

David: May I interject a question here?

Machaelle: Yes.

David (to Machaelle): When you shift the dome to mission go in July, would it be better if I have present here those who are in charge of the different areas of the mission?

Machaelle: I don't know. I'll have to ask.

Pan: *I'll leave that up to you, David. I think your understanding of the picture will be more than adequate to enable you to make that shift. In terms of energy, I suggest that the mission-go energy Machaelle moves into the dome and site come directly from you. If at that point you feel that having the individuals (each in charge of his own area of the mission) in the room with you will clarify your intent and your understanding of the mission more than being by yourself—if that feels better to you, then certainly that should be done. But to facilitate the process, so as not to overwhelm Machaelle, I suggest that the actual shift to mission go come directly from you to Machaelle and through her into the site.*

Hyperithon: Certainly with the practice landings we're having, nature will more than understand that part of the mission by July.

Pan: *That's correct. That will be a major part of the mission we need to know, and by then we'll know. What we need is the shift of intent from preparation to mission go, and you do not personally need to be present unless David wishes that to be a function of the group leaders at the Cottage.*

David: I'll be talking to Machaelle about it and will make a decision—as long as we know that whatever decision we come up with is fine with you.

Pan: *There is no issue here.*

Machaelle: The question arose awhile ago about whether or not I could include in the protection dome for July different elements such as the sensation of an enclosed, protected environment so that when the people arriving by foot enter the site they would have a sense of enclosure and protection. What do you think?

Pan: *Again, there's no issue here. That would be an ingredient you can add in July, if you so wish. The domed site has within it the characteristic of an enclosed environment. When you get to the mountain in July, the kind of detail and refinement you are now bringing up can be added easily when you shift the environment to mission go.*

Machaelle: Just to check, do I understand correctly that this protection can hold indefinitely? David has the landing scheduled for anytime between the 14th and the 17th, with the 15th as the target date. Do I need to be concerned about the site once it's set for mission go if it is postponed for whatever reason, for example, until the 17th?

Pan: *There need be no concern on your part. The dome and its environment will hold until you return to the mountain to release it.*

Machaelle: Good. I'd like to shift the topic to the actual landing on the mountain.

Pan: *That's fine.*

Machaelle: We want to make sure that the people coming to the mountain both by craft and by foot maintain a strong stability throughout this entire landing, and the question arose as to how nature might help facilitate this. We thought of creating a team with nature and myself, for the express purpose of responding to any needs during the actual landing. What we need is your input on this.

Pan: *I have already taken that situation into consideration. Remember, when the question of the expanded mission first arose, I was part of the coning; therefore, I understood the situation from our perspective. What I've been devising throughout this particular meeting addresses those needs. When you add both group realities into the protection dome prior to the landing itself, their stability will be met by your introducing the needed flower essences into the environment. What we will be doing is maintaining those essences as part of the atmosphere of the protected site. When they enter this environment, the groups will receive the assistance they need for their stability. That's one of the beauties of this protected environment: We can create, and have been creating, something completely separate and apart from the mountain specifically to address the needs of the Mt. Shasta Mission.*

Machaelle, you can have complete confidence that each group assembled at the mountain will have available to them what they need for their stability as a group. That is one reason your trip to the mountain prior to the landing is so important. This is also assuming that Salvesen will have done her work with the people prior to their coming to the mountain by foot so that this group will be entering into the site having had their individual needs met. As a group their needs will be met within the dome itself. Don't forget that in terms of energy, a collection of individuals is very different than a unified group. Therefore, it will be equally important that Salvesen provide the individual needs prior to coming to the mountain for the mission.

Machaelle: Okay, that took care of that situation. I take it I'm to bring the Perelandra Rose Essences.

Pan: *They will be the primary essences that will be used on the mountain. Most likely the need for Bach and the FES essences will show up in the individuals through their work with you and Salvesen.*

Machaelle: With everybody coming to the mountain for this landing, it seems important that nature somehow be represented by something other than the actual physical location of the mission site.

Pan: *Let me interrupt here because you're jumping the gun and getting into our next order of business, which has to do with the grounding process of the mission. I strongly suggest that your Mt. Shasta Mission four-point coning be another element added into the dome environment prior to the landing. This includes the Deva of Perelandra, the Deva of the Mt. Shasta Mission Site and the Deva of the Mt. Shasta Mission so that there will be three devas representing the devic point of the coning. I will be happy to continue to represent the nature spirit point. I suggest that David, Lorpuris and Hyperithon together represent the White Brotherhood point and that you, Machaelle, continue to represent the Earth level human point, the connection that bonds the entire four-point coning.*

By including the coning, you consciously add a unique balance and grounding into the environment. The Mt. Shasta Mission coning creates a balanced involution/evolution phenomenon, and when you include it in the site, you include a functioning, all-encompassing nature/human unit that will maintain balance and, therefore, grounding. Everything and everyone will be fully grounded by this coning unit. You need not be concerned beyond this about grounding the mission.

The energy that will be released—the shift from (as you call it) the Piscean to the Aquarian dynamic that's going to occur on the mountain in the arena of government and military will occur within an environment that is grounded; therefore, the shift will be grounded. The energy that will be moved from the site to the lead craft and then spread into the leyline system will be grounded. It will have grounding energy as part of its makeup and be fully infused with not only nature's grounding but also (in this particular case) the strong involution/evolution grounding tool, which is the coning unit you will introduce into the protection dome. I point out that you must introduce the Mt. Shasta Mission coning specifically and activate it within the site and that also can be done at the time you make the shift to mission go. Once this is done, you needn't be concerned about grounding what's going to happen at Mt. Shasta in terms of the people, the mission or the activation of the leyline system—everything will be grounded.

Machaelle: Well, that takes care of that, too. You seem to have this under control.

Pan: *You're right.*

Machaelle: Is there anything else that you see now that I need to add to the coning?

Pan: *Yes. This is most likely going to be our last suggestion to you in terms of the site shift to mission go. Your position as liaison with nature has to be taken into consideration because you will be entering the mountain not just as a representative of man, but in the role of* nature's liaison as well. In this particular mission, that's been a key role from the beginning in terms of your work—your understanding. Also your presence on the mountain during the landing will represent, among other things, man and nature come together. You are the bridge between the intelligence of nature and the intelligence of man. You are the one who has brought man and nature together in this mission.

I recommend that when you come to the mountain to shift the site and dome to mission go, you enter that environment as Machaelle, the human, but at some point early on you shift your presence in the site to that of nature's liaison. At this point, activate that connection within you and add it as an element into the site. That addition will give more stability to those coming to the mountain, particularly those coming by foot. But there is another side to this: You will be coming to the mountain with these people and be functioning in this mission as nature's liaison. By virtue of your having added your reality to the protection, the people entering the site will sense its presence and be relaxed around you as you work. You will not strike an alien note in them because your working reality will already be present in the environment.

I have one more suggestion regarding grounding—not the grounding in the site, but the grounding within the mother ship coming in. I recommend placing the crystal/topaz that is currently at the Cottage in the mother ship in a prominent position and using it for the purpose of grounding during its positioning and descent into the site. Now, "using" does not mean doing anything in the ship other than recognizing the crystal's position and its function. You need not tell the historic leaders coming for this mission the crystal's purpose, but the ship's crew, those involved with planning the mission, certainly Hyperithon and David should understand what that crystal is doing. The crystal/topaz that originated at Perelandra has been split 100 percent/100 percent and shifted to the Cottage *from the Perelandra garden, and during this mission it will be returning to Earth—the same level as the Perelandra garden. Because of this, it will function as a grounding honing device. It will move you into the site, physically ground you, and connect the reality of the ship and the guests on the craft into the site. Another way of saying this is that it will function as a fusion device.*

David: Is there a specific area of the craft in which the crystal/topaz should be?

Pan: *We'll leave that up to you.*

Hyperithon: I think I know where it belongs.

David: Do you want to say it now?

Hyperithon: No, I'll…well, wait a minute. Am I allowed to borrow the crystal? I think I need to ask Machaelle that.

Machaelle: I think I need to ask Pan that. Pan, the buck has been passed to you. Can Hyperithon borrow the crystal out of the Cottage between now and July?

Pan: *Yes, as long as the crystal is in the Cottage for the coming summer solstice, its removal from the Cottage is fine. However, I recommend that the crystal not be taken for a long period of time.*

Hyperithon: I can have the crystal out and back to the Cottage within the same day.

Pan: *That is best. Machaelle physically feels the crystal's presence in the Cottage, and it would be good not to remove it for any length of time.*

David: Then you'll have to have it out and back within a day.

Hyperithon: Yes. (To Pan) Then would you recommend that we continue our simulations with the crystal present?

Pan: *I recommend that the crystal be shifted to beyond five-senses form along with the ship as well.*

Hyperithon: There's not a problem with that. In fact, I can possibly use the energy of the crystal without removing the crystal from the Cottage.

Pan: *No. Remove the form, have custody of the form in your presence and then shift it to the site with the ship.*

Hyperithon: Fine.

David: Should the crystal be kept in the wooden box?

Pan: *Not while it's being used for the mission during preparation and mission go. It must be exposed to light on the spacecraft.*

Hyperithon: Need it be natural light? We're going to have difficulty with that.

Pan: *No, it must simply be exposed to the craft's interior light.*

David: Just to be clear, are you saying we need to transport the crystal back and forth in the box?

Pan: *Yes.*

Hyperithon: I had a feeling that crystal was coming with us.

Pan: *You'll find that the crystal is going to make quite a difference not only because of its function as a crystal/topaz combination but also because the topaz itself links one with the devic realm in nature. The other important aspect is that because the crystal/topaz originated from Perelandra's garden, it has been infused with the Perelandra-level energy, which is the level you're coming into.*

Hyperithon: Yes, I understand that. It makes all the sense in the world.

Machaelle: I'm through my list of questions. Is there anything else we can think of at this point?

Pan: *I am also finished with the information I held for this meeting, unless you have specific questions.*

Hyperithon: No, I think I have what I need for now.

David (to Pan): I think we should have another meeting with you just prior to Machaelle going to California to make sure we have all the information we need at that point.

Pan: *That's not a problem. We're available at any time, as you know.*

David: That sounds fine. Do we all feel it's a wrap?
(All indicate yes.)

I closed the coning, then David, Hyperithon and I talked about the information Pan had given us. Prior to this meeting, the three of us had tossed around ideas on how we could address the different issues we had just raised with nature. To be honest, Pan gave us a completely different way to go, and it was a simpler and better way, as well. So much for our trying to figure out nature's job. I left this meeting not only understanding what I was to do on the mountain for the mission-go shift, but feeling confident about doing the work. Perhaps the Cottage men had found the right "nature girl" after all. There goes my rototiller.

Chapter 25

Gettysburg Battlefield

PHASE THREE

It was now early spring, and for the next four weeks I concentrated on the Perelandra garden. Salvesen asked me to give a flower essences workshop at her office at the end of March, and on the day of the class my neighbor's cows busted through the fence and spent the morning tromping around my garden. Work wise, this set me back some.

In mid-April, I received word from nature that it was time to go to the Gettysburg Battlefield for phase three. Once again, Salvesen was going to accompany me, and we decided on April 22 for our adventure. On April 21, I opened a coning meeting and included Igor to find out what I was to do for phase three.

U.L.: *Phase three will be simple tomorrow. There are actually two steps to phase three. Step 1 will be accomplished tomorrow. Step 2 will be done by you at Mt. Shasta when you are there in July.*

Step 1: The many souls who have had karmic ties to the Battle of Gettysburg have answered the call to return to the battlefield this past year. Once there, they either consciously or unconsciously experienced a shift that allowed them to free themselves from the battle. For the most part these souls returned, experienced a change in insight either around war in general, Gettysburg specifically or their relationship to their country. As this shift occurred, as we've said, their karmic bonds to the battle were broken. Not only were they set free from the battle, but the battle was set free from them. This was vital if we were to continue forward with phase three.

For Step 1, first go to the area where you planted the comfrey. For this phase, you will be working with the Copse of Trees and the High Water Mark areas. In each, you are to conduct the final "mop-up" phase of the karmic release process the souls have been going through this past year by infusing each area (Copse of Trees, then the High Water Mark area) with Comfrey essence that will be released to you from the plants. Infuse the entire area with this Comfrey essence (you'll see the full area included in each spot in your mind's eye once you get there tomorrow), then do an Energy Cleansing Process and use the comfrey energy to form the cleansing sheet five feet below the ground surface. This will clear both areas of any karmic energy that may still be present.

Next, proceed to the Battle Energy Release Process, releasing the energy of the final stage of the Gettysburg Battle that has been held in custodianship by nature for over 100 years. Once released, test each area for essences. This will complete the job in these two areas and bring you full circle with the job you began in phases one and two. The battlefield will be fully released.

There's more to do however.

We suggest you do this last part from the Eisenhower Tower. Once there (at the top), connect with the Overlighting Deva of the Gettysburg Battle and ask for a balancing and stabilizing reading to facilitate the final healing of the Gettysburg Battle. For that work, test the battlefield using your flower essences and your full soil balancing kit as both your balancers and your stabilizers. Each needed element is to be administered to the battlefield by nature, which will be poised and ready to infuse them throughout the entire battlefield area. Once this is complete, the Gettysburg Battle will be raised to its higher level and ready to be linked into the Mt. Shasta Mission's protection dome this July.

And finally, there will be a gift given to you from nature. You and Salvesen will be directed from the Eisenhower Tower to the gift. You are to take the gift with you to Mt. Shasta and physically place it into the protected site during the mission-go work as part of the linking of the battle to the mission.

Machaelle: Who should be included in the four-point coning for this work at the Copse of Trees and High Water Mark?

U.L.: *The coning you have been using for the Gettysburg Battlefield work plus David, Hyperithon, the Deva of the Copse of Trees and the Deva of the High Water Mark.*

To answer your thoughts about the gift: The gift should be kept in your cabin at Perelandra until your trip to Mt. Shasta. It should be kept with you during travel and in your custody once you arrive in California. It will be carried to the mountain by you, and you will place it into the protected site area.

Nature will "guard" (if you will) the gift the entire time it is in your custody. Once placed into the site, nature will receive its presence and assure its clarity. You need not be concerned about the gift absorbing any inappropriate energy—especially during the trip to Mt. Shasta.

Here's what the Gettysburg tour map has to say about the High Water Mark, the area I would be working in for phase three:

On July 3 [1863] Lee's artillery opened a two-hour bombardment of the Federal lines on Cemetery Ridge and Cemetery Hill. This for a time engaged the massed guns of both sides in a thundering duel for supremacy, but did little to soften up the Union defensive position. Then, in an attempt to recapture the partial success of the previous day, some 12,000

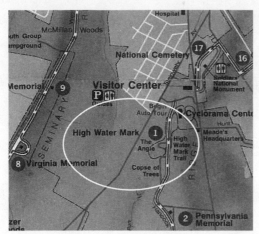

Confederate soldiers advanced across open fields toward the Federal center around the Copse of Trees, The Angle and the Brian Barn, in an attack known as "Pickett's Charge." More than five thousand soldiers became casualties in just one hour.

With the repulse of Pickett's Charge, the Battle of Gettysburg was over. The Confederate army that staggered back into Virginia was physically and spiritually exhausted. Never again would Lee attempt an offensive operation of such magnitude. And Meade, though criticized for not pursuing Lee's troops, would forever be remembered as the man who won the battle that has come to be known as the "High Water Mark of the Confederacy."

Total casualties for the three days of fighting were 23,000 for the Union Army and as many as 28,000 for the Confederate Army.

❖◆◆❖

Salvesen and I arrived at Gettysburg just before noon and found the place full of tour buses and school kids. It was a heavy kiddie tourist day.

First we decided we needed to eat lunch to muster the nerve and strength for going out there and doing what we had to do amid the horde.

The Copse of Trees
and High Water Mark

There were buses and people everywhere at the Copse of Trees. We walked over to where the comfrey had been planted the previous June and, lo and behold, much to my relief, the three plants were still there. While trying to look as nonchalant as possible, I opened the coning. Almost immediately, an area stood out to me visually, and I knew I would be infusing the Comfrey essence into an area that included the Copse of Trees and the land extending some forty-five feet beyond the copse fence. *(Fig. 5)*

This is where you insert "And a miracle occurs here." Everyone had cleared out of the High Water Mark area. There were no people, no buses and no cars. Salvesen mumbled something about the extraordinary clout I must have. I, on the other hand, felt that out of the many amazing things that had occurred during the Gettysburg work, this had to be the most amazing of all. I walked over to the copse to begin my work.

First, I worked with Pan to infuse the area that stood out to me with the essence from the comfrey plants. According to Pan's instructions, I only needed to wait fifteen seconds while this infusion took place, and, as it occurred, I could feel a change in the atmosphere.

Fig. 5: The Copse of Trees and extended area receiving
the first phase-three Comfrey essence infusions.

Once the infusion was completed, I set up the area for an Energy Cleansing Process. Normally the energy sheet that is used for the cleansing is a simple sheet of white light. This time, as the sheet formed five feet below the surface, I asked Pan to infuse it with Comfrey essence. The Comfrey essence ensured that the Energy Cleansing Process focused only on the energy related to the karmic issues we were working with. In comparison to the many other Energy Cleansing Processes I had already done, this one moved exceptionally quickly and smoothly. The whole process was over in about three minutes.

As per instructions, I did not test the area for essences after the energy cleansing. Instead, I set up for the Battle Energy Release Process, which moved as easily as the Energy Cleansing Process and was completed in three minutes, as well.

With those two processes finished, I tested the area for needed essences to stabilize the work. However, none of the essences I brought with me tested positive. But I kept sensing something was needed. Then Pan told me to test for the new Rose Essences. Luckily, I remembered the names of the roses in the set, and I was able to test a mental list. Royal Highness tested positive. Here's the definition nature gave me for this essence. (But instead of addressing a person, it now applied to the environment I was working with.)

Final stabilization. Royal Highness relates to the full stabilization one must experience when an evolutionary step or movement has been completed. In gross terms, one might say that this is the mop-up essence. Once a conscious process has been completed, the individual has moved all aspects and levels of himself into a position of new perspective, new balance and new awareness. There follows a period of adjustment during which the individual is completing the integration process and becoming acquainted with the results of the shift. Royal Highness helps insulate, protect and stabilize the individual and the shift during this period when both are vulnerable.

None of the roses had bloomed yet and I had been unable to make any of the essence tinctures. So, right there on the spot, Pan created the essence from the Royal Highness bush growing in the Perelandra garden. Then, when I gave the go-ahead, Pan shifted the essence into the Copse of Trees area. And that's when Salvesen said she saw a cloud of soft pink light. The Royal Highness rose is soft pink, something Salvesen didn't know.

For the next work, I was told to go to The Angle, just north of the Copse of Trees and right next to the road to work with the rest of the High Water Mark area. *(Fig. 6)* Still there were no people, cars or buses. This time, I infused the Comfrey essence and did the two processes for a larger area that extended south past an obelisk. And again everything went smoothly—and fast.

Fig. 6: High Water Mark area.

That area needed Royal Highness also. But just as I was about to call for the release of another "batch" of Royal Highness, a Wilson Tour Bus pulled up. I knew my luck couldn't hold out much longer. Salvesen said, "Here come the troops!" The bus parked beside us and, to my amazement, my luck still held. The people were facing away from me, the door remained shut and there were no sounds coming from inside the bus. The people just sat there quietly and paid no attention to me. So I finished the work, and Pan infused the area with Royal Highness. This time, both Salvesen and I saw the pink cloud.

After the infusion was completed, the bus pulled away. On the back of the bus was a huge mural of a bald eagle landing on a ridge. I said to Salvesen, "The eagle has landed." With that, three more buses pulled up, a bunch of tourists got off and began wandering around, and cars started driving down the road.

THE EISENHOWER TOWER

Going back to the Eisenhower Tower was like returning to an old friend, although I wished my friend was shorter and had fewer steps. We made the climb to the top and—you guessed it—no one was there. I have to admit we laughed a lot throughout this entire adventure. I mean, really…what is there to say about these things? I got down to work and added the Deva of the Gettysburg Battle to the coning. I now did the final essences and soil kit tests for the entire battlefield to facilitate its healing process. The battlefield needed Royal Highness essence, and the soil needed Nitro-10 (an amendment that adds nitrogen to soil) and greensand. Pan infused Royal Highness first, giving the battlefield a beautiful pink glow (in my mind's eye) and then applied the two soil amendments to the battlefield soil.

THE GIFT

With this accomplished, I was now faced with finding my mysterious gift from nature. Let's see…where in this big battlefield was my gift? It felt like we would be hunting for the proverbial needle in the haystack. We were leaning against the tower railing facing the battlefield and discussing what we should do next, when suddenly Salvesen said, "I wonder why those trees over there are glowing?" She pointed to something across the battlefield that looked to me like a short line of Redbud trees in bloom. I could barely see them, but I checked with Pan and found this was where we were to begin our hunt: Little Round Top. We climbed down from the tower, got into the truck and headed to the other side of the battlefield.

At Little Round Top, Salvesen told me to sit on one of the handy humongous boulders while she walked down into the overgrown field just in front. Hey, she found where we were to start the search. Why would I start arguing with her now? The field where she was walking was filled with more monster rocks. It was definitely not a field for farming. *(Fig. 7)* She moved slowly and headed down the field until she was out of sight. I just sat there—for half an hour or so.

When I finally caught sight of her, I felt I was to join her. She had tried to move back up the hill toward me, but the snakes crawling around near her feet stopped her, and she figured they were hinting that she was moving in the wrong direction. I was thinking, "Snakes. Great." (That's "great" read with a deadpan voice tinged with dread. You can cross your eyes while reading it for special effect.) So I walked slowly down the field to meet her, and we continued moving wherever the snakes weren't slithering. I guess you could say we were taking the path of least resistance.

Fig. 7: The field of snakes.

Fig. 8: The gift from nature.

Further down the field, we climbed over some more rocks and came upon a huge, hidden boulder that sat low to the ground with a large hollowed out circular "garden" in its center. The garden had beautiful, healthy plants growing in no more than an eighth-inch of soil. In some places I could see no soil, and the plants just grew out of the rock. (Ten years later, I learned I had been looking at the miracle of chelation.) In the very center of the garden were some small stones and a small piece of wood. It was clear that no human had placed them there because the arrangement looked too natural, almost random in how they laid in a circular shape.

As I looked at this amazing garden, Pan told me that this was the fairy ring of the Gettysburg Battlefield—nature's office for the battlefield. True to the tradition of fairy rings, the boulder, its garden and the center arrangement were extremely powerful— powerful enough that the hair on my arms stood up. Salvesen leaned down and carefully picked up the piece of wood from the center arrangement, held it in her hands and said, "Here's the gift." I checked with Pan and, sure enough, it was.

When receiving a gift such as this, it's important that the recipient not reach out to *take* the gift. Rather, the one giving the gift must place it into the open hands of the recipient—that is, the recipient must *receive* the gift. When Salvesen placed the gift into my hands, I made sure I didn't move toward the gift or her.

The gift was a piece of weathered wood measuring five inches long and shaped like a long-barreled Civil War gun. *(Fig. 8)* At least, that's what it looked like to me. After examining it, I reluctantly wrapped the gift in clean paper for protection and put it carefully in my backpack where I knew it would be safe. Actually, I didn't want to let the gift out of my hands, but I was afraid I might damage it if I didn't protect it for the rest of the trip.

We stayed at the fairy ring a little longer, then headed back to the truck. Guess what? We didn't have any problem with snakes as we walked out of the field, and we walked right through the middle of the snake area.

By the time I got to the Cottage that evening, David had already received word from Hyperithon that the Gettysburg work was successfully completed, and I found everyone pretty elated about it. Personally, I was just relieved that everything had gone so well. I told them about my gift and that I had placed it in my cabin at Perelandra with the paho.

I now had a wooden gun and a feather on a string to take to Mt. Shasta. I was getting quite an interesting little collection. (Thank god, I didn't have to go through post–9/11 airport security with this stuff. It would have been hard to explain.)

Chapter 26

Runway to Liftoff

I NOW HAD TWO AND A HALF months before I would be flying to California. I returned my attention fully to the Perelandra garden, and on May 4, I received word from nature that I was to add several items to the mineral ring that encircles the crystal/topaz sitting in the center of the garden. On top of specific quartz rocks that formed the circle, I laid an agate, a malachite, an azurite, a piece of amber, a small piece of coral and a piece of petrified wood. When I got everything in place, I felt a shift, and for the first time in many months, I felt relaxed.

That evening I told David about the garden changes, and he asked me to test with nature if the additions to the mineral ring were to be split (a nature process where something from Perelandra is duplicated and then shifted to the Cottage) for the Mt. Shasta Mission. When I checked, it was a yes—and they were to be placed in the wooden box with the crystal/topaz at the Cottage. My assumption was that these new items would enhance the grounding effect of the crystal/topaz on the ship.

On May 16, I wrote the confirmation letter that I was to send to Peter's witnesses on behalf of the Cottage and the Mt. Shasta Mission. I knew that Peter had already given them a brief description of the mission, so I felt comfortable being candid, but I also didn't need to give too much detail since I would be talking with these people at Mt. Shasta prior to the mission. I think it's fair to say that I was naive when I wrote this letter and I certainly had no idea what it would lead to.

16 May 1985

Dear_____,

Peter Caddy has informed me that you have been invited to witness a mission that is scheduled to take place on Mt. Shasta in California this July. I am the liaison between those of you who are coming to the mountain by foot and those who are coming by craft.

The purpose of this mission is focused on the global government framework and its shift from the Piscean dynamic to the Aquarian dynamic. Part of what will occur on the mountain is the creation of the global leyline system for the Aquarian government framework and the activation of that new system. The leyline shift, as well as the entire thrust of the mission, is being fully planned and organized by those working in the government/military "branch" of the White Brotherhood.

Undoubtedly, Peter mentioned several things about this mission to you. One is that a mother ship will land at the mountain site between July 14th and July 17th, with the primary target date as July 15th. Two: the landing will be attempted on the physical plane rather than the etheric. Work has been going on this past year for the purpose of assuring in every possible way that the meeting be experienced by the witnesses through their five senses. As part of the preparation, you are asked to contact me at Mt. Shasta (Finlandia Motel, 916-555-5555), on July 13th or 14th in order to go through a body balance. It is a painless twenty-minute procedure and will be done by a holistic chiropractic physician and myself. For the success of the mission and your own well-being, this work must be completed prior to going to the mountain site.

We are asking that you come prepared with a flashlight (the craft arrival will be around dusk), a bottle of water, hiking boots or good walking shoes and cool weather hiking clothes. We also ask that your physical condition be such that you can easily walk two miles.

I am requesting that we meet as a group in my room at the Finlandia Motel on July 14th, at 3 P.M. At that time, I will be able to give you the details of the mountain meeting, its purpose, timing, etc.

I am also including information about the motels in the town of Mt. Shasta in case you need to book a room. If you were planning to stay with the Caddys during this time, perhaps I should say (if you haven't heard), that they are now living in San Francisco. I will be in Mt. Shasta at the motel by July 11th if you wish to get in touch with me. Prior to then, you may contact me at Perelandra: 703-555-5555.

Looking forward to seeing you at Mt. Shasta.

Sincerely,
Machaelle Wright

I printed twenty-two copies of the letter on Perelandra stationery and mailed them two days later.

On May 18, I made my first Perelandra Rose Essence: Gruss an Aachen. The other seven bushes had buds, and I knew I would be making those flower essences shortly. I breathed the proverbial sigh of relief.

Three days later, I had a three-hour interview at Perelandra with a reporter from the Virginia Biological Farmers Quarterly on co-creative gardening and agricultural techniques. As I was showing the woman around the garden, she asked, "Don't deer come into the garden and cause damage?" I explained that deer did come into the garden, but they just moved on through and were considerate enough to use the garden paths. I could tell she was skeptical. But I told her it was the truth—which it was—until the next morning. I came into the garden and found that deer had walked around the rose ring and eaten the buds off a number of the bushes—including the Ambassador rose bush. I needed Ambassador roses for one of the Rose Essences. Now it was going to be a race to see if that bush could produce flowers before I left for California. If you think I took this calmly...

During this period, the Cottage was a hotbed of activity, and every day it seemed to me that the intensity there increased. In early June, David sat down with me for a "little" talk. First, he told me who would be coming to the mountain on the mother ship. Besides the crew of about thirty-five and David, there would be Hyperithon, Lorpuris, John, Butch, Tex, Mickey and St. Germain. David's invited guests who would be participating in this mission were Winston Churchill, Franklin Roosevelt, Harry Truman, Charles de Gaulle, Joseph Stalin, Cardinal Richelieu (Armand-Jean du Plessis), Mao Tse-tung and three political advisors whose names were completely unfamiliar to me. One advisor was American, one Egyptian, and the other advisor was French. They were three eighteenth-century men who operated behind the powerful rulers of their day and who were considered inconsequential at the time. As a result, they were lost to our history. But in truth, they had been important to their governments.

David explained that these ten men were members of a large group of individuals who were the guardians of the governments around our globe throughout the Piscean Era. The ten coming on the mother craft had been chosen by this group to represent them on the mountain at Mt. Shasta. David explained that it was an honor for them to have been chosen, and, as he spoke about it, I could feel what an extraordinary honor this really was.

I will readily and humbly admit that back then I knew next to nothing about history. (Until I started going to the Cottage, I thought D-Day was the end of World War II.) But I had heard a little about the brutal activities of Stalin and Mao, and I wondered why these two were included in the honored group of ten. David pointed out that there is a difference between the actions of a person's mind and personality and the quality of his consciousness. If I understood him correctly, he was saying that the level of consciousness in each of these men was so great that they functioned as guardians of government for our planet throughout the entire Piscean Era. But like us, each was responsible for his individual conduct and acts and remained responsible for whatever occurred during his respective periods of leadership. David pointed out that these two leaders who were coming to the mountain embodied the broader consciousness of their souls and not just the personalities we knew as Stalin or Mao. I was not to see them solely as personalities with questionable histories.

By using the specific bodies these ten men had already used on Earth while functioning as leaders, they would be able to move into the Earth level as if pulled by a magnet. Although coming to the mountain was still a tricky exercise for them, this movement back into the familiar would help ensure their stability and balance during the mission and while on the mountain.

Finally, David let me know that there would be 7,834 spacecraft positioned around the planet for the primary mission and 7,834 spacecraft paired with them for the expanded mission.

You're probably wondering my reaction to this discussion. Well, I was excited…and it gave me a bit of a headache. Now I *really* understood the issue about keeping Peter's witnesses conscious, alert and focused.

--------◆●◆◆--------

Throughout the final two months, I continued my regular medical sessions with Lorpuris. My body, head and mind were being adjusted and shifted every which way. Sometimes it was painful. Sometimes it was exhilarating. Sometimes enlightening. Sometimes I had fairly difficult reactions to the work and threatened to punch out Lorpuris' lights. But all the time, I could tell I was getting stronger in every way and there was a noticeable increase in my receptivity, intuition and creativity.

By June 19, all the Rose Essences were produced—except Ambassador. There were new buds on the bush, but I couldn't tell if they were going to pop open before my trip.

The summer solstice that year arrived at 6:44 A.M. on June 21. Since beginning the co-creative garden and my partnership with nature in 1976, I have acknowledged and diligently observed the precise moments of each solstice and equinox, no matter what ungodly hour they occurred. These moments fuse me with nature's rhythms and the seasonal rhythm of the garden. I also work with nature to infuse the solstice/equinox energy into Perelandra, the garden and my Perelandra research. This conscious intent heightens the impact of those energies, making them especially strong and supportive. Each summer solstice, I received a color from nature that best represented the tone and intent of the solstice for that year, and I placed bows in that color in the center of the garden and on each of the Perelandra buildings. As you can see, it was and is an important time for me.

I felt this summer solstice heading into the Mt. Shasta Mission to be critical. The only problem: I missed it. I slept through it. In fact, this solstice completely slipped my mind. I woke up several hours after the moment, and before I even got out of bed, it hit me right in the gut. I missed the solstice. I couldn't believe it.

I opened a coning right away and set Perelandra up for the solstice, as I would normally, to see if there was anything I could do to rectify my mistake, but I was told there was nothing for me to do. Around noon, I opened another coning to have a session with Pan about what was going on. I was still especially interested in knowing if I needed to do anything to reverse what I felt was an obvious and potentially serious screw-up on my part.

We realize that this is a most unusual summer solstice for you, and one that would evoke questions. As you have noted, there are no solstice colors displayed at Perelandra for the first time in eight years. And you were asleep for the actual moment of this solstice. One other obvious difference you have noted: When you attempted to open Perelandra several hours after the solstice moment, thus attempting to make the grounded solstice energies available to Perelandra, you were not able to accomplish this. We point out all of this to verify your sense that this is indeed a most unusual summer solstice for you.

This solstice is going to be one of the key elements at the Mt. Shasta Mission this July. The solstice energies were grounded into the Perelandra garden center at 6:44 A.M. and shall be held there by us until you go to the mountain for the landing in July.

As you know, the summer solstice is the celebration of spirit and form fully come together and made visible as one unit. It is the celebration of nature within five-senses form. This is what is being held within the garden center at Perelandra and what will be released by you at Mt. Shasta at a specific moment as the ship is moving through its time and space zones. At that moment, you will call into your focus the crystal/topaz in the center of the Perelandra garden and from this point of focus, you will call for the release of the solstice energy. You will then direct the energy from the center of the Perelandra garden and into and through the crystal/topaz in the mother ship. From that point, you will direct the energy through the ship and release it to the universe. It will then be made available to all the other craft involved in both the primary and expanded mission, as well as to the universe at large. What you will be directing will be similar to what you have already done at Perelandra when you receive and ground the solstice/ equinox energies and direct their release through the garden crystal. The same principle is involved. Only this time these specialized grounded energies will be released from Perelandra by you at the mountain to the advancing mission and ultimately into the universe. This action will not only infuse the mission with the nature energy that celebrates the coming together of spirit and matter, but it will also consciously release to the universe a strong five-senses form ingredient that will enhance the environment surrounding the mission, thus enhancing the mission itself.

We feel you need take nothing from Perelandra to the site in order to accomplish the release from Perelandra. However, check with us just prior to leaving for Mt. Shasta in case there is a change and there is something for you to take along to assist this work.

You also need not move the solstice energy into the site itself as you release it from Perelandra to the mother ship. The solstice energy will automatically become part of the site environment once the energy is available to the universe. The principle focus of your action, the energy release, is the marriage of the solstice energy to the incoming mother ship, the surrounding mission craft and their environment.

About the expanded mission: The solstice energy will be received by the expanded mission's lead craft once the energy has been released into the universe beyond. This will make the energy available to the expanded aspect of the mission operating beyond the universe. We suggest that David be informed of what you will be doing and that he brief those in the expanded mission so that they will adjust their actions accordingly in order to receive the solstice energy. You need not concern yourself once the energy is released into the universe. Your job, as it were, will then be over.

We wish we could be exact about the timing for this work at Mt. Shasta. We understand that it would ease your mind to know now when the release *is to be activated. But you will have to receive that timing on the moun-tain. We can say now that this action will be directed by you at the site the evening of the landing, not before. You will receive a clear indication from us that the time for the release of the solstice energy has arrived. Do not worry. We will not let it slip by you.*

As for your concerns about "missing" the solstice this morning: Hope-fully you now understand that you missed nothing. You did exactly what you were supposed to do. If any questions arise once you share this informa-tion with David, we'll be glad to expand on what we've said here.

Later that day, I met with David. Besides talking about this new development, he questioned how I might facilitate receiving in-formation from each of the mission "department heads" while I was in California, in case they needed me (and nature) to respond to any incoming mission x-factors. For an answer, I consulted Pan. Any time I went to the mountain, whether I was working or not, I was to open the Mt. Shasta Mission coning. That coning would allow each of the mission leaders to have direct communi-cation with me. Pan also told me the signal to activate the summer solstice energy movement from Perelandra would also come through the coning. In short, the Mt. Shasta Mission coning pro-vided me with an intercom system that was connected with nature and each of the mission department heads.

The day after the summer solstice, I got a call from Gary Dunlap, one of Peter's invited witnesses. He wanted me to explain the mission to him. After I talked to him about the primary mission, he informed me that anything Peter Caddy was connected with was a disaster because of the glamour he brought to it. Gary also told me that he had gotten "guidance" that the mission would be attacked on the mountain by "dark forces" and that it would fail. Well, that thrilled me. It added a new wrinkle to things, and now

I wondered if I needed to pack my laser six-shooters for the Mt. Shasta Mission.

I really didn't know what to say to this fellow. He used to be a member of the Findhorn Community, and, when I visited Findhorn in 1977, he was highly respected and considered by many, Peter included, to be someone to listen to. He was also supposed to be Peter's friend. Had I been someone who had casually heard about the mission and knew nothing else about it, I might have felt his information was important. But I had been involved in this mission for well over a year, something Gary was dismissing as unimportant. I knew how carefully it was being put together and how much consideration was being given to everyone's safety. And, quite frankly, I didn't think there were "dark forces" stupid enough to attack an Eisenhower operation.

Really, there was nothing I could say to Gary. Besides, it was clear that he considered me inconsequential and was flicking me off. I told him that I would pass along his information to David. Gary said he and his partner, who had also been invited by Peter, had not made up their minds about witnessing the mission because, he reminded me, they had serious concerns about Peter's involvement. He ended the conversation by telling me he would get in touch with me when I arrived in California.

That evening I talked to David about Gary's phone call. Here's all that David said: "Don't listen to him. He's a fool." And with that, I took my laser six-shooters out of my suitcase and put them back in my underwear drawer.

It was as if Gary's call was a warning: "Attention. Things are about to spin out of control." I began getting some odd phone calls from strangers from all around the country. It had to do with the twenty-two letters to Peter's invited witnesses that I sent out in May. Some of the invitees (actually most of them) had unexpected and unusual responses to that letter. A few of the letters were xeroxed and posted on community and college bulletin boards; some invitees sent copies to friends; some "conveniently" left their letters in books that they then loaned out to others; and some actually announced the mission, giving names, dates and phone numbers from the letter, in classrooms, workshops and meetings. . . . I kid you not.

The calls I received were from people who saw or heard about the mission and felt "guided" that they were to be at the site. Not one of them asked me if they could participate. They just informed me they were to be there. And they each made it clear that they, and they alone, would be *the one* responsible for the success of the mission. They didn't want to hear about the Cottage team or anything else, for that matter. They didn't even want to hear about the mission. Each said they already knew about the mission from their "guides." No one would admit the little they knew about the Mt. Shasta Mission was actually from my letter. One of them said she was the walk-in for Benjamin Franklin and, of course, "he" had to be at the site. Each of them, including "Ben Franklin," had been told by their "guides" that, for the mission's success, they were to do such things as toss programmed crystals into the site and conjure up energies to be released at the site during the mission.

Now, as someone who had been working with nature to develop the balance of the site, the thought of these fine, "well-guided" people lobbing crystals around and unleashing who knew what into the site made my skin crawl. Let's just say I got concerned. (Hmm. Do you think these people were the "dark forces" that were going to attack the mission on the mountain?)

And who were these people Peter was inviting anyway? These well-disciplined, educated, experienced, mature ones who were passing their letters around. Out of all the options they could have chosen for reacting to that letter and the mission, being discreet and keeping their mouths shut apparently wasn't one of them. Were these people morons?

In today's jargon, I would have called the Cottage and said, "Houston, we have a problem." David calmly told me to say nothing to them. Let them blather on. I was to go to the mountain and see who showed up. He felt most of them would not put out the effort or the money to get to the mountain, and we'd figure out later what to do with any who did make it.

As for my reactions to all this? Obviously, I wasn't prepared for this screwiness. Working with nature at Perelandra and at the Cottage had insulated me from these kinds of things. I was angry. I was angry that these people could be so arrogant and disrespectful—to the mission, to those who were planning the mission and to me. And I was embarrassed. What kind of screwball, crackpot level was I living on? After venting my anger at the Cottage, I decided that the only way I could function was to concentrate on the mission and let the witness chips fall where they may.

By now, everyone at the Cottage (myself included) was running full steam taking care of the final preparations for the mission. I made sure I had copies of my notes and sessions for the mission and the Gettysburg work, and put together a notebook with all the information I would need for the mountain.

I was still getting odd phone calls at Perelandra from people who felt they were guided to take over the mission. But, out of all the craziness, one phone call stood out as different. It was from Sarah Wheatley. What caught my attention was her demeanor. It was completely different from the others I had talked to. She was polite, soft-spoken and willing to listen to what I had to say. She explained that she had been told about the mission by a friend who heard about it in Colorado and who had recently traveled to visit her in … (insert organ music here for suspense) … Gettysburg, Pennsylvania. Sarah asked if there was anything she could do to help the mission. Now, that was a different approach. I told her a bit about my nature work at the Gettysburg Battlefield and about

David's work at the Cottage. Then I gave her my regular brief description of the primary mission. For a few seconds, Sarah was quiet. Then she said, "I'm in my office and you'll never guess who I'm looking at right now." When I asked who, she said…(more organ music)…"President Eisenhower." She worked for the U.S. congressman from the Gettysburg district and kept a framed picture of Eisenhower on her office wall. There were so many "coincidences" with Sarah that I told her, "Look. I don't know what you can do to help. But I'll talk to David about your offer and get back to you." Unlike the other calls that sometimes left me with a creepy feeling, Sarah's call made me feel comfortable…and safe.

I presented Sarah's offer that evening. David liked what he heard. He suggested I tell her to go to the Gettysburg Battlefield while the mission was going on in California and just stand there to hold the presence of the mission at the battlefield. I called her back the next day and asked if she would be willing to do this. She was thrilled to help. I gave her the projected touch-down date in July and any other details that might help her. As we talked, it was clear to both of us that she would know where on the battlefield to go once she got there. I told her it was certainly a quiet job that she was being given, but she said she was glad to do whatever we needed. I said I'd call her once I got back from California and we'd exchange tales of our respective adventures. She made me smile and gave me hope for Earth's humanity.

At the end of June, Salvesen and I met with Laura and Albert Townsend and Clarence to do a round of landing procedures. Clarence's body responses showed he was going to need two additional processes once we got to California and before going to the mountain. His nervous system was still having difficulty identifying what was going on. Albert had just had minor surgery, and it tested we were not to do the procedure with him until he got to California. Then it was Laura's turn. She was structurally aligned and needed no adjustments, but her adrenal glands were weak and she needed Eclipse, the new Rose Essence. (I was now testing the Rose Essences set along with Bach and FES for the mission work.) When we moved the mother ship into her body, everything held.

Salvesen's husband, also a chiropractor, was with us this time to work with her for the landing procedure. Before the ship was shifted into Salvesen's body, her structure and systems tested fine, but she needed one essence. When I moved the ship into her body, she had a B-vitamin drain. Otherwise, her body held. It tested that she was to take two Glycodyne (B-vitamin supplements) at the motel prior to going to the site for the mission.

The morning of July 6, I had a dream. I was at the site on Mt. Shasta and thick clouds overhead began to swirl and form a large cone that rotated inwards and counterclockwise toward the ground. I could see the mother ship, and it was descending toward the site through the clouds. I watched as it touched down and stayed with what I was seeing for the longest time. It was a clear visual experience that I could feel viscerally. The dream and those feelings stayed with me all day.

July 7, three days before my flight to California, was a red letter day. *I made the Ambassador essence!* Finally. The Perelandra Rose Essence set was now complete. I was one happy, relieved, grateful camper, believe me. Lorpuris surprised me by asking me to split several of the sets to the Cottage for him to use with those on the mother ship.

On July 9, I opened the Mt. Shasta Mission coning and went through a list of last-minute questions. I asked if the crystal/topaz and Genesa crystal (a three-foot in diameter, three-dimensional circular shape made of thin copper tubing) in the center of the

Perelandra garden were oriented properly and ready for the mission. I was told they were. I also asked if the Perelandra garden was ready for the mission and was told that it was, as well.

For the past couple of days, I had been seeing in my mind's eye an ivory satin bow. Now I asked the question: Was an ivory bow to be taken to Mt. Shasta to assist with the solstice energy work I was to do? Pan said yes. I was to place a bow at the site when I did the work to shift to mission go. I was to use the ivory bow as the focal point for grounding the solstice energy into the site after it was released through the mother ship and into the universe. This was a change from the original information I had gotten.

To end the session, Pan told me to make sure I did an Energy Cleansing Process for my motel room when I arrived. And finally, I was to have a medical session with Lorpuris the next evening to prepare my two bodies for the time zone changes and trip. The coordination between the two bodies while at Mt. Shasta would be especially critical. Throughout my trip, I was to continue splitting my day at both locations—Mt. Shasta and the Cottage—so that each body would maintain its strength and energy.

The next day, I met a close friend for lunch. She knew about my trip and why I was going, and she gave me a gift. She said she did not know why she chose this thing to give me, but she felt I was to have it. It was a small, simple, hand-carved spoon made from cherry wood, and it was beautiful. *(Fig. 9)* The pattern of the

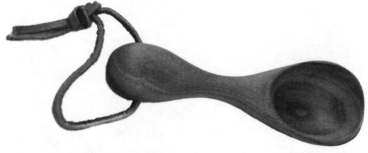

Fig. 9: The cherry wood spoon.

wood grain in the spoon's bowl had concentric circles that looked like the swirl of the clouds in my dream. Other than to remind me of the dream, I didn't know why I should have the spoon either, but I told her I would take it to the mountain anyway— just in case. Besides, it was small and light.

That night, after the medical session with Lorpuris, the pressure around the mission hit me, and I cried. Eventually, I pulled myself together and packed for the trip. My "site kit" backpack included a box of the Perelandra Rose Essences, the four boxes of Bach Flower Remedies, two boxes of the FES Flower Essences (Stocks One and Two), my soil balancing kit (two boxes), pens, a binder notebook, my work notes and records, a regular table-spoon, a wooden "gun," a feather on a string, a small wooden spoon and a yard of ivory satin ribbon. The kit was weighty. I decided I would be taking this stuff on the plane with me. I was not going to let that backpack out of my sight.

Chapter 27

Wednesday, July 10

Departure day. I traveled to Mt. Shasta with my partner, Clarence. Over the previous year, I talked to him about the work at Gettysburg and the mission. I didn't give him details, but it was enough to give him an idea about what I was doing. I had told David that Clarence expressed interest in both the Gettysburg work and the mission, so David suggested I invite him to the mountain. It was an invitation that Clarence accepted quickly with appreciation and enthusiasm.

Mt. Shasta

The mountain came into view as we drove the hour and a half from Redding, California, and neared the town of Mt. Shasta. I stared at it for the longest time as Clarence drove along. I decided I wanted to talk to this mountain and ask if there was anything in my range of ability that I could offer it—a gift of thanks for its unique support of the mission. I made a mental note to get back to that later.

The Finlandia Motel was small, simple, clean and inexpensive— twenty bucks a night. Clarence and I each had our own room, and I could see the mountain from the window in my bathroom. Once I was settled in, I connected with the Deva of Mt. Shasta (mountain) and asked if there was a gift I could offer. My offer was accepted immediately, and I was told that it would be best to wait until after the mission for the information on the gift that was most needed from me. I made a paper note to get back to that later.

Clarence and I had dinner in town and headed back to the motel. In all, it was an uneventful day. I remember thinking, "So far, so good." And with that, I headed to the Cottage.

I could feel purpose in the Cottage air that evening, but other than this the Cottage felt quiet, even calm. David had already told me that they were ready. Their primary focus would be my work on the mountain, attending to a few last-minute details on their end, and getting the spacecraft paired and in position.

Chapter 28

Thursday, July 11

At seven in the morning, we found out why the Finlandia was so inexpensive. It was across the road from a sawmill, and they started their saws and belts and whatever else operated with loud motors at 7:00 A.M. Alarm clock optional, but not needed at the Finlandia.

After breakfast and shopping for hiking boots for Clarence, we drove to the mountain. This was going to be my first big test, and I wasn't sure what I'd do if I failed it. I had to find the site. It had been ten months since my trip to the mountain; I was only there once and it was with Peter and Karen, two people who knew the mountain well. Karen sent me a hand-drawn map to the site that couldn't have been more minimal. Basically it showed we were to go past the upper entrance to Sand Flat, go right when the road forked and walk up about three-quarters of a mile above Horse Camp. Hey, if none of this means anything to you, it didn't mean anything to me either. I suggested to Clarence that we find the upper entrance to Sand Flat and hope my memory kicked in from there. Actually, Karen's map, minimal as it was, gave me a general direction, and I was able to find a trail that looked like the one Peter had led us down from the site. Remember, we didn't walk up that trail, so now I was trying to recognize the landmarks backwards.

But once I stepped onto the trail, something happened. It was as if I had a rope tied around

Fig. 10: The survey
tape at the site.

my waist and someone was gently pulling me up the trail, then off
the trail and through the woods, right to the site. I looked around
and there was the ring of large fallen trees. I thoroughly checked
out the site from every angle to identify landmarks that I remembered from September. But at times I didn't recognize what I was
seeing. The September vegetation looked a lot different from the
July vegetation. And the mid-morning July light was quite a bit
different from the late-afternoon September light. I opened the
Mt. Shasta Mission coning and tested to make sure I was in the
right spot. The test was positive. This was the site. And that's when
I noticed something. Right in the middle of the site, as if to verify
my test, was a yard-long piece of bright red surveyor's tape loosely
draped over a pile of dead branches. It looked like it had blown
there from another location. Or maybe one of the crew on the
mother ship left it there during a practice run just to mess with
my mind. Being left by a hiker or a surveyor, however, were the
two things it did not look like.

On the ground next to the branches and red tape was a relatively flat rock that was about a foot wide and two feet long. It was
in the center of an open, protected space at the base of a huge
tree. I chose this area, almost exactly in the middle of the site, and
that rock as the center or base for the work I would be doing
there. Clarence and I cleared away some branches and generally
tidied up the spot. I tied the red surveyor's tape to a stick and

stuck it in the ground in front of my work area so that I could easily recognize the spot when I returned. *(Fig. 10)*

While Clarence hiked around the mountain, I sat on one of the logs at the site. The mountain and the site were incredibly quiet and peaceful. This moment, this first time alone at the site is one of those special memories I hold in my heart.

Clarence returned and we walked back down the mountain, placing a couple of sticks and small rocks at strategic spots along the trail so that we would not have to rely on a miracle to find the site again. *(Fig. 11)* At the motel, I worked on my notes for the next day because tomorrow I would be shifting the mountain site and dome from mission prep to mission go.

Then I went back to the Cottage and let them know I found the site (something I had expressed concern to them about that morning) and the location of the rock I had chosen for my work base. Finally, to bed.

Fig. 11: One of our trail markers.

Chapter 29

Friday, July 12

We ARRIVED BACK AT THE mountain at 10:30 A.M. I hiked to the site, and Clarence headed out to explore the mountain while I did my work. I told him I would leave my jacket draped over the log nearest the trail when I was finished to give him the all-clear to come up to the site.

It was a gorgeous morning—sunlight pouring through the trees, comfortably warm and quiet. I was always struck by how quiet that mountain was. I cleaned my work rock to prepare for the testing, then I set out the four sets of essences, the soil balancing kit, paper, pen and the notes I made the previous evening on what I was to do. All was now in order.

First, I opened the Mt. Shasta Mission coning. I needed to be present both at the Cottage and at the site, so I activated my body at the Cottage in the room where David and Hyperithon were already seated. I checked essences to make sure I was fully seated in both bodies and tested clear, no essences needed. I then tested the site to clear it before beginning, as well. It needed two drops of Gruss an Aachen, one of the Perelandra Rose Essences (PRE). I placed the drops on the work rock and set up with Pan to shift the essence from the rock and infuse it into the site. The infusion took about fifteen seconds. It was the first of many such shifts I would be doing with Pan from that rock for the mission. I was clear, the site was now clear, and I was ready to move on.

THE SHIFT TO MISSION GO

The evening before, Pan gave me the order in which I was to do the different steps for this morning's work.

1.   David's physical reality had to be shifted into the site to prepare for his presence on the mountain. We needed to see if that would change the site's balance or if he needed something added to the site environment that would assist his balance during his presence. Although David was already part of the coning, it was not the same dynamic as physically standing on the mountain. We did a process similar to the one I had originally used with Hyperithon to move the ship's reality into Peter Caddy's body. David grasped my left hand with his left hand and moved the energy of his physical reality and presence into my hand. I then moved the energy through my Cottage body, into my body at the site and into my right hand, which was resting on the work rock. Finally, I shifted that energy from my hand into the rock. Immediately, I saw the energy radiate out from the rock and into the site, move twenty-five feet beyond the site's perimeter, then move up from ground level and infuse the entire dome covering the site. I waited twenty seconds after all movement had stopped, then tested David for essences to see if being present at the site had altered his balance. He tested clear. I tested the site and its soil for anything it might need as a result of his presence or for supporting David when he arrived on the mountain. There was no site or soil change.

2.   I needed to test the dynamic David and I created together since we would be working and coordinating as a team at the site. This time, instead of moving David's energy cleanly through me and into the rock, I commingled it with my

energy first—the energy in my body at the site—and moved this mix into the work rock. The energy radiated out and infused the protection dome just as it had done before. Once completed, I waited the twenty seconds and tested. David tested clear. The site and its soil also tested clear, meaning that our working partnership did not change the balance of the site and soil. However, I needed PRE Royal Highness. While I was in the site working with David, the site would need to make Royal Highness available to me. So I placed the two drops onto the rock for Pan to infuse into the site and watched a pink energy fill the dome.

3. Next, I was to move David's full understanding of the mission into the site. Earlier, he made the decision that we would use his knowledge of the mission and not gather the mission "department heads" at the Cottage for this step. He felt it would be an unnecessary trip for them to make at that critical prep time in the mission. Once again, we clasped our left hands and I moved the energy of his knowledge of the mission as a single, unified package from my body at the Cottage, into my right site hand and into the rock. The energy moved out and infused the dome area. This time I only tested the site and its soil because the impact was with the site and not with David. Everything tested clear. The soil maintained its balance and the dome environment was clear. To me, this verified that the site was now fully prepared for the mission. We were ready for the big shift.

4. David was now to shift the site from mission preparation to mission go. I had wondered how he was going to do that, but the obvious never occurred to me. He commanded it. He simply ordered the site and mission to shift from preparation to mission go. His command moved through both of my bodies and into the work rock. This time, in comparison

to the other shifts, the energy moved out from the rock and into the dome in a quick, "snappy" fashion and with a different clarity and purpose. Apparently an Eisenhower command still had some clout in that neck of the woods. Pan told me to wait two minutes for the soil and dome environment to complete the shift before testing.

The soil needed liquid seaweed, which meant that when David shifted the site to mission go, that new intent drew nutrients from the soil, creating a drain. Had we not added liquid seaweed (which supplied these needed nutrients), the mission-go intent would have continued to deplete the soil and the mission itself might have been compromised. Pan infused the drops of liquid seaweed into the site's soil, and I waited another two minutes for the infusion to finish.

5.   We had to move my position as liaison with nature for the mission into the site to see if that had any impact. It was another working partnership that would be active during the mission. For this, I was told to hold my left site hand out and request that I be linked with Pan. I did that and instantly felt a strong pressure and warmth in my hand. I felt our energies commingle, and I moved our mixed energies through me, into my right hand and into the rock. This shift was powerful for me, and as I felt the significance of my partnership with nature, emotions rose and my eyes filled with tears. Much to my surprise, I tested clear for essences. Because this had been such a strong experience for me, I expected I would need something. The soil also tested clear. However, the site needed PRE Ambassador, which needed to be available anytime I was working with nature/Pan during the mission. I put the drops on the rock and waited while Pan infused the site with Ambassador essence.

6.   Next, I was to marry the people coming on the mother ship to the site. I again connected with David, and we did this shift in two stages.

First, I moved the ship's crew, David, Hyperithon, Lorpuris, Tex, Butch, Mickey, John and St. Germain as a group to the site. For this, David envisioned them as a group and moved that energy mix to me. I then moved it into the site, waited twenty seconds after the infusion completed and tested. The group tested positive for two drops of Royal Highness. The soil and site tested clear. Hyperithon explained that the crew members who had been to the site during the practice runs had not gotten out of the ship, so technically, their personal presence, individually or as a group, had not yet become part of the site—until now.

Second, we added the group of ten Piscean government leaders. Once again, David formed the group dynamic by visualizing them together. The energy shifted smoothly through the two of me and into the work rock, then from the rock and into the site. The site and its soil tested clear, but the leaders, as a group, needed Royal Highness. Remember, the point of these infusions was to determine ahead of time what each group would need and make it available to them in the site's domed environment and/or soil while they were on the mountain. This was not just to ensure the mission's success, but it was also to ensure the participants' safety. I put the drops onto the rock and the essence infused into the site.

7.   Now we turned our attention to Peter's invited witnesses. David had gotten a list of the people Peter had invited from St. Germain. To this, David added the six people he had invited: Salvesen, Peter, Clarence, Albert Townsend and his

wife, Laura and Paul Botski. Although we didn't know who was actually going to show up on the mountain, David visualized everyone in these two groups to cover any combination that would come to the site. He combined the two groups (witnesses and guests) into one, thus forming the combined group I called the "Foot People" (those coming to the site by foot), moved this package to me, and I moved it into the rock. I watched the energy shift into the site, then I tested. I was a little startled by the results. The soil and site tested clear, but for the Foot People themselves, we needed to infuse the following into the site:

Agrimony: For those who suffer inner torture
    with a cheerful façade.

Mimulus: Fear or anxiety of a known origin.

Yarrow: For vulnerability to psychic or emotional
    "attack," to harmful environmental influences
    or energies.

Gruss an Aachen (PRE): Stabilizes body and soul
    while moving forward in evolutionary process.

I placed two drops of each essence on the rock and was told to wait another two minutes after the infusion completed before moving on.

8.   Next, I married the people coming on the ship *with* the Foot People. Time for the big face off! We needed to see what was going to happen when these two groups looked at one another. But before I did this, Hyperithon suggested I test myself for essences to make sure I was still clear. I was fine, my balance was holding.

To marry the two groups, Pan instructed me to see these two groups facing one another. Then as they looked at one another, I was to mix the energy of each group and move these mixed energies into the rock. By doing it this way, the mixed energies would include whatever impact the two groups seeing one another might bring. I followed the instructions and watched the energy move from the rock into the site. Then I tested. Again the soil and site tested clear, but the two groups facing one another were having a problem. For their use as they looked at one another during the mission, I needed to infuse the site with the following:

Agrimony: For those who suffer inner torture with
a cheerful façade.

Mustard: For gloom, depression and melancholy
that descends for no known cause.

Saguaro: Clarity in relation to parental/authority
images; appreciating the wisdom of true
spiritual elders and tradition.

Gruss an Aachen (PRE): Stabilizes body and soul
while moving forward in evolutionary process.

I placed the drops on the rock and watched the infusion for two minutes. It was clear to me that the Mt. Shasta Mission might be a bit of a challenge when these two groups meet. I sat with my thoughts for a few minutes before moving on.

9. I now realized more than ever how important this next infusion was going to be for the people present at the site. I was to create the energy of a closed, protected, safe environment. As soon as I set up with Pan for this step, I saw in my mind's eye a painting: Mary Cassatt's *Mother and Child*. It had everything I needed: The mother and child were in a room, presumably in their home, and the mother was holding her child, giving the child the safety and protection only a loving mother can give. If I could have, if Pan had hands, I would have given him a high-five right then. This wasn't

just perfect for achieving what I needed, it was très cool. I maintained my focus on the painting, allowed the energy from all the elements in the painting to form and moved that combined energy into my work rock. It moved out into the dome and instantly I felt the environment around me soften. I tested the soil and site, and both were clear.

10. I needed to add the special dynamics of the Mt. Shasta Mission coning to the site. The coning was already activated but solely for this work. Now it had to become part of the site itself in order to add its unique grounding, stability, purpose and intent to the dome. To do this, Pan told me to envision the coning and see it move through my body at the site, into my right hand and into the rock. When I asked for help on how to envision the coning, I saw the clouds in my dream rotating counterclockwise and forming a large cone shape that moved through me and touched down into the rock through my right hand. And, just like the dream, I saw the mother ship slowly descend through the swirling clouds and touch down into the rock through my hand, as well. The strong energy created by the combination of the swirling clouds and the mother ship moved from the rock and quickly infused the entire site. The soil and the site tested clear.

11. Now it was time to deal with the Gettysburg Battle. I asked, "Does the Battle of Gettysburg in its higher purpose and intent get connected into the mission and the site now?" The answer was yes. I then was told to get the wooden gift I had received from the battlefield. However, the gift was now in two pieces, and, needless to say, I was concerned about it. I had carefully wrapped it in tissue paper and bubble wrap and packed it in a box for the trip. I felt it would survive a plane crash. But when I unpacked it at the motel,

Fig. 12: The gift in two pieces.

it was broken. A small portion of the "gun barrel" had broken off. *(Fig. 12)* So here was the moment of truth. I was
expecting at least a bit of a tongue lashing for my careless-
ness. Instead I was told that to do what we needed to do,
the gift had to be in two pieces. (Insert a major sigh of relief
here.) Pan instructed me to place the larger wood piece on
the rock and hold the smaller piece in my left hand. Then I
connected with the Deva of the Battle of Gettysburg and
moved that battle's higher intent and purpose as energy
into the smaller piece. I placed the smaller piece on the rock
next to and touching the larger piece where it broke off,
making the "gun" appear whole again. The energy moved
from the smaller piece into the larger one, then into the
rock and into the site. I waited two minutes for this infusion to complete. Finally, I saw a gold cord move from the
gift on the rock to David and wrap around his right wrist.
Pan said it would remain there until a specific moment during the ceremony on the mountain. I tested the site, the soil
and David. All were clear.

12. I asked about the paho, which I also had with me at the site,
just in case. Pan told me to bring the paho to the landing.
There I was to present it to one of the ten leaders. I would
know who at that time. I was also told that it might be possible that I would not present it but would need to deal
with it differently. So, here's the bottom paho line: I may or
may not present the paho to one of the leaders during the

mission ("Hello, President de Gaulle, sir, here's a feather on a string for you."), or I may have to deal with it later, but I won't know anything until…whenever. (I hate these little mysteries.)

13.   The last thing to check was the ivory ribbon, which I had with me, as well. Pan told me to tie it in a simple bow and place it on the rock. I was to weigh it down with a small rock, leave it in place, and at some point during the mother ship landing, I would be using it. They'd get back to me on this also. (Another mystery. Great.)

Machaelle dwarfed by the Mt. Shasta site.

That was it, so I closed down the coning and pulled myself together, as we like to say in this trade. It took about two and a half hours to complete everything. It was clear to me that the site's environment had changed. It had both strengthened and softened at the same time. Or perhaps instead of being softer, it had become smoother. I checked my notes and made sure I had everything, then sat there in the site for awhile thinking about what had just happened. I *loved* doing this work. It required an amazing amount of focus, but I hung right in there. I was in my element. I was working in direct partnership with nature, something that always excited me, and we were moving through new territory together. It was interesting, educational, amazing and even comforting. And it was another special moment on the mountain that I tucked into my heart. After about twenty minutes or so, I draped my jacket over the log, and shortly after that, Clarence showed up at the site.

◆❖◆

Clarence and I left the mountain, had lunch in town and headed back to the airport at Redding to pick up Salvesen and Paul Botski. I first met Paul during a visit with Albert and Laura Townsend. He had read a photocopy of the confirmation letter that was tucked inside a book that was loaned to him by "Ben Franklin." He had come to the Townsends to meet me and plead his case. He talked about why this mission was so important to him and asked if he could go to the mountain. I told him I'd have to talk to David and get back to him on it. David listened to my take on Paul and told me to say yes and see if he made it to Mt. Shasta. Well, he made it. Technically Paul wasn't an "interloper" (what I was calling the people who had not been invited by Peter or David), but was one of those extended an invitation by David. Hence, he was a Foot Person.

We drove Paul and Salvesen to the Finlandia Motel where they were staying as well, and then the four of us headed out to dinner and talked…a lot. I was heartened to see that Paul didn't act pushy and he didn't seem to feel he personally was the key to the mission's success. He listened well and was willing to do whatever was needed. One thing he needed was the medical work, and we scheduled his first session for the next day. He would need at least two landing procedures before the mission, depending on how his body responded. We went back to the motel and called it a night. I got my notes set for the next day's work at the mountain and left for the Cottage.

Because David and Hyperithon had participated in the day's work on the mountain, I didn't have to recap what I had done. I just needed to give them my opinion of Paul, eat another dinner (each body needs its own set of meals, folks) and head off to bed.

Chapter 30

Saturday, July 13

AFTER BREAKFAST, WHICH WAS pretty early thanks to the sawmill, Salvesen and I met with Clarence and Paul for their medical work. We were a little concerned about Clarence because his body reacted strongly the first two times he received the landing process. Basically it was telling us that it never heard of a mother ship, didn't want to know about such things and wouldn't know what to do with the experience if you paid it. Now we were giving his body a third shot at this. Right away we saw that climbing around the mountain while I worked was doing Clarence a lot of good. When Salvesen cleared him before the landing, he only needed one adjustment. I did the usual hookup with Hyperithon, and we landed another ship into his body. Well...that ole body of his must have been studying up on spacecraft because it now knew what to do with the experience. He needed only one cranial adjustment—a *big* difference from his other landing processes.

This gave Salvesen and me new confidence that we would get everyone through the medical work and ready before they had to go to the mountain. Only two of Peter's witnesses—Jack and Ann Winslow—had the landing process done on them at Perelandra. None of the other witnesses had contacted me, and now they would have to be moved through this preparation pretty quickly.

Paul was a bit like Jack Winslow. Apparently the two of them, whether they consciously knew it or not, could not get enough spacecraft experience. However, Paul needed a lot of work before we could land the ship: a pelvic adjustment, two vertebral adjustments, three essences (including one Rose Essence), B-vitamins and 30 mg of zinc. Salvesen administered everything he needed, then tested again to make sure he was clear. When the mother ship was moved into his body, he held. Everything was fine. Paul's body liked mother ships—a lot.

Finally, Salvesen checked me to make sure everything was in place for the work I would be doing on the mountain that day. I needed just one cranial adjustment and that was it. Considering everything I had done up to that point and the stress I felt, I was pleased with the results.

I arrived back at the mountain site around 1 P.M. I wasn't sure what I would be doing, so I set up the coning, connected with Pan and was told we would be figuring it out as we went along. Today, for our dining and dancing pleasure, Hyperithon and his crew were going to bring the mother ship into the site while I was present. It was a practice run for, among other things, coordinating my work during the actual landing and providing the final mission-go stabilization. To start, I was told to sit on one of the logs around the circumference of the site while the ship descended. I found a large log with a nearly flat top, decided I would use it as my "desk," took a seat and spread out the sets of essences and soil kit boxes on the log beside me. I tested the site and soil, and found both to be clear.

I sat on my log for about a half hour. Nothing seemed to be happening until, suddenly, the atmosphere became tense, alert. It was a palpable shift. Hyperithon called to tell me they were now descending into the site. I was to wait ten minutes for touch down and another five minutes for their on-site shifts. As he said this, I saw the trees and rocks in the site begin to fade out. They were just slowly disappearing. I could feel the ship coming through several stages of its descent because the atmosphere kept changing, and, with each stage, the trees and rocks became less visible. At this point, I began to feel a tremendous heaviness and pressure in my head and neck, and hoped they weren't landing on me. I checked myself for essences, but needed nothing.

Once the ship touched down, my ability to see it was about the same as my ability to see the trees and rocks. Both were faded, but both were there and equally visible. (Or perhaps I should say they were equally invisible.) When Hyperithon told me that the ship had completed its touch down and was now moving through its final stages, the trees and rocks became less visible and the ship more visible. To my mind, the ship was huge. But since I didn't have anything to compare it with, it could have been the mother ship version of a Volkswagen Beetle, for all I knew. It nearly filled the entire site. I sat on my log and watched several people looking out the mother ship's windows at me, and Hyperithon was waving. Besides being friendly, he was checking to see if I could see him. So I waved back.

The trees and rocks weren't totally gone (I could still see a faint outline around everything), and the ship was still a little fuzzy when he told me to check the site and soil. The site tested clear, but the soil needed two drops of liquid seaweed, 30 mg of zinc, 400 mg of potassium and 45 mg of iodine/kelp.

I asked why I was getting such a dramatic readout after all the work that had gone into the site and soil balance prior to this. Hyperithon explained that they had not brought the mother ship into the site this far into five-senses form during the practice runs, plus they wanted me there for the testing when they made the final five-senses practice touch down. The site was now adjusting to a new level of the ship's reality.

Before the mother ship had begun its descent, Pan told me I still needed to release anything that was needed for the site and soil from the work rock. Well, now I needed to put the liquid seaweed, zinc, potassium and kelp on that rock, but there was a

mother ship sitting on it. Before I could finish the thought—
"What the hell do I do now?"—Pan said to walk slowly through
the mother ship and over to the rock.

Back in 1985, we didn't have the Harry Potter stories. But I can
now compare this experience to Harry going through the wall at
the train station to get to Platform 9¾ for the train to Hogwarts.
He just had to suck it up and run headlong into a wall that, for all
normal intents and purposes, was solid. It took a leap of faith on
his part, especially that first time. On the mountain, I took a similar leap of faith, got up from my log and walked slowly into and
through the ship.

Like Harry's wall, it appeared solid, but it wasn't. Not really. It
was like walking through a deep, dense, slightly chilly fog. Once I
entered the interior of the ship, I only saw white fog and, except
for a few lights, none of the ship's details. With every step I took,
I was feeling more head and neck pressure and, added to this, I
now felt nausea.

It's funny what we think at odd moments. But at this particular
odd moment, I hoped I wasn't going to vomit on the site and in
the ship. It just seemed too embarrassing. I could see the headline:

Virginia Woman Hurls in Mother Ship Grosses Out Crew

Determined to maintain dignity, I moved to the work rock, put
everything the soil needed on it and called for Pan to infuse the
soil. I watched the energy move on the surface of the soil without
"bleeding" into the ship's surface, then "soak" into the soil to
about five feet in depth. This took about ten minutes.

One of the things they were checking with the practice run was
my position at the site relative to the interior of the mother ship.
As luck would have it, the ship's main bathroom was positioned
right over my work rock area, and I was now standing next to a
toilet, which I thought would come in handy if I actually vomited.

Laughing, Hyperithon told me to move slowly back to my log. He said they would position the ship differently for the actual mission so that I wouldn't be standing in the toilet! At this point, we were all laughing. (Details. Details.)

By this time in the practice run, I really understood that their target for the mission was a *range* of five-senses form. My sensory system was clearly responding to what was happening at the site, but I couldn't say I was experiencing the same degree of form as you would experience looking at a teacup sitting in your hands. I knew that David was shooting for the cup-in-the-hands sensory experience, but now it was clear to me that all they needed for a successful mission was for everyone's sensory systems to be *activated*. The witnesses didn't have to see it with sharp edges and intense colors. If the sound was faint and the scene fuzzy, it didn't matter. As long as their sensory systems picked up what was happening, the witnesses would still be hearing and seeing.

I also realized that for the mission, the two worlds, the two realities (the ship and the mountain site) were going to fuse and become one so that, at any given time, the crew, the government leaders and the Foot People would experience both realities simultaneously. And this was how the ship, the crew, the leaders and the Foot People were all going to fit at that site. I had no idea that the work I was doing with nature since September 1984 was, in part, leading to the fusion of these two realities.

The ship stayed at the site for about forty-five minutes. I sat on my log and watched men and women move around inside, and every once in a while, someone would wave hello to me—and I'd wave back. By the way, they all still looked like regular people, the kind of people you and I would recognize as people. No one looked like what we see in the movies. In fact, none of this looked like the movies. (I definitely need to talk to Steven Spielberg.) At a certain point, I noticed an increase in activity going on inside the ship with crew rushing back and forth. Then Hyperithon told me they would be lifting off. I was to wait for him to contact me again to give me the all-clear, and then I was to test the site and soil one last time.

While waiting for his call, Pan talked to me about the actual landing. The practice run had given nature the information it needed for setting up what I was to do for the landing.

For the mission, the mother ship will descend to the site as it did today and will be in place and ready to begin its final shifts to become physically perceptible. At this point, you are to walk to the work rock as you did today and, from there, while holding the summer solstice ribbon in your left hand, move the solstice energy from Perelandra through the ship and into the universe. You are then to direct the solstice energy to expand and infuse the entire dome environment, including the ribbon being held in your hand. Once this is completed, set the ribbon back on the rock, which will complete the grounding process for the rock, the focal point of the site. You will then leave the area and go to the log you are using as your "desk." I will be your partner for this summer solstice grounding process, and since you received communication so clearly from Hyperithon today during the descent, he, as well as I, will let you know when the solstice shift is to occur.

You will be monitoring the site and soil at least three times as the ship completes its final shift into five-senses form, and the trees and rocks complete their shift to form beyond the five-senses range. We expect few imbalances in the soil makeup at this point, but to be sure, we suggest you monitor the site and soil every five minutes during this final stage. For the monitoring, test the four sets of essences and the full soil kit. If anything is needed, release whatever is needed to us from your log desk. At this point, do not walk into the site. Hyperithon will determine how long this final stage will take and what degree of sensory form they will take on.

While the final stage is going on, Salvesen will need to monitor the Foot People. She and they need to be assembled at least fifteen feet outside the perimeter of the site dome and away from you while you are doing your work. Let Salvesen know that monitoring the Foot People during the final stage will be critical to their sensory adjustment.

Ten minutes after completing this session, I received Hyper-ithon's all-clear. The ship was gone, and the site's trees and rocks were back in normal view. The site and the soil tested fine, nothing needed. I, on the other hand, was not in good shape. The pressure in my head and neck was intense, and I still felt I was going to vomit at any moment. I tested myself for essences again, and again I tested clear. I really didn't understand why I kept testing clear when I was feeling so bad. I decided to pack up and head down the mountain. Perhaps the walk would help.

About three-quarters of the way down, I ran into Salvesen and Paul. She looked at me and said, "Who sat on your head?" She told me the blood was drained from my face and I didn't look good at all. After filling her in on what had occurred and how I felt, she checked me right there on the mountain. My cranial occipital tilt action was jammed, my cervical vertebrae were fine, but my diaphragm had been kicked by a mule (hence the nausea), even though I needed no essences or supplements. I told her she was *really* going to have to monitor the Foot People on the mountain, especially during the final stages as the ship shifted into five-senses form because what she was seeing now with me was what it was like to deal with that mother ship in person.

After my checkout, Salvesen and Paul told me they had come up with an idea on how to deal with the interlopers (the gate crashers) who showed up. The issue was that none of the inter-lopers had been included in the preparations at the site. Only the invited groups had been planned for. And now that we had an idea of how intense the mission experience was going to be, we couldn't just let the interlopers mosey on into the site. For one thing, it could be dangerous to them and their health. And then there was the issue of their impact on the site and mission.

So Salvesen and Paul had a plan: create a second site somewhere else on the mountain especially for the interlopers to use during the mission. Their role would be to support those of us attending the mission itself. Actually, this seemed like a decent idea. They had not been invited, but they were there because, I assumed, they were interested. The support role seemed ideal for them. And then there was this other thing: What if all the Foot People disintegrated into little piles of ash on the mountain, or passed out, or dropped dead or something? There was no one at Mt. Shasta who would know something had gone wrong and inform their families that their loved ones had just blown up on a mountain during the landing of a mother ship carrying a bunch of dead government leaders. Finally, I could see how the interlopers could be helpful. The only question was whether these people, who believed they were each the only essential ingredient needed for a successful mission, would accept a secondary, support role.

When I got back to the Finlandia Motel, I talked to David about the new interloper plan. He saw no problem in keeping them corralled and focused on the mission at another site, and reminded me to impress on these people that no one was to chuck crystals around *anywhere* on the mountain. The site that Paul and Salvesen thought would be ideal for the interlopers was Sand Flat, the original site Edith had chosen for the Mt. Shasta Mission. David agreed this location would be fine. Their presence at Sand Flat would not impact anything going on at the mission site. He told me to identify and prepare the Sand Flat site tomorrow. (I'd have to balance and stabilize it for mission support.) It was clear that as long as the interlopers were controlled, and all the

Foot People were comfortable with this new development, we would be fine.

I then set up for a medical session with Lorpuris. By this time, I was exhausted—drained to the bone, actually. But I was only a little nauseous, and the pressure in my head and neck had dissipated dramatically, leaving just the echoes of my former discomfort. Lorpuris said, contrary to what I was thinking, my body held up well and that I took a lot of pressure from the ship as it was coming in. They had already discussed ways to minimize this for the Foot People and to adjust the final stages so that no one would feel kicked in the diaphragm. Lorpuris and I agreed that I was the mission guinea pig that morning. After the hour-long session and a nap, I was fine.

I awoke thinking a quiet, solitary walk was just what I needed. Instead, Salvesen told me that three interlopers had arrived and were anxiously waiting to meet me. I had to admit that they had followed the instructions in the witness's confirmation letters and arrived according to schedule. Here it was, July 13, and there they were all eager and wide-eyed, and staying at the Finlandia. Our little motel with the saw-mill ambience was turning into Ground Command Central.

I spent the rest of the afternoon speaking to each interloper separately so that we could get to know one another a little. I talked to them about the mission and told them about the new support site and the job they could do for us. They each said they would be happy to help in any way.

You might remember one of the three interlopers: "Ben Franklin." She was someone I had already spoken to on the phone in May. At that time she made it clear that if anyone should be at this mission it was Benjamin Franklin, and, lucky for us, she was Ben Franklin's walk-in. I wasn't overly impressed. I figured if Franklin was to be at the mountain, David would just invite him and he'd be on the mother ship like the others. She also let me know then that she had been "guided" to "save the mission" by tossing pre-programmed crystals around the site at the "given" time (according to her "guidance") during the mission. Now that she had actually shown up at Mt. Shasta, I spent a good amount of time talking to her about the work that had gone on to balance the site and tried to impress on her that it was critical that she not bring her crystals to any location on the mountain. They were to stay in her room. By the time I left, she was telling me she "completely understood," while at the same time she was looking at me with an I'm-tolerating-you expression on her face. But other than her Ben Franklin fetish and her unmistakable look of forced tolerance, I found her to be a reasonable, well-spoken, polite person, and I had high hopes that she understood the need to behave.

Each of my discussions ended with smiles from the interlopers coupled with grand statements that they were "eager to do any-thing—*anything* to help the mission." But I was left with a nagging feeling that they weren't being up front with me and were actually eager to do *anything* to be included at the mission site as witnesses. We all went out to dinner together and, by the time the evening was over, Salvesen, Paul and Clarence said they liked the interlopers and felt the three were being sincere with me. I, on the other hand, continued to have doubts. I decided to let it ride and see where the interloper situation would lead us.

My first big meeting with the Foot People—Peter's invited witnesses and David's handful of invited guests—was scheduled for tomorrow at 3 P.M. at the Finlandia. When I got to the Cottage, David and I went over what I needed to say at the meeting and how I was to present the interloper situation. If any of the Foot People felt uneasy or uncomfortable about the interlopers, the whole second-site plan was off and the interlopers would be asked to leave tomorrow.

Chapter 31

Sunday, July 14

SALVESEN, CLARENCE, PAUL AND I took the three interlopers ("Ben," Traci and Janice) to the Sand Flat site ("the Flat") in the morning. Time was becoming a serious issue since the mission was scheduled for the next day. Salvesen and I decided the quickest and best way to get the interlopers set up at the Flat was for me to balance and stabilize it this morning and for Salvesen to check the interlopers for body balancing at the Flat site right after my work was completed. That way we could quickly see how the Flat and the interlopers interacted with one another.

The goal for my work was to create this second site as an independent location that would be *related* to the mission without being *directly linked* to the mission site in any way. I didn't need the Flat to help stabilize the mission. No matter what, the Mt. Shasta Mission site was to remain untouched.

I opened a new four-point coning set up specifically for the Flat and stated that my intent was to establish a balanced foundation for the non-intrusive support activity that these folks would be providing for the mission's Foot People. When I tested the Flat site and soil, I found they needed no soil amendments, but the site needed three essences:

Royal Highness: Final stabilization.
Zinnia: Laughter, lightness and release of tension.
Mustard: For gloom, depression and melancholy
     that descends for no known cause.

Compared to the work I had done at the mission site, achieving the Sand Flat balance was easy. But guess who showed up at the Flat carrying a small bag of crystals? You guessed it…"Ben." I couldn't believe it when she whipped out her cloth bag filled with about fifty quartz crystals that she announced proudly were "preprogrammed" with different intents. She thought that since crystal lobbing was her specialty, I might want her to toss a few around at Sand Flat. It was as if the hour-long conversation I had had with her the afternoon before had never happened. By this time, I considered grabbing the bag and stuffing it up one of her orifices, but, instead, I was a relatively good girl and told her to put the bag away and leave it in her room for the mission. And then I finished with the thought, "Or I'll break your arms."

Salvesen set up her paraphernalia for working with the interlopers at the Flat. All she was aiming for with these people was a general body balance and alignment in preparation for their support role. Unfortunately, this took a lot of work.

Janice needed two pelvic adjustments, two vertebral adjustments, two Glycodyne and a trace mineral for her B-complex deficiency, a gall bladder pump, several additional trace minerals and two essences.

"Ben" needed two pelvic adjustments, two thoracic vertebral adjustments, one flower essence, and she tested she had an adrenal weakness.

Joining "Ben" for this adventure was her twenty-something daughter, Traci, who worked for the forestry service somewhere in the Northwest. Traci needed two pelvic adjustments, five vertebral adjustments and a left heel tension release. Plus she had lower back/sacral weakness. But she needed no supplements or essences.

Of the three, Traci was the most down to earth, plus she was young and physically strong, despite all the work Salvesen had to do just to get her balanced and aligned. So we chose her to be our go-between in case we didn't get down from the mission site within a set time frame and she needed to come up to locate our little piles of ashes. To do this, she needed the landing process, which we did later at the motel. Well, her body knew exactly what to do with a mother ship, and she tested clear. We had chosen the right person as our go-between.

Fig. 13: The Sand Flat site.

The work at Sand Flat took a little over two hours. Before heading back to the motel, we spent time walking around the Flat, and because it looked like a big, open meadow, it was unanimously decided that the interloper/mission support group would be called "The Meadow Muffins." *(Fig. 13)*

By the time I got back to my room, I was feeling a lot of discomfort in my neck. Salvesen checked me and found that all seven of my cervical vertebrae were out of alignment. She felt it was a delayed reaction to the work I had done at the mission site with the mother ship the day before and said it looked like someone had rolled a bowling ball down my spine. It was another indication to us both that she was going to have to watch diligently over everyone at the site.

I had a quick lunch in town and then it was back to the motel for the first meeting with the invited witnesses and guests scheduled at 3 P.M. Peter Caddy, who was staying with friends in town

that week, arrived a little early and let me know that he was keeping his presence at Mt. Shasta quiet so that no one would question
why he was there. He understood that this was not a public event.
I spent a few minutes filling him in on the development with the
three interlopers-turned-Meadow-Muffins.

At 3 P.M., Peter, Salvesen, Albert and Laura Townsend (who had
arrived that morning and were also staying at the Finlandia),
Clarence, Paul and I were sitting in the room waiting for Peter's
witnesses to show up. We waited fifteen minutes, then twenty,
then a half hour. No one showed.

  Of the twenty-two people who Peter had invited to the Mt.
Shasta Mission and who had received confirmation letters, no
one bothered to come. Both Peter and I were surprised. These
people were well educated and experienced in "unusual" events
and work. It was remarkable that they just dropped out without a
word. Did they think the Mt. Shasta Mission was a two-bit operation run by some hacks? Or some lark? What was going through
their heads? In June, I received a letter from one of the witnesses
saying he would be unable to make it due to other commitments.
Aside from this, I heard nothing from the others. Nor had Peter.

Ah, yes…there were two exceptions. Gary Dunlap, the fellow
who called me at Perelandra earlier to tell me the mission was
going to be "attacked by dark forces," and his partner were in Mt.
Shasta at a campground at the base of the mountain. They called
Peter earlier that day and let him know that they had not yet
decided if they wanted to be part of the mission. Ten months to
think about it and come up with a decision just wasn't enough
time for these two. Also, for some reason unknown to Peter and
me, they did not wish to speak to me; they would only speak to
Peter. And those evil, dark forces Gary had warned me about
were still on for an attack.

Back in June, when I told David about the "potential attacks" on the mission, he just rolled his eyes and told me to dismiss this crap. But I must say, hearing it again gave me concern. This mission was big and complex, and none of us needed to waste time and energy dealing with that kind of information, even if it was trash. Plus, I was surprised that these two people were acting this way. They knew better.

I felt I needed to give them some wiggle room rather than just tell them to go away and stop bothering me because they were invited witnesses and not interlopers. So here's how I handled the latest Gary Dunlap wackiness:

1. I decided I would check with David to make sure the impending "attack" on the mountain was still trash.
2. I told Peter I didn't care if they didn't want to talk to me, as long as they followed my instructions on the mountain.
3. I told Peter he would have to call Gary and tell him and his partner they had until 3 P.M. the next day to decide about the mission. If they wanted to participate, they needed to "come in from the cold" and have their landing processes done at 3 P.M.
4. They needed to agree to join the mission and not conduct themselves independently on the mountain. If I didn't hear from them (through Peter) by 3 P.M. the next day, they were out of the mission.

The night before, David told me to explain the mission fully to the witnesses and guests at this meeting. So, to begin the meeting, I launched into the Mt. Shasta Mission. I talked about the goals, the primary mission, who was involved, and gave them the names of the ten government leaders who would be coming to the mountain on the mother ship. I told them that the group that had held the custodianship of governments for the past 2,000 years had chosen these ten leaders to represent them for this mission, and that the ten would be releasing their Piscean government custodianship so that the Aquarian government leylines could be set up and activated. I must say, every time I thought about what these men were going to do on the mountain, I thought about what an extraordinary moment this must be for them. They had been entrusted to develop and head our planet's governments for over 2,000 years, and now they were going to release that responsibility right before our eyes. To me this was a huge moment for them *and* for us on the planet.

I talked about St. Germain, why he was part of the mission and what he would be doing at the mountain. Peter helped me explain St. Germain and his role in establishing the Aquarian leylines that he had activated back in the 1950s. These leylines, a grid that is different from the government/military leylines being addressed in the primary mission, support us all as we change our goals and actions in each area of our lives to reflect the new Aquarian principles. I let them know that after the primary mission was completed, St. Germain would be using the framework and process David had set up for the primary mission to shift the energy from our five senses into his leylines. This would result in fully grounding the impulses and information carried within that large umbrella grid, thus enabling us to better and more easily understand and work with the Aquarian dynamic in our personal lives.

Then I told them about the expanded mission and how it would be mirroring the primary mission and moving its accomplished goals and dynamics into the levels of reality beyond our universe. I gave them the number of spacecraft that would be positioned for the primary mission and the number for the expanded mission and talked about the issues of pairing the craft. I let them know that, according to what David had said to me the previous evening, all 15,668 craft were already paired and in formation beyond our solar system and holding. They would move in formation around our planet just beyond our atmosphere the next day and be in position two hours before the mother ship descended into our atmosphere and into the Mt. Shasta Mission site at 9 P.M., give or take fifteen minutes.

I explained my work on the mountain, why it was needed and what support it would give them during the mission. David estimated we would be spending about four hours on the mountain for the mission, so I warned them they would be spending a considerable amount of time at the site and that we would probably not be coming off the mountain until after 1 A.M.

I talked about the Meadow Muffins, who they were, how they pushed their way into the picture and what they would be doing. Several said they appreciated the fact that people would know we were on the mountain and would be prepared to help, if needed. Based on their reactions and their unanimous vote, the Meadow Muffins were now an official part of the mission.

I told them about the crystal situation and, as I had already done with the Meadow Muffins, warned the Foot People not to bring any crystals or other "power objects" to the mountain.

Since none of the invited witnesses had shown up, the six who were present for this meeting were now the official mission witnesses. I told them that great care was being taken to have everything on the mountain in five-senses form. Their job as witnesses was to do just that, bear witness: accurately perceive what was going on and allow the event to activate their sensory systems. Their sensory activation would be part of what was to be shifted into the leylines, and in the future, this will allow all to more easily identify the new dynamics and move them through their own sensory systems as they seek to effect changes in the government/ military arena.

I then asked Salvesen to explain her medical balancing work and what their bodies were going through with the ship landing process. Everyone in the room except Albert had already had at least one landing process by this time. We scheduled the remaining round of work and made sure Albert had at least two processes before going to the site the next day. Salvesen also let them know that, besides testing them for flower essences on the mountain, she would be supplying them with cell salts whenever needed. She knew that cell salts contained those elements that the nervous system, muscles and bones would use up quickly during the mission.

Salvesen told them that, in light of what I was experiencing on the mountain, everyone would probably need several spheno-basilar pump procedures during the mission and especially while the mother ship was descending. We now knew that the descent itself changed the barometric pressure at the site and this would affect the action between the occipital and sphenoid cranial plates (see drawing on p. 15), which ensures that the movement of the cerebrospinal fluid is equal and even.

She had a little issue with the spheno-basilar pump procedure, however. Normally this is done by a chiropractor in their office while the person is lying on the table. Salvesen didn't have this kind of luxury at the site. Since necessity is the mother of invention, as they say, she came up with a different approach to the procedure. We'd be doing it standing, thus eliminating the need to lie down on the ground, something she wasn't sure some of the Foot People could do comfortably. Whenever any one of us needed a spheno-basilar pump procedure, we'd stand on a rock, balanced on our toes and with our heels facing out from the rock. Then we'd stick our thumb in our mouth. The procedure was timed to our breathing: On the exhale we'd lower our heels and press our thumbs against the roof of the mouth. On the inhale we'd raise our heels and release the thumb pressure. At this meeting, she had us stand up on chairs to practice the procedure. It wasn't easy, and for most of us it required a concentrated effort for coordination. But, after a few tries, I'm proud to say we each got it.

> NOTE: Now, don't be goofy and try this in the comfort of your home, or anywhere else for that matter. Salvesen was monitoring us at all times to make sure we did it correctly. To find out if you need a spheno-basilar pump, you must be tested by a professional, and it's safer, easier and less clumsy to just lie on the table and receive this procedure the normal way.

We discussed the merits of pairing off and using the buddy system during the mission. The buddy could help them with the spheno-basilar pump procedure by steadying their partner as they balanced on the rock. But more importantly, as the mission unfolded, their buddy could verify what they were experiencing.

> Buddy 1: "Do you see a mother ship?"
> Buddy 2: "Yes, I see a mother ship. Do you see that it's silver with a green racing stripe?"
> Buddy 1: "Yes. Is that an ad for Coke on the side?"

Salvesen felt this would help keep anyone who felt so inclined from blacking out at the site. So they paired off. I remained independent because I would be operating in a different capacity and a partner for me would have interfered with what I needed to do. Besides, I was used to being around the Cottage men, and I had already seen the mother ship. I already knew there was no racing stripe or Coke ad.

Finally, I reminded everyone about the items I had listed in their confirmation letter that they each would need: a jacket, since the mountain site could get chilly at night even in July; hiking boots or good walking shoes; a flashlight because we would be coming down the mountain in the dark; and a bottle of water.

Immediately, they began organizing themselves for trips into town to buy their jackets, boots/shoes, flashlights and bottles of water. Apparently only Peter paid attention to that section of the confirmation letter and was prepared.

We agreed to meet in the motel parking lot the next night at 6:15 P.M., having already eaten dinner and ready to start to the mountain.

I think it would be fair to say I was able to get their attention in this meeting. But I can't say that each one of them actually *heard* everything I said. Sometimes it seemed that my words were falling into a bucket in the middle of the room or bouncing off the walls. I tried to work around the bucket and walls by explaining what I had just said. Finally, Clarence and Albert announced they now realized how big and important this mission was, and this gave me hope. By the end of the meeting, I felt everyone had some understanding of what was going to happen and how they were to participate.

Of course, Peter already knew enough about the mission to understand its importance, so the meeting wasn't a revelation to him. It was obvious to me that he was the most experienced and disciplined of the group (myself included) in these kinds of events. He was calm, he listened carefully for what needed to be done and offered his help with anything. He made himself completely available to the Mt. Shasta Mission, never challenged the schedule and showed up prepared for anything. And he did everything that was asked of him. All of this was contrary to what Gary Dunlap had said to me.

One of the things Gary had "warned" me about was Peter's "propensity for taking charge." I never saw any such inclinations. Peter would offer assistance whenever I asked for advice or help, but he never tried to function as the leader with the Foot People and Meadow Muffins, nor did he attempt to shove me aside and take over. He knew about the Cottage and the fact that I was talking everyday with the David and the Cottage team, and I felt he not only respected but understood my position in the mission. He wasn't a fool, nor was I. More and more, I found myself looking to Peter for support and advice.

I didn't get to the Cottage until later that evening. I asked David about Gary's warnings, and again he rolled his eyes and told me to ignore what that fellow was saying. It was still trash. I let David know I had put my foot down: If I didn't hear from Gary and his partner by the next afternoon, I was going to make an executive decision and exclude these two from the witness list. David smiled and said, "That's fine with me."

Chapter 32

Monday, July 15

Aʀᴍᴇᴅ ᴡɪᴛʜ ᴊᴜsᴛ ᴀ ғᴇᴡ hours sleep, an early breakfast and some last-minute pointers from David, I left the Cottage and arrived back at my motel room in time to discover the wheels were spinning off the Foot People cart. There was a loud, somewhat frantic knock at my door and when I opened it, Laura and two other Foot People tromped into my room.

Sometime between last evening when I left for the Cottage and this morning when I arrived back, these three Footers decided that the three Meadow Muffins should now join the Foot People ranks. In an attempt to justify their decision, Laura told me she had gotten "guidance" that the Meadow Muffins were to be included. This didn't really impress me since I suspected that Laura's "guidance" came from Laura and had been inspired by the Meadow Muffins themselves. It turned out that these Footers had dinner the night before with the Meadow Muffins. Since I had suspected all along that the Muffins were not happy with their support job, despite all the things they were saying to the contrary, I now suspected that they used the dinner to convince the Footers that they, the Muffins, should be included in the mission at the site. Oh, call me cynical all you want, but I was watching this whole manipulation scene unfold right in front of me.

I didn't need that laser six-shooter I had in my underwear drawer for astral attacks. No sirree. I needed it to control these three Footers and the Meadow Muffins. They were nuts. Laura was standing in my room insisting I let the Muffins come to the mountain site as the other two Footers joined in by telling me it was the only fair thing to do. They reasoned that the fact that the Muffins made it to Mt. Shasta "proved" they were deserving of being included at the site.

This is about the point in their absurdity when they were all lucky I wasn't packing those six-shooters. I felt ambushed by the Footers and was completely caught off guard. I had entertained the possibility that the Muffins might try something to get to the site, but it hadn't occurred to me that they would get Foot People to act as their emissaries—their irate, pushy, indignant emissaries. Did the three Footers not understand anything that was said at their meeting the day before? Did they not get that this mission was being carefully put together and was not to be played with? Did they not understand that their only role in the mission was to watch and listen? And that this did not include restructuring the mission for their personal pleasures and entertainment? To me, it all seemed so simple and easy to understand. But, obviously they weren't getting it.

I reminded the Footers that the Meadow Muffins were gate crashers and they had not been invited to the mission in the first place. I felt including them in the support role rather than telling them to get lost was already a considerate response. But the three Footers dismissed everything I was saying. They felt that since Laura had gotten "guidance" this should be enough for me to act on. I needed help, so I told them I could not make such a decision about the Mt. Shasta Mission and that I would have to discuss it with David. I let them know that David was already on the mother ship and it may be difficult for me to get him now. They didn't seem to care.

I told the Footers to leave my room while I talked with David. Once alone, I set up a coning and asked to be connected with him. Luckily, it worked. I told him some of the Foot People were staging an uprising and that they strongly felt the Meadow Muffins should be included at the mountain site. I then tried to give him an accurate picture of what was being said, including Laura's "guidance," and the prevailing attitude among these people. I also told him I suspected the Meadow Muffins were behind the uprising. He wasn't surprised. I had discussed the interloper/ Meadow Muffin situation several times with him, and he knew we had reached a fragile peace yesterday.

He said his major concern was any or all of these people angrily stomping out of Mt. Shasta, running their mouths and causing a major problem with the mission. God knows who would show up at the mountain then. I was to meet with the three Footers again and remind them once more that the Meadow Muffins had never been a part of the original plans, and in order to include them, I would have to go to the site and adjust the protection dome to accommodate the inclusion of the Meadow Muffins. These three would also be required to have two landing processes before going to the site, as well. This procedure was now complicated by the fact that Hyperithon and Lorpuris, who were needed for the work, were on the mother ship with David and moving through space and time. Also, I was to impress on them the serious time factor we were now facing. David and I both felt this was a long shot, but perhaps understanding what was involved might back them off and settle them down. If not, he did not want them leaving town disgruntled. He wanted them under control, and Salvesen and I would need to do the work to get the site and the three Muffins ready for the mission that evening.

At 10 A.M., I called the three Footers back into my room and gave them the information just as David suggested. Well, they didn't care how much work it took or how inconvenienced anyone was. They wanted the Meadow Muffins included. (Somebody pass me my six-shooter, please.)

When I told the Meadow Muffins about the change of plans, they had very pleased and all-knowing expressions on their faces, which verified that they had manipulated the three Footers and convinced them it was a mistake not to be included. (Can someone *please* pass me my six-shooter?) However, having gotten what they had been angling for all along, they were now willing to cooperate.

I had to find Salvesen and tell her what had happened. She wasn't surprised, nor was she happy about the extra work. We had the first round of landing processes right away, and I'd love to be able to say to you that these three former Meadow Muffins hardly needed any body balancing and that their bodies loved the landing. Actually, this was Traci's second round and her body responded well. She only needed a couple of spinal adjustments prior to the landing and tested clear after the landing. But the other two required a lot. As soon as we finished, I left with Clarence for the mountain to adjust the site and dome.

Even today, twenty years later, I clearly remember how it felt to go back to the mountain and site that morning—comforting and soothing. And it was still quiet. Blessedly quiet. Once again I felt surrounded by sanity. This world made sense to me. What had just happened with the Footers and Meadow Muffins was all nuthouse stuff.

Physically, I was really tired and felt like an old, broken down pack mule who should have been retired to pasture four years prior. Clarence took pity on me and hauled my backpack to the site, then headed off to explore the mountain again. Once I got settled in, I opened the Mt. Shasta Mission coning and asked what I needed to do to prepare the site and include the three Muffins into the protection dome. I needed to:

1. Bring forward and reactivate the two groups coming by mother ship:
   - David, Hyperithon, Tex, Butch, Mickey, John, St. Germain and the ship's crew
   - The ten historical leaders

2. Restructure the Foot People group to include the three Muffins.

3. Marry the people coming on the ship with the new Foot People group.

4. Call for the new Foot People dynamic to commingle fully with the other elements that had been included in the complex mix of dynamics in the protection dome: David's presence on the mountain, the dynamic of David and me working together, David's full understanding of the mission, the mission-go dynamic, my position as liaison with nature, the Mary Cassatt *Mother and Child* dynamic, the Mt. Shasta Mission coning dynamic and the Gettysburg Battle dynamic.

THE WORK

1. In order to "bring forward and reactivate the two groups coming by mother ship," I did not need to go back to square one and reform the groups by linking with David as I had done the first time. Their dynamics already existed within the site's dome, and all I had to do was ask Pan to move these two dynamics "forward" from the larger dome mix.

Perhaps the easiest way to explain myself here is to have you picture each dynamic that is included in the dome (such as everything that is listed above in #4) standing before you as chairs—a bunch of chairs lined up in a row in front of you. I then asked Pan to move forward the chair holding the dynamics of the first group (the crew and David's guests). And I did the same for the second group (the ten leaders).

We now have two chairs sitting in front of the others. At the site, this allowed me to work with these two "chairs," apart from the other chairs. To make sure everything was still balanced with the two groups, I tested them. They were clear.

2.   Still using the chair metaphor and still keeping these two chairs forward, I asked Pan to bring forward the chair representing the original Foot People. Well, this chair needed to be restructured completely. The people who were invited by Peter as witnesses could be removed, and the three Muffins had to be added to the remaining group that included Peter, Salvesen, Clarence, Laura, Albert and Paul.

Once I had my new chair, I needed to test the site and soil for balancing and stabilizing in light of this new group. The site needed a few essences (she says, tongue in cheek): Gruss an Aachen, Ambassador, Royal Highness, Chestnut Bud, Clematis, Gentian, Holly, Rock Rose, Larch, Oak, Star of Bethlehem, Impatiens, Vervain and Nasturtium. It also needed potassium, magnesium, phosphorus, molybdenum, copper, manganese, zinc and iodine. What a difference three people can make. I put all the needed drops and supplements on my work rock and asked Pan to release them to the site. I watched the energy move out from the rock and into the air above me, permeating the entire protection dome area.

I then turned my attention to the soil for testing. It needed Eclipse, White Lightnin', Royal Highness, Cherry Plum, Chicory, Clematis, Holly, Willow, Scotch Broom, Shasta Daisy and Yarrow. For nutrients, it needed silicon, sodium, potassium, chlorine, magnesium, potash, molybdenum, copper, manganese, zinc and iodine. Drops and supplements for each of these were placed on the rock, and once again I watched the energy move out from the rock and then plunge down into the soil.

3. Now I had to let the two groups coming in by ship face the new Foot People group. I saw the three group dynamics touch, as if the three chairs moved together until they touched, and was told to wait two minutes before testing. I stood there, and I have to admit that I was hoping the new Foot People group would behave itself and not pick a fight. But I wasn't too worried. I felt confident these old dead men could take out the Foot People with little effort.

    When I got the go-ahead, I tested the site first: Gruss an Aachen, Eclipse, Ambassador and Royal Highness, plus nitrogen, zinc, magnesium, phosphorus, molybdenum, manganese, and iodine. Everything was put on the rock and released. I tested the soil and the following were released: Ambassador and Royal Highness, plus potassium, nitrogen, magnesium, potash, copper, manganese and zinc.

4. To explain how I fully mixed in the new Foot People group with the site, I'll continue to use the chair metaphor. I was told to move the two chairs representing the groups coming in by ship back in line with the other chairs. I then called for the new Foot People chair to move in line with the others. To reconstruct the fully integrated dome dynamic again, the chairs needed to "explode," forming "liquid waves" that then mixed together to create one unified dynamic field.

    Once the dome's dynamics were reformed into a new, cohesive unit, I tested the site and soil again. Both tested clear. This told me we had successfully accomplished our goal of including the Meadow Muffins. The entire job had taken an hour and a half.

I put my jacket on the log facing the trail, and enjoyed the tranquility at the site while I waited for Clarence to come up. There were a lot of conclusions, some of them mean-spirited, that I could make about the new Foot People group, but I remember sitting there and thinking about how interesting it was to see the different impact each group had on the site and soil. I guess it's fair to say that I had morphed the Meadow Muffins and the new Foot People group into a petri dish and I found what I was looking at to be extremely interesting. For the moment, at least, I was not considering shooting people.

After we left the mountain, Clarence and I stopped in town for a quick lunch. Then I had a meeting with the others about the new Foot People group. They were all happy campers—finally.

Salvesen and I set up for the second round of body work for the former Muffins. Thankfully, this second round went better. "Ben" needed one leg adjustment before the landing. With the ship, she was fine. Janice also needed a left leg adjustment, plus one spinal adjustment and one essence. The good news was that the effects of the gall bladder pump that Salvesen gave her the day before were holding. With the ship landing, she only needed Gruss an Aachen and Peace. No other adjustments were needed.

We then worked with Laura, Albert and Clarence to give them their final round of landings before the mountain. They each handled the landing well. I must say, this round of work showed us once again just how quickly the human body can learn.

By now it was almost 4 o'clock. We had a little over two hours to eat dinner and get ready for the hike to the mountain. I met Peter and the two of us went into town for dinner together. Among other things, I got him caught up on that morning's uprising and all the extra work Salvesen and I had to do that afternoon. Peter told me that Gary Dunlap and his partner did call him back to tell him they now wanted to be part of the mission because they had gotten new "guidance" that the mission was not going to be attacked. I called David about their decision, and he told me to have Peter tell them they were no longer included in the Mt. Shasta Mission. David had just had enough with these two people.

Peter and I were standing in the parking lot at 6:15 and ready to go. Unfortunately, none of the others were there. We waited about a half hour. We talked it over and decided that if the others didn't show up by 7 o'clock, the two of us were going to the mountain alone. Finally, two cars full of Foot People pulled into the parking lot. I asked Clarence what the hell happened to them, and he just looked at me and said, "Don't ask." They all rushed to their rooms for a last pit stop and to get ready.

By 7 o'clock they were back in the parking lot, and I was more than surprised at what I saw. I guess shocked might be an apt description. First of all, there was "Ben," bedecked in a Smokey-the-Bear baseball cap with two felt "paws" that stuck out in front of the cap. When she pulled a string, the felt paws clapped. But this wasn't all. For her part in the mission that she had manipulated so hard to have, she also had sitting on her shoulders a stuffed puppet that was about three feet tall who she introduced to us as "Reverend Absurd." It looked like a tall, male version of a Raggedy Ann doll, complete with a top hat and long legs striped like two barber poles that hung down her chest.

I took one look at her and I wasn't even bothering to look for my laser guns. I was just going to choke her with my bare hands. Salvesen grabbed me by the arm before I could say anything and said, "Ignore her." I looked over at Peter, who had been staring at "Ben" and her outfit, and he nodded his head ever so slightly at me in agreement with Salvesen. So now I worked to ignore the fool with the clapping bear cap and three-foot-tall puppet. I needed my naked man.

Janice was standing there dressed for our mountain hike in polyester slacks, nylons and shoes fit more for an office than a dirt trail. Traci, who worked for the forest service, knew how to dress for a mountain hike, as did the others, but only a few had jackets for the cooler nighttime air.

If I had occupied myself choking "Ben," I wouldn't have had time to notice the paper bags everyone was clutching. If you'll remember, they were supposed to bring bottled water. Well, this group not only brought water, they brought dinner. They each had a grocery bag stuffed with boxed fried chicken dinners, bags of chips, pretzels, crackers, packaged cheese and cookies that they were going to be eating as soon as they arrived at the site because ... I can hardly say this to you... *none of them had eaten dinner!*

And that's when I found out why they were late. They had gone off together into town to find a restaurant for dinner. But they spent two hours arguing over which restaurant they would choose. (Okay. This job is too big for just hand choking. I'm now going to go look for my laser guns.)

I figured if I could control myself enough not to do bodily harm to "Ben," I could control myself about their lack of preparedness and bags of crap. I just said, "Let's go," and we all piled into cars. I rode with Peter and Clarence, and en route Clarence filled us in on the colorful details of the strange and tortured search for the perfect restaurant.

I needed to get to the site and set up, so I walked up the trail ahead of the others, something I was more than happy to do. Clarence walked with the Foot People and Peter brought up the rear. By the time they straggled into the site carting their dinners with them, I was sitting on the log with my stuff spread out beside me. I told them they needed to be fifteen feet outside the circle of logs until after the mother ship docked, so they settled in a relatively uncluttered area off to my right.

They immediately set up for dinner, which necessitated opening a bunch of cellophane bags. Imagine the noise. And they were
talking, joking and laughing with one another. A rambunctious
picnic was being had by all. I was still in my "ignore mode" and
busy testing the site to see if everything held as they arrived, so I
said nothing to them. But when Peter arrived, he told them they
had to be quiet. He could hear them and their noisy bags all the
way up the trail. He explained that sound carried easily and far on
the mountain, and we were not supposed to be attracting other
hikers to the site. Immediately, the noise level lowered.

Now they were creating muffled noise—muffled voices and
muffled bag rattling. Peter settled into a spot away from the group,
leaned his back against a tree and closed his eyes. He was waiting
for the mission to begin. Salvesen went around to everyone and
checked them for any needed alignment or supplements. They all
tested clear. She found two large rocks that were relatively flat and
designated them as our "spheno-basilar [SB] pumping rocks."

Amidst the greasy smell of fried chicken and the charming
muffled sounds of crunching chips and pretzels, we waited for a
mother ship to land. We didn't have long to wait.

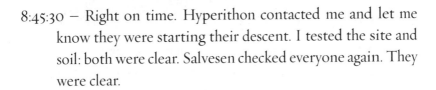

8:45:30 – Right on time. Hyperithon contacted me and let me
know they were starting their descent. I tested the site and
soil: both were clear. Salvesen checked everyone again. They
were clear.

9:04 – The mother ship touched down into the site. None of us
could see anything yet (several of the Foot People were still
busy eating), and the trees and rocks were still fully visible.
The ship now had to go through the various stages of shifts
to come into five-senses form. For the ten leaders on the
ship, this was the trickiest part of the descent process. I
tested the site and soil again: both were clear.

9:08 — Salvesen tested the Foot People again. Nearly everyone's body was now responding to the ship. In a very real way, this was good news. The ship was descending, and their bodies weren't ignoring it. In fact, their nervous and sensory systems were working hard to identify what was happening.

> *"Ben"* needed to do the SB pump procedure. (I don't know if she did this with Reverend Absurd still sitting on her shoulders or not.)
> *Paul* needed Gruss an Aachen and five cell salts.
> *Traci* needed six cell salts.
> *Laura* needed Eclipse and four cell salts.
> *Clarence* was clear!
> *Albert* needed Gruss an Aachen (twice), a pelvic adjustment and three cell salts.
> *Peter* was clear!
> *Janice* needed a hip adjustment, six cell salts and Eclipse.
> *I* needed Royal Highness and my six-shooters.

The cell salts indicated to us that their nervous and sensory systems were working overtime to identify and sort what was happening in front of them. I couldn't even begin to imagine what would be happening to these people had we not done the preliminary landing work for their bodies.

9:21 — Site check: liquid seaweed needed. I set up with Pan and administered this into the site from my log. Hyperithon told me that everyone on the mother ship was okay and that the descent process was on time. But they were now holding the descent in order for Lorpuris to check the ten leaders. Each time the ship and everyone on board went through a descent level, more pressure was experienced. And, like Salvesen's checks with the Foot People for problems caused by the ship's descent, Lorpuris was also checking for problems with the leaders. When he described it to me, it sounded like what deep sea divers experience as they surface. If they surfaced too quickly, they would be in trouble. In the case of the leaders, there was a problem if they moved "too deeply" and too quickly into the stages of our level's form.

9:32 – Hyperithon let me know the leaders were fine and they were continuing through the final stages of the ship's descent process.

9:34 – I could see an opaque fuzzy appearance in the site. By now, the Foot People were standing and looking into the site for evidence of the mother ship. Some saw fuzz, and the others were quietly straining to see something, anything.

9:36 – I needed two cell salts. Several of the others were doing the SB procedure on the pumping rocks. It was an interesting sight. Grown people rocking up and down on stones with their thumbs stuck in their mouths while a mother ship was descending into form.

9:40 – The descent stopped again for another check with the leaders. I tested the site and needed to release greensand into it.

9:50 – The descent was still holding. I needed to release liquid seaweed into the site. It felt like I was balancing two realities that were constantly moving and adjusting, almost like two different liquids adjusting to one another.

9:52 – Nothing needed in the site.

9:56 – Liquid seaweed released to the site. I needed a shot of Royal Highness.

10:04 – Site and soil holding.

10:30 — The descent continued. The site now needed 198 mg potassium, 5 mg copper, .15 mg iodine and Gruss an Aachen.

10:35 — Hyperithon told me some of the leaders were now experiencing considerable physical distress as they moved into the final stages. He asked me to work with him in order to test them for the final shift to five-senses form. We were going to set up a process similar to what we did for the landing process into the bodies of the Foot People. Using our focus, each leader and I would be linking my left hand with their right hand. With this, his electrical makeup would move into me. He would then experience the five-senses form at the site because I was in five-senses form at the site: horizontal compatibility. Salvesen would use me as a surrogate and test each leader through my body. I set up with Pan to make sure this process worked properly and that the leaders and I would be protected. When I gave the go-ahead, we began. The first person I linked with was Winston Churchill.

Winston Churchill: He needed 90 mg of zinc. Also he tested that he was a weak link among the leaders that would prevent full materialization for the others. Although he personally was not a weak link, his connection with the other leaders created a weak link and full five-senses form for him and the others would be difficult.

Franklin Roosevelt: He needed a T-5 spinal adjustment, which Lorpuris administered. Although it was clear to me that he was strong and no longer used a wheelchair or crutches, Salvesen tested that he should not come any further into five-senses form.

Harry Truman: He needed a sacral adjustment and Sweet Chestnut essence. Both were administered to him on the ship by Lorpuris. And this was when we picked up a most unexpected factor-x. As we tested President Truman, Salvesen and I could feel a vibration building around us that almost felt like a rising storm in the trees in the site. There seemed to be a problem with Truman's relationship with the trees. I let Hyperithon know what we were picking up, and he told us to set it aside for now and continue with the testing. Harry Truman tested positive for coming all the way into five-senses form.

Charles de Gaulle: President de Gaulle needed six drops of Rescue Remedy in a glass of water right away. Salvesen said he needed to be alone in a room and to drink the Rescue Remedy solution while we tested the others. With that, he and I were disconnected and he left for another room.

Joseph Stalin: His body held fine, and he tested positive for coming the rest of the way into five-senses form.

Mao Tse-tung: His body held, as well, and he tested positive for coming the rest of the way into five-senses form.

At this point, Hyperithon asked me to tell Salvesen not to bother with the full readouts and just to check the others for whether or not they should come the rest of the way into five-senses form. That made the testing go a lot faster, and I suspected that Hyperithon had an idea what the testing results would be. Cardinal Richelieu and the three eighteenth-century political advisors all tested that they should go no further. Lastly, I reconnected with President de Gaulle. Salvesen tested that he had a weak heart and that his heart would weaken even more if he continued into five-senses form.

David told me he and the team now needed to decide if it was advisable to continue the mission tonight in light of the seven leaders who were having physical difficulty. They may have to make changes and try again the next night.

Salvesen and I used the time to tell the Foot People of the difficulties. Peter and Clarence took the news well and expressed
concern for the leaders' well-being. I can't say the same about the
others. (God, keep me away from these people. Every time I had
to deal with them that night, I wanted to inflict bodily harm.)
They didn't care about the difficulties the leaders were experiencing, nor did they appreciate the care in which the mission was
being handled. They came to see a spacecraft, dammit, and now
they were not happy. They made condescending and insulting
remarks about the mission, and a couple of them even declared
that *they* could get that mother ship into form. That's when I
turned to "Ben," who was still wearing her clapping hat and puppet, and said somewhat menacingly, "Did you bring those crystals?" She said no. Her life was saved.

10:50 — David decided they would abort the mission this night
          and return to the mountain the next night, bringing just the
          three leaders who tested positive for coming the rest of the
          way into five-senses form. Then he told me the Foot People
          were now to leave the mountain first. The mother ship
          would lift off once we were about halfway down the moun-
          tain. I realized this was one adjustment they made to elimi-
          nate the head and diaphragm stress on the Foot People that
          I had experienced at lift-off during the practice run.

It was now well after 11 P.M., and those who hadn't brought
jackets were quite cold by then. (When I stepped out of the dome
area, something odd happened to me. I began to shiver uncontrollably. I had a good jacket on and had been comfortable throughout
the evening, until that moment. I hoped more Indians weren't
trying to get in touch with me.) A couple of the Foot People also
didn't bring their flashlights, so getting everyone down the mountain was going to take more time than expected. I packed up my
testing stuff while the Foot People packed up the trash from their

dinners. (Hey, they were being environmentally conscious.) But all the way down the trail, several of them just could not resist discussing what had "gone wrong" with the mission and how they could have done it better.

Other than listening to the griping, carping and boasting, I was focused on what was next for the mission. David had always said that the mission had a window—July 14 through July 17—so I wasn't bothered by this one missed evening. And it made sense to me that they had to get the leaders who would be adversely affected off the ship before they could complete the landing. I questioned what was going on with Harry Truman and the trees. And what were we going to do with some of these Foot People? I found their attitudes to be much more disturbing than the aborted mission. I was looking forward to getting back to my room and going to the Cottage for some answers.

Chapter 33

Monday, July 15

CONTINUED

I HAVE A PERSONAL RULE: The day doesn't end until I go to sleep, and the next day doesn't begin until I wake up. Technically, it was now the wee hours of July 16, but I still considered it July 15. On the mountain, David told me that he would be meeting with the team at the Cottage and he wanted me at the meeting. I got back to the Cottage around 2 A.M., and David, the Cottage team, several heads of the mission departments and the ten government leaders arrived a half hour later. You know, it was taking me almost as much time to get to and from the mountain site from the Finlandia Motel as it was taking these people to get from the Cottage level (wherever that is) to our planet Earth and the site. I was trying not to hold a grudge against them.

This was the first time I met a lot of these people, including nine of the leaders. I had already met Charles de Gaulle at the Cottage two years prior, so now it was like seeing an old friend. I asked him how he was feeling, and he told me it was a little bumpy there for a moment but he was fine. Introductions were made, and I shook hands with the others. It was one of those moments when something was happening that couldn't be more ordinary (meeting people), but the people and the context in which it was happening were extraordinary. After coffee and wine were served, we got down to business.

When everyone sat down, they were upbeat, and it was clear that they were convinced this mission was going to work—barring something totally unexpected. I told them I had a couple of Foot People who absolutely knew how to get this mission to succeed. Just give me the word and I'd be happy to unleash their "expertise." And while we were on the Foot People, several men asked, what in the world was that one woman wearing? I asked, were they referring to the clapping Smokey-the-Bear cap or the big stuffed puppet sitting on her shoulders? It felt good to laugh.

The purpose of the meeting was to put together Plan B. Plan A was still the first goal of the primary mission, which was to settle into the site and for everyone to have a relatively "normal" five-senses experience. But they did not need to scrap the mission if Plan A wasn't possible. They had discussed contingency plans over the past few months, and this meeting was to put together the best approach from those plans now that we knew exactly what we were facing, thus creating Plan B.

Right away, the seven leaders who tested weak for continuing into five-senses form at the mountain stepped back from their part of the mission with extraordinary grace. This moment touched me because I knew that it had been an honor for each of them to be chosen for the mission. But now there wasn't even a hint of debate about what they should do since their focus was on the success of the mission. It was understood by all that only Truman, Stalin and Mao would be on the ship the next night representing the Piscean government leaders, and I had a feeling it didn't surprise anyone that some of the leaders may have needed to step back. There were congratulations and good wishes to the three, as if they had been the lucky ones who "passed the test."

By the time the meeting ended at 4 A.M., Plan B was fully outlined and I knew what I would have to do for Plan B. It was going to take more focus and concentration by everyone on the mountain, but I felt confident it would work. However, first we were going to try again for Plan A and bring the ship into what you and I would consider cup-in-the-hand form. Then, if needed, we would shift to Plan B.

I finally crawled into bed around 4:30 A.M.

Chapter 34

Tuesday, July 16

IT WAS 10 A.M. AND I WAS not yet awake at the Cottage. As if coming through a long-distance telephone with a bad connection, I heard the static sounds of someone beating on my door at the Finlandia. Was the motel burning down? I left the Cottage and switched back to my motel room in time to answer the door. It was Laura. She rushed into my room and was frantically telling me everyone was leaving Mt. Shasta and it was "all a disaster" and I needed to do something about it "right away."

I sat her down and tried to make sense of what she was saying. Just then, I saw Peter pull into the parking lot and asked him to join me. And Clarence poked his head out of his room to find out what was going on, so I asked him to join us as well.

Laura said that "Ben" and her daughter, Traci, had packed up and left already. As you might imagine, I didn't find this turn of events bad news. In fact, I was delighted by it. Laura was also saying that this morning at breakfast, a bunch of the other Foot People were griping about the previous night's events—or lack of events—and also threatening to leave. She rambled on about it being my fault and that I was going to be responsible for the mission's failure. At one point, she was lying across my bed on her stomach, beating her fists into the bed and shouting that she was my "ersatz mother" and I needed to listen to her. She lost me a bit there because I was busy trying to figure out what in the world an "ersatz mother" was.

I wish I could say that I remained above Laura's tantrum, but I had just been "pulled" out of the Cottage, I had had little sleep and I was now getting hungry. Her shouting and beating pounded against me and I was also beginning to feel nauseous. Clarence and Peter tried to calm her down, but there was nothing they could say either. She was out of control.

Finally, I told her she had to go away. I still needed to get dressed and I was hungry. She immediately offered to go get me some food, but I didn't want her anywhere near my food. To give her something to do, I told her to find the others and tell them we would all be meeting in Clarence's room at 1 o'clock. I would listen to what they had to say then. She got up quickly and, with new purpose, rushed out the door.

Laura's tantrum was the proverbial straw that broke my camel's back, and all the frustrations I had felt over the past few months about the Foot People, the interlopers and the Meadow Muffins welled up. I didn't just cry, I sobbed. Then Peter said something that put the whole mess into perspective: "Now you know what I've been dealing with for the past twenty-five years." I stopped crying and looked at him, "I don't know how you did it." He just smiled. I realized I had joined some elite club and I now had friends who understood what I was dealing with. We talked a little longer, then the two men left while I got dressed. They took me to town for lunch.

———————— ◆●◆● ————————

The meeting wasn't particularly pleasant for me. I was now faced with another uprising, and they came to this meeting with an attitude. I started by letting them know that I wasn't upset about "Ben" and Traci leaving the mission. In general, they agreed with me. Well, actually they were a little sorry to see Traci leave. She was quiet, dependable and didn't sport around puppets and weird hats. "Ben" was another story. I told them I had heard they were considering leaving, as well, and if they had something to say to me, now was the time to do it.

Peter said he had no complaints with how the mission was being run and what I was doing. Clarence and Salvesen said essentially the same thing. Only Salvesen wasn't being supportive at this point. She was angry. Actually, she was pissed at me. She had nothing to add because she did not want to talk to me. I didn't understand what was going on until later when she told me what Laura had done when she spotted Salvesen on the street that morning. Salvesen had made an appointment with a chiropractor in town, and the only time she could get in was that morning. Laura saw her walking across the street on her way to the doctor's office, stopped the car, jumped out, grabbed Salvesen by the arm and shoved her into the car saying, "Machaelle wants to see all of us *now*." So Salvesen arrived at the motel ready to clobber me.

The remaining Foot People complained. They didn't like the way David excluded Gary Dunlap and his partner from the mission. They felt it was mean-spirited and that they should have been in on the decision. Many of them indicated they were disappointed that the "lesser" government leaders were now coming to the mountain. They preferred Churchill, Roosevelt and de Gaulle to Truman, Stalin and Mao. They wanted me to give them a rundown on what would be happening that evening to see if it met with their approval and expectations, and they were not pleased that I had not given them this vital information before the 11 A.M. checkout time. (Damn, I left my guns in my room.) And some didn't like that there were blocks of time in the day where they had to figure out what to do to entertain themselves.

When we got to Albert, he pointed to Clarence's copy of my book *Behaving as If the God in All Life Mattered* sitting on the table and said that I needed to start acting like my own title. This was insulting, but I'm assuming that was exactly the impact he was going for by saying it. Little did he know that when I didn't punch him out at that moment, I was behaving as if the God in all life mattered. Rather than inflicting bodily harm, I asked what he felt they needed. He told me the group should be attuned at the mountain, and he proclaimed I was the appropriate one to lead them in their attunement.

I might explain here that I first heard of "attunements" when I visited the Findhorn Community in Scotland back in 1977. To begin a meeting they would attune: stand or sit in a circle, hold hands and have a moment's silence or one of them would say a few prayerlike words. Often they would end the meeting the same way. Albert and Laura had strong connections with Findhorn and were familiar with attunements.

Albert's suggestion was greeted favorably by the others. I remember smiling at this point because it was obvious to me that they wanted me to attune them because they had disgusted themselves on the mountain the evening before with their lousy attitudes, loud talking, laughing, smart-assed comments and crappy dinners. They wanted to act differently this evening, and apparently they felt I was the one who was going to save them from themselves by leading an attunement.

I had a little problem with this. The point of an attunement is to focus the group and bring them into harmony with the matter at hand. That's fine, but I kept thinking that if they could not gather their own focus for the landing of a mother ship, seeing dead government leaders and witnessing a historic shift of ley-lines, something that had never before occurred on this scale, I didn't think there was any magic act or dance I could do to get their attention or help them overcome their wandering minds and lack of concentration. Plus, I felt that out of everyone involved in this mission—and there were over a quarter million people participating, counting the crews on the 15,668 craft—the only people who needed attuning were five Foot People. This seemed odd to me. But an attunement on the mountain would be easy, and if this is what they wanted, this is what they would get.

As I listened, it seemed to me that they had come to the Finlandia Motel anticipating a "Mt. Shasta Mission Conference" or a Findhorn-like Experience Week with a schedule for meetings, talks, discussions, meals and play. Based on everything they were saying, I felt it all boiled down to their feeling they weren't getting enough attention. I explained the mission's goals again, hoping its mere importance would sink in and settle them down. And I again explained that I had work I needed to do with the site and the mission, and I didn't have time to hang out with them. When we finished the meeting, everyone, including the disgruntled Foot People, said they would be going to the mountain that night. However, I had made a decision. If the mission was aborted again that night, I was prepared to ask David if we could winnow down the Foot People for the final attempt to just four: Peter, Clarence, Salvesen and me.

No more emergencies or catastrophes occurred that afternoon. The Foot People went off to continue discovering how to entertain themselves. Peter left to take care of other business and said he'd be back at the appointed time: 6:15 P.M. I went to my room for a quick medical session with Lorpuris, then rested and met Clarence for dinner.

A LITTLE SIDE NOTE HERE: It has occurred to me that you might be thinking I'm one of the more dangerous people around and all I did was run around shooting, choking and punching out the Foot People. Let me assure you I didn't lay a hand on anyone, nor did I draw any weapons on them. I'm just letting you know the moments when I *wanted* to do these things. The most dangerous weapon I had at Mt. Shasta was a nail clipper. Really, the laser six-shooters I have are in my head—actually they're in my imaginary underwear drawer. Another thing: I'm pretty sure the only time I raised my voice with any of these people was to blow off steam with Salvesen or Clarence. They were aware of the craziness that was going on, and we had several no-holds-barred gripe sessions that went a long way to helping me keep my equilibrium.

Back to the Finlandia: It was an evening of miracles. Everyone arrived back at the motel parking lot on time, dressed properly and carrying their water bottles, flashlights and jackets—and they had managed to eat dinner! Things were looking up.

THE MT. SHASTA MISSION

7:03 — All the Foot People were present and accounted for at the site. I opened the Mt. Shasta Mission coning, then told the Foot People to prepare for their attunement. They formed a circle and held hands. Since this was Albert's idea, I told him to lead the attunement. I no longer remember what he said, except that it began with "Mother/Father God . . ."

7:15 — The Foot People settled in the same spot they had used the night before outside the log perimeter. I set up on my log desk and did my first check. Both the site and soil were clear and ready to go. Salvesen checked everyone and gave them whatever was needed. Generally speaking, they were in better shape this evening than they were for the first check the evening before.

The first order of business that came out of the previous night's Cottage meeting was to address the issue between Truman and the mountain's trees. We had learned at this point that it had to do with the complete annihilation the trees in Japan experienced when Truman ordered the dropping of the A-bomb in 1945. It wasn't that the bomb left burnt and severely damaged trees, but, rather, the bomb destroyed the very essence of these trees. Where a tree had once stood, there was no longer any evidence that it had ever existed—not even ashes.

Pan explained that the shift that was to occur between the mother ship and the trees at the site had *trust* as its foundation. The trees would release from their five-senses form as the ship took on that form, *trusting* that they (the trees) would be able to return to their natural state once the mission was completed. The rising storm that Salvesen and I felt from the trees the night before had to do with this trust. With Truman on board and once again representing his position as leader, would the trees be able to return to their natural, pre-mission state? Or, as in Japan, would there no longer be any evidence that these trees ever existed?

Harry Truman was prepared to do whatever was needed to resolve the situation. At the Cottage meeting, he had written a statement that he wished to make in the sincere hope that this would do the trick. I now needed to find out from nature when and how Truman was to make his statement.

First, I connected with the deva of the mountain's trees and asked if there was something I could do to assist in this situation. I was told that President Truman needed to initiate the release and resolution for the problem between himself and the trees. Then, I was asked to work with the trees again before leaving Mt. Shasta and returning to Perelandra. This was to be the gift to the mountain that I had asked about when I first arrived. I agreed to return to the mountain for this, and Pan then gave a few instructions on what I was to do to facilitate the statement that Truman would be making a little later.

Pan: *President Truman's statement will have to be shifted to us* [the Deva
of the Mt. Shasta Trees and Pan] *in energy-form. You may do
this prior to releasing the summer solstice energy to the mother ship
and into the universe. At that point, you will know what to do with
Truman's statement, we are sure. Use the site's work rock to aid you.
Once you have left the dome and returned to your log, check the
trees for balancing and stabilizing in light of their adjustments to his
statement.*

I called Hyperithon to tell him what I would be doing. He
said they would be touching down shortly, but he would
hold the ship's final shifts until after Truman made his statement and I completed my work.

8:23 — Salvesen got up and headed to where the Foot People were
sitting. She said, "Here they come," right at the same time I
received a call from Hyperithon telling me they were hovering in position over the site. She felt the barometric pressure
change and decided to check everyone again. An hour before, they were all clear. Now their bodies needed help.

Paul, Laura, Albert, Peter, Clarence:
     two spinal adjustments (T-5, 6)
Janice: Five spinal adjustments (T-5, 6, 7 and C-2, 3)
     and a gall bladder reflex
Salvesen: one spinal adjustment (T-6)

[Salvesen told me later she thought the common spinal
adjustments that everyone needed—thoracic vertebrae 5
and 6—were connected to the hit their diaphragms were
taking and related to the X on the human body that she
observed Lorpuris working on with me during the summer
of 1984.]

8:52 — Hyperithon confirmed they were close to touch down. I tested the soil and site and found both still testing clear.

TIME OUT FOR A MOMENT OF INSANITY: For some reason unknown to me, several of the Foot People came over to where I was working. This was fine, until they began moving my testing boxes around on the log to make room so that they could sit. I had the boxes in a specific order so that I could test the bottles in the dark. This didn't seem to concern them, so I told them to get off my log and leave my boxes alone.

8:59 — The descent was on schedule, but Hyperithon gave me a heads up that they were descending more quickly into the site than they had the night before. He said Salvesen needed to know this for monitoring the Foot People.

9:01 — Touch down.

9:02 — As instructed, I walked to the center of the site to my work rock and connected with Harry Truman just as I had done on the mountain the night before. As he delivered his statement, he "moved" its energy and intent to me, and I shifted it into the rock. Then directing my words to nature, I asked that the heart and intent of his statement be released to the Deva of the Trees and Pan. The whole thing— Harry Truman's statement, the shift and the release—took less than five minutes.

I don't know what he said because I felt this was a private moment and I had deliberately not listened to his statement. When I received the energy and moved it into the rock, it did not feel like what I felt with the other work I had done at the site. But since I was working with a human, Harry Truman, and not solely with nature, I assumed that this might account for the difference I was feeling. I asked the Deva of the Trees and Pan if the shift was complete and was told yes. I then tested the trees to see if any balancing and stabilizing were needed and was told to release Yarrow and Gruss an Aachen to the trees. For me, this was verification that a shift had taken place.

9:07 – I told Hyperithon that the shift was verified and my work was completed. He let me know they would now begin the ship's movement through the final stages and into full five-senses form.

9:11 – They stopped the descent for Lorpuris to check the leaders. Truman needed Orange Ruffles. Stalin and Mao were clear.

9:17 – The soil and site tested clear. However, I needed Elm and one Glycodyne (B-vitamin supplement). At this point, the ship was visible but hazy, and I could see Mao, Stalin and Truman looking out the window at me. Salvesen could not see the ship, but she could see that I was having a problem and tested me again. I now needed Borage. These two test results were out of my usual pattern, so she did some further testing and found that I was picking up emotions from the three leaders: a lack of confidence in facing danger and challenge (Borage) and overcoming discouragement (Elm).

I told Lorpuris what was happening and that Salvesen and I suspected that as the three men watched me, they were inadvertently linking with me and transferring their emotions to me. Immediately, I saw a flurry of activity and a shade was lowered at the window in front of the three leaders. Salvesen tested me again and I was fine.

TIME OUT FOR ANOTHER FINE MOMENT OF INSANITY: Salvesen decided to sit on the log next to me, which meant she had to move my testing boxes further down the log to make room. I just stared at her, then said something like, "What the hell are you doing?" Whatever was going on with these people and my boxes was driving me nuts. Peter had been watching, so he came over and, without a word, sat with me on the log to my left (the side opposite my boxes). I thanked him, put my boxes back in order, and from that point on, until we went into the site, Peter functioned as my guard dog.

9:40 – Lorpuris checked Mao, Stalin and Truman again. They were clear.

9:50 – The three leaders began showing some signs of stress as the ship continued to descend into five-senses form. Hyperithon told me that Truman and Mao were experiencing labored breathing and the color had drained from the faces of all three. Lorpuris was particularly concerned about their labored breathing. They stopped the descent again, and Lorpuris worked with the leaders to eliminate their physical stress.

After a few minutes, David verified that the ship's form level was compatible to the mountain's form level and made the decision to come no further into five-senses form. He announced we would be working with Plan B for the mission. At this point, several of the Foot People said they could see haze and light where the ship was sitting. Others saw nothing, but most of them could feel a strong and clear presence.

PLAN B

Here's a thumbnail description of Plan B: The two groups of people (those coming on ship and those coming by foot) needed to be on *compatible levels* of five-senses form—that is, the Foot People would be able to sense unmistakably the other group's presence and visa versa. It was always understood that the ship's people would have a broader range of sensory function and, therefore, would more easily hear, see, smell, touch and taste what was happening on the mountain. But it was the clarity and function of the Foot People's sensory systems with their more limited range that was the important issue. As the Mt. Shasta Mission's witnesses, their systems had to be activated and functioning in order for them to accurately perceive and understand what was happening around them. With Plan A, we would have had *identical levels* of cup-in-the-hand form, and the ceremony on the mountain would have been witnessed and experienced by the Foot People in the usual fashion. ("I see it. I hear it, and…yikes, I just licked Stalin's face, and boy, does he taste salty.")

For Plan B, we were going to move each element of the mission's primary phase as an energy "package" directly into each person's sensory system. I would then use the summer solstice energy (nature's strongest and highest expression of five-senses form) from the solstice ribbon to ground each mission element— that is, I would move the solstice energy into their bodies right after they received each mission package. The solstice energy would mix with the mission energy and, because of the inherent nature of summer solstice energy, that combined and now-grounded energy would automatically activate their sensory systems. With this, we would be activating their sensory systems for each element of the mission. Get it? There will be a test later. If you're confused, hang on. I think it will clear up once you see how we did this.

At 10 o'clock, Lorpuris told me to escort each Foot Person, one at a time, slowly through the ship to a central position near my work rock. First, I gathered my testing boxes and put them on the ground next to the rock. As I moved through the site, I noticed that the ship was oriented differently than it had been for the dry run. They were making sure we wouldn't all be huddled in the bathroom for this most extraordinary and important event!

The Foot People were standing around the outside perimeter of the logs. I went over to Salvesen, told her to climb over the log, then took her arm and moved slowly with her to the center of the site. Whatever I needed to do for Plan B, I always chose to do it with Salvesen first. She was the most aware of the group when it came to the human body and picking up problems her body might be experiencing. And she had a keen sense of what was happening, whether she could see it or not. If anything went wrong, she would pick up on it right away, not panic and work to remedy the problem before we went on to the others. In short, Salvesen was the safety net for all the others.

We waited a minute or so to make sure everything was okay with Salvesen, then I went back to the log perimeter and escorted the next person in. I did this for each Foot Person, making sure I moved them into the ship's reality slowly and watching for any discomfort they might be having. I think their experience the previous night gave their bodies good practice because none of them were experiencing distress as I moved them through the ship. They could tell something was different, but they weren't having bad reactions to the changes.

I also noticed something else that, to me, constituted the second miracle of the night. As soon as I began escorting them through the ship, they were totally different people. They were quiet, focused, aware, alert, sensitive to the need to cooperate and willing to follow instructions. I couldn't believe it. This rowdy group of Foot People had morphed into our mission witnesses.

Once I moved all seven Foot People into position, Salvesen checked each of them to make sure their balance held now that they were standing in a mother ship. Albert needed Nymphenburg essence and Janice needed Royal Highness. The rest, including Salvesen and myself, were clear.

Then David escorted each person from his group, one by one, into a large conference room on the ship. That room was positioned right where the Foot People were standing and, as David brought each of his people into the room, they were standing with the Foot People on the mountain as well as with the ship's people in the conference room. The two realities, the mother ship and the mountain site, had commingled. First, he escorted Truman into the room, then Mao, Stalin, Hyperithon, Lorpuris, Tex and John. These seven were now facing the seven Foot People. David and I were paired and would be working Plan B together. (I found it interesting that with all the shuffling of people in both the ship's group and the Foot People's group, we ended up with an equal number of people from both groups in the room. I don't think anyone planned it that way.) We then gave everyone a few minutes to acclimate to everyone else in the room. Once again Salvesen checked the Foot People while Lorpuris checked the ship's leaders and guests and, much to our delight and surprise, everyone tested clear.

The others on the ship, the crew and St. Germain, were watching what was happening in the conference room/mountain site on what we would call "closed-circuit monitors" in the next room. Their presence in the conference room would have overwhelmed the small group of Foot People.

Phase One: Primary Mission

Summer Solstice Energy Release and Shift

The summer solstice energy was key to the success of Plan B and this shift was more important than ever. I walked over to my rock and went through a four-step process with nature.

1. I set up with Pan, picked up the ivory bow, focused on the crystal/topaz in the Perelandra garden and called for the release of the summer solstice energy. I saw golden energy shoot up from the center of the garden, high into the sky.

2. I then directed the solstice energy into and through the crystal/topaz sitting on a small table in the ship's conference room in which we were standing. As I said this, I saw the energy from Perelandra move into and through the ship's crystal/topaz, and that crystal/topaz lit up and glowed.

3. I asked Pan then to move the solstice energy through the ship and release it into the universe. I saw the energy shoot out of the ship in all directions. The crystal/topaz in the room continued glowing.

4. Finally, I asked that the solstice energy from the universe infuse the mission's domed environment and that the solstice energy from the ship's crystal/topaz infuse the ivory bow in my hand. And with this, I felt a shift in the dome and saw the bow light up. I felt there was now a direct triangular link between the crystal/topaz in the room, the crystal/topaz at Perelandra and the bow in my hand.

After returning the bow to the rock, I waited two minutes for the solstice energy to seat. Then I checked the balance of the site and soil (both were clear), picked up the bow again and went back to where the others were standing.

Gettysburg Battle Energy

David needed to set the tone for the primary mission, transfer the energy of the higher intent and purpose of the Gettysburg Battle to the Foot People and activate their sensory systems with it so that it could become grounded in five-senses form. He was still linked to the raised battle energy by the gold cord wrapped around his right wrist from the work I did on Friday. Now with our attention on the Gettysburg Battle energy again, the cord lit up and could be seen.

David stood directly in front of each Foot Person, and one by one (beginning with Salvesen), I told them to hold out their left hand. He placed his right hand on top of their outstretched hand, clasped it and moved the energy from the cord into his hand, and then into their hand. He did this simply: He stated that the energy from the cord was to move into his hand and then directed where he needed it to move from there.

I stood next to whomever he was working with, monitoring the energy shift. After the energy was "comfortably" seated in each Foot Person's body, I held the person's left hand and directed summer solstice energy from the bow that I now was holding in my left hand to move into my right hand. From there, I transferred it into the person's hand I was holding and directed it to mix with the Gettysburg Battle energy. We waited a minute or so for the now-mixed energy to move automatically into the person's sensory system. I asked each person to focus attention on their different senses in order to pick up how the mixed energy was activating the system. Once completed, I told them to "hold" the mixed energy until it was time for the release and said that the easiest way to hold energy in the body was to trust it will stay there and then ignore it—for now.

When all seven Foot People had the mixed energy seated in their sensory systems, David stood before them as a group and let me know he was ready. I told them to focus on David and to send the Gettysburg Battle energy from their systems back to him. For this, all they needed to do was request the shift while focusing on David. They did this, and I was able to see the energy move from each person back to David's outstretched right hand.

Finally, David called for the release of the Gettysburg Battle energies from his hand to our universe. The energy shot straight up through the mother ship, and I saw it move rapidly into and spread throughout the atmosphere above the ship. Our universe now had as part of its makeup the higher intent and purpose of the Gettysburg Battle. For the Mt. Shasta Mission, this signaled to all our readiness for what Stalin, Mao and Truman were about to do—shift the underlying dynamic and principles of governments around the world from the old to the new.

After infusing the battle energy with the solstice energy and watching it move into everyone's sensory system, it was clear to me that the battle energy's dynamic, intensity, color and perhaps even weight changed once mixed with solstice energy. I now understood that because of Plan B it didn't matter if we could see, hear or smell the mission in the conventional manner. What mattered was that the seven Foot People, representing us on planet Earth, allowed their sensory systems to be infused with the mixed, grounded energy, thus making that energy and all that it contains available to the rest of us and our sensory systems.

As I watched what was happening, I knew I had the verification that Plan B was going to do the job. And I fell in love with Plan B right then and there. It was a more complex plan to pull off than Plan A, but I loved the fact that we would not be depending on each witness's personal intellectual and emotional interpretation of what was stimulating their sensory system. Accurate interpretation had always been a major concern whenever the mission's witnesses were discussed. Instead, this new

sensory stimulation was clean and uncontaminated. It would ensure that when any of us—you, me and anyone else—wishes to
understand and work with the higher intent and purpose of any
battle, and in particular the Gettysburg Battle, we will touch into
a clean, unadulterated dynamic that has not been put through the
lens of another's interpretation.

With the successful completion of the Gettysburg Battle energy
shift, the Foot People provided their third miracle of the night.
Plan B was not only more complex than Plan A, it was also much
more subtle. Yet these people hung in there beautifully. They
did everything they were asked to do. They didn't try to question anything or suggest we change what we were doing. They
paid attention throughout the entire time we worked with
them—and they were quiet. On top of it, everyone held their
balance as they worked with David and then me. Salvesen carefully monitored them in case she needed to jump in, but they
were fine.

   Except for Janice. She had a reaction while David and I
worked with her that concerned me. From the moment David
grasped her hand and until I released her hand after the solstice
energy shift, her body shook, like she was shivering. I noticed
that the solstice energy infusion smoothed her out a lot and
reduced the shaking, but I was still concerned. I asked if she was
okay and she said she was fine. I asked if she was cold, and she
said no, she was fine. Salvesen checked her and she tested clear.
She quietly explained that sometimes she shook when energy
entered her body, so I chalked this up to Janice's personal style in
these matters. As long as she held her balance during the mission
and she was comfortable, I didn't care if she needed to shake,
rattle or roll.

Release of the Piscean
Government/Military Custodianship

It was now time for the three leaders to release their government custodianship. Essentially, we repeated the same process David and I used for the Gettysburg Battle energy shift. All three leaders had been briefed on Plan B the night before and knew what to do on the mountain.

We began with Joseph Stalin. Would it be politically incorrect of me to mention that he was short? Perhaps if I told you all three leaders were short, I'd only be accused of equal opportunity political incorrectness. Salvesen not only found him to be short, but businesslike and formal, as well. He wasn't cold, just serious and purposeful. And another thing, I heard from some history buff somewhere that Stalin was born with a deformed left arm. I did not see any signs of a left-arm problem on the mountain, and he clearly didn't hesitate to use his left hand.

But I digress. Stalin stood in front of Salvesen, and I stood to her left facing both of them. Salvesen held out her left hand and Stalin grasped it firmly with his right hand. He looked directly into her eyes and with quiet purpose and conviction, made the statement he had come so far to make:

> On behalf of all leaders who have worked in the arenas of government and the military around the world and throughout the era that is coming to an end, I release full custodianship and pass on to the government/military leaders of the new era all responsibility inherent in their positions and goals.

He directed the energy of his words to move through his body and into his hand and, from there, into Salvesen's hand. Salvesen then moved it from her hand and into her body. It was important, in releasing the custodianship, that Stalin fully extend his gesture and Salvesen fully receive the gesture. That's why Salvesen, not Stalin, moved the energy from her hand and into her body once he placed the energy into her hand.

Next, it was my turn. I held Salvesen's left hand and followed up Stalin's shift by moving summer solstice energy into her body. As with the battle energy, the solstice energy mixed with Stalin's statement. And, with this, the mixed energy moved right into her sensory system. Once completed, I told Salvesen to hold that energy mix, and we moved onto the next Foot Person.

We repeated this entire procedure with Stalin and each Foot Person. Stalin's release of custodianship and the movement of the mixed energy into the other person's sensory system was clear and clean, and easy for me to watch with each Foot Person— except with Peter Caddy. Beginning with his work with David, I noticed something odd with Peter. The energy that was directed to him flowed into his body, but then it disappeared. When I moved the solstice energy into him, I noticed that it felt like the energy was moving straight through his body and exiting out his back. With everyone else, I could see and feel the energy enter the body, hit a wall or backstop (pardon the pun) and then stay inside the body. Peter's backstop was missing. I knew Lorpuris was observing us and he wasn't indicating to me that there was a problem, so I figured it was just another personal style thing.

The Foot People held Stalin's energy in their sensory systems as we moved on to the next leader—Mao Tse-tung.

Mao stood before Salvesen and she again held out her hand. But he didn't grasp her hand. Instead, he held her wrist and it was clear he was refusing to touch her hand. Salvesen looked at me and I looked at her with that "now-what-do-we-do" expression on our faces. Later, when she and I were sharing notes, we both admitted that right at that moment when Mao placed his fingers around her wrist, we had the strangest feeling he was thinking,

"Ewww, ca-ca." On the mountain, we figured his reticence had something to do with some Chinese custom, and decided to ignore it and move forward. As it turned out, he moved the energy into her wrist effortlessly and smoothly. His statement to release custodianship was the same as Stalin's, and I now understood the three leaders were being careful to represent the larger group at the mountain and not themselves as individuals. I assumed (correctly, as it turned out) that the statement, simple though it may have been, was written by the larger group and not just by these three men.

Mao's release-and-solstice mix combined with Stalin's release-and-solstice mix in the Foot People's systems, thus creating a larger, unified, more complex package of grounded energy. Everyone was comfortable, relaxed—and still attentive, alert and focused on what was happening.

Finally, it was time for Harry Truman. He stood before Salvesen, she held out her hand, he placed his hand over hers and grasped it firmly. It was obvious he didn't have a problem with touching women's hands. He repeated the same custodian release statement. As with the others, I coordinated the energy shift by saying, "Move the released custodianship as energy to Salvesen." I waited. Salvesen waited. About fifteen or twenty seconds went by. Salvesen and I looked at one another and, at the same time, said aloud, "Nothing's happening." Immediately, my mind went nuts. Was he refusing to release custodianship? Was this a protest? Did the others know what he was doing?...And then the pertinent question hit: Did he know what to do? Is this why he had been watching the others so intently?

Just as I was about to call for help, I saw David walking over to us. He and Truman had a quiet conversation, and then David turned to me and said, "He doesn't know how to move the energy." I couldn't believe what I was hearing. Out of all the things that

were carefully thought out for the mission, no one, Truman included, had considered asking about this little issue. Of course,
we had not put Plan B together until the evening before, and only
Plan B required the energy-moving skill. Plan A had circum-
vented this completely.

David said to me, "Go ahead and teach him what to do." Now I
was mentally scrambling around for an easy and quick way to
teach Harry Truman how to move energy from point A to point
B. I thought I'd try visuals. Maybe he was a visual man. So I told
him to imagine he was holding a white Ping Pong ball in his right
hand. I asked if he could see it and he said yes. I told him to hold
the ball up to his mouth and speak the release statement into the
ball. He did this very well, and I could see that now the statement's energy was in the ball. That's when I got a little too confident (sloppy) and said, "Place the ball into Salvesen's sensory
system." It was the wrong thing for me to say at that moment.
And it wasn't even accurate. I wanted him to place it into her
hand and then she would put its energy into her system. But I
totally screwed up the instruction and he took me literally. All of a
sudden, I saw him try to push the ball up Salvesen's nose. First one
nostril, then the other. She started laughing and we were both
telling him to hold on a minute. We had to try this again.

I decided I'd try a different, safer image, and one that he might
be more comfortable with. I had Pan neutralize the custodianship
release energy in the Ping Pong ball so that we could start over. By
now I was becoming fond of this Truman fellow—he was trying
so hard to do what he needed to do. It seemed like he was over his
head with the energy thing, but that wasn't going to stop him. No,
sirree. So, here he was, listening to me, of all people, giving him a
lesson on how to move energy. In the meantime, I could feel supportive cheerleading coming from everyone else in the room.

Knowing he had been a baseball fan, I chose a clean, white
baseball as the new image. Now I really had his attention. He saw

the baseball in his hand and spoke the statement into it. I watched as the energy flowed easily into the ball. The baseball was too large to fit into any of Salvesen's sensory orifices, so I felt she was safe. And, to make it even more safe for her, this time I gave him the correct direction. I told my new friend, Harry, to place the baseball in her left hand. And with that, he enthusiastically slammed the ball into her hand. She winced, said a quiet, "Ouch," and started laughing again. It was in her hand now, of that we were sure, so I had Salvesen direct the energy from the ball into her body. Then I followed up with summer solstice energy, and I watched the two energies mix and move into her sensory system.

We had six more Foot People to go, and I was a little concerned about Truman's happy enthusiasm with the baseball. I pointed out to him that none of us had baseball gloves, so he'd have to ease up a little. And with the rest of the Foot People, I made sure I reminded him to place the ball gently into their hands. By now, Harry Truman was having a good time and we were all smiling with him.

The problem with Harry Truman and energy movement explained why I didn't feel anything happening when he was supposed to shift his statement to the trees to me. He didn't know how to do it and just gave it his best shot. But because Truman clearly intended to offer his statement to the trees, Pan saved our butts by capturing the heart and intent from his spoken words and moved that energy directly to the trees, thus bypassing me and my work rock altogether.

The Foot People now had the combined energy from Stalin, Mao, Truman and the summer solstice. I directed them to spend a moment experiencing this unique energy package in whatever sensory manner they could. When each indicated they were finished, I told them to look at David (I pointed to where he was standing for those who couldn't see him) and move this energy package from their sensory systems back to him. I reminded them that all they needed to do was request this shift to occur and see or feel it happen. The energy shot out of the seven Foot People and came to a stop in David's outstretched, cupped hands.

Immediately, David called for the energy to be released to the command ship that was hovering above our ship. There the energy package experienced a 100 percent/100 percent split, thus creating two equal packages, and one package was shifted into the expanded mission's command ship that was paired with ours. The energy package being held by our command ship expanded and swiftly moved to the waiting 7,834 primary mission craft positioned above the Piscean government/military leylines. Once completed, the second package of energy being held by the expanded mission's command ship expanded and moved to the paired 7,834 expanded mission craft. The entire process took fifteen seconds. You read that right: fifteen seconds. The grounded energy was now being held in place on all 15,668 craft—similar to the Foot People holding that energy in their bodies—to be used as the foundation for the deactivation of the old government/ military leyline system and as part of the foundation for activating the new leyline system.

> At 11:23 P.M., after receiving word that everyone was ready, David Eisenhower ordered the deactivation of the Piscean government/military leyline system and the formation and activation of the new Aquarian government/military leyline system.

At this moment, Salvesen was resting against a large rock in the site/room and looking at the stars. She swears that when David ordered the shift, the stars instantly moved en masse in the sky to the left and then quickly shifted back. For me, I felt a sudden, crisp, clean change in the air, almost like another barometric shift.

The Cottage team later explained to me what happened once David gave his command. Six seconds after the command, the team of leyline experts on each primary mission craft deactivated and released the old leyline system. The paired craft then shifted their positions around the globe to the new leyline pattern. Gold energy circuits shot from each of the craft, linking with the other craft, crossing circuits and forming an intricately patterned grid. The Aquarian government/military leyline system was formed and was now held by the 7,834 primary mission craft just outside our atmosphere. Then, with a single, swift, smooth motion, the leyline teams moved the new grid into our planet's atmosphere and seated it deep beneath the Earth's surface. And lastly, in a matter of just a few seconds, the teams activated our new Aquarian government/military leyline system.

After David gave his command, he told us we had a thirty-second wait before he would receive word from the command ship that the leyline shift and activation was successful. Thirty seconds. Several of us looked at one another. Is it possible this whole thing was going to take just thirty seconds? It took us almost an hour and a half to complete our part on the mountain, and it was taking 7,834 spacecraft thirty seconds. But I have to admit that under the circumstances thirty seconds felt like thirty hours. No one said anything as we waited and Salvesen continued to stare at the stars. Then, suddenly there was movement and talking among the ship's people in our site/room, and David announced, "We've got it."

Phase Two: St. Germain

We weren't finished yet. So while there was some restrained cele-bration and genuine happiness going on among all of us, David left the conference room. In less than five minutes, he returned with St. Germain. Salvesen told me later that when St. Germain came into the room, she felt an overriding presence, like "big daddy had just come in to join us kids at the party." St. Germain has been around a while—hundreds of years—but he looked just fine. There was a bounce in his walk and a quickness to his step. He was around 5 feet 10 inches and had an athletic build—strong looking and slender at the same time. He had dark hair and blue eyes. And he was dressed in a wine-red cassocklike robe. From David's preliminary reports, the primary mission was a resound-ing success, and St. Germain wanted to build on this success.

The arrival of St. Germain quelled our celebration and focused us on the next order of business. I swear to you, I picked up a dif-ferent feeling from the Foot People now. Besides still being well behaved, they had success under their belts—and they had confi-dence. This was now an experienced group, and they were ready to give St. Germain whatever he needed—even though none of us knew exactly what that would be.

St. Germain was there to complete the work that was done thirty years prior when he had activated the overall, "umbrella" leyline system for the Aquarian era. Those leylines had been suc-cessfully activated then, but its impulses were beyond normal five-senses range. St. Germain felt it was time to bring that system into full, human five-senses form. The primary mission had been perfectly set up for just this kind of job. I was curious as to how St. Germain was going to accomplish his goals. Although he would be building on the process we had just used for the primary mis-sion, I had a feeling he was going to come up with a different approach.

Beginning with Salvesen, he stood to the left of each Foot Person. As they had done for the primary mission, I told them to hold out their left hand, palm up. And he showed us a new variation on passing energy through the hands. Instead of just placing his hand over theirs or holding their wrists or slapping them with baseballs, St. Germain lightly touched the fingertips of their left hand with the fingertips of his right hand. He then moved energy from the leylines he was working with right into their spines and spiraled it up toward their heads. They were instructed to hold that energy in place. Nearly everyone felt what he was doing and how he was moving energy in their bodies. I was amazed at his efficiency and power, along with the extraordinary clarity and crispness in which he moved the energy. I had never seen anything like it.

Next, it was my turn. I moved a new round of summer solstice energy from the ribbon I was still carrying into their bodies. I did it the old-fashioned way by standing in front of them and grasping their left hand with my right hand. Taking my direction from St. Germain, I gently moved the solstice energy into their spines and saw it commingle with his leyline energy. When we had completed working with each of the Foot People, I told them to spend a few moments experiencing this new grounded energy from St. Germain.

Finally, the Foot People focused on St. Germain—the spot in front of them where I told them he was standing—and directed the energy from their spines, into their bodies, then hands and back to him. He held the energy in his hands for just a moment, then I saw it shoot out from him horizontally in all directions. In about fifteen seconds, he lowered his arms and pointed to the ground with both hands. And with that, the energy disappeared into the ground. All of his work was amazingly powerful and efficient, and I felt honored just to have been able to watch him, let alone work with him.

David told me we would be waiting another thirty seconds for confirmation that St. Germain's work was successfully completed. I told the others what David had said, and we relaxed against the rocks while we waited. Sure enough, St. Germain received word that the infusion of human five-senses form into his Aquarian leyline system was a success. I could tell he was one happy man. He didn't dance around in a jig or high-five anyone, but he had a big smile. He thanked us all and stepped out of the conference room again.

For St. Germain's work, I set things up a little differently with Peter Caddy. I knew he wasn't feeling, seeing or hearing anything, which wasn't unusual for him. And I could still feel the summer solstice energy that I was moving into him pass straight through his body and exit out the back. I wanted to give him the best shot I could for experiencing something with St. Germain because these two men had worked together for over thirty years. Yet in all of this, Peter had never tangibly experienced St. Germain, and I knew that it was something he very much wanted. For so many years, Peter depended on others telling him what St. Germain wanted or needed from him. Peter always acted on faith—faith that he would do whatever someone said St. Germain wanted him to do, and faith that whatever Peter was told was indeed from St. Germain.

Now here we were on the mountain and St. Germain was standing just to Peter's left—less than two feet away from him. I asked David to join us and stand behind Peter to act as Peter's backstop. I could tell that St. Germain knew what I was aiming for and worked with Peter carefully and deliberately. I could see the energy enter into Peter's body and spiral up his spine. But Peter felt nothing. I kept David behind him while I shifted the solstice energy, and Peter still felt nothing. I looked at Peter after we finished with him and said, "I'm sorry. I don't know what else to do." He replied, "Don't worry. It's fine." But I could tell this was a personal disappointment for him. I had really hoped that with St. Germain, David's backstop and the solstice energy infusion, Peter could have a tangible experience with his friend.

The impact of the summer solstice energy was interesting and had a twofold effect on all the Foot People, Peter included. First, it added the five-senses grounding to whatever other energy they held. Several Foot People told me that the solstice energy took the edge off the other energies and it relaxed them. Second, it provided them with the strength and support from nature as they did the work on the mountain. We were now two hours into the mission, and everyone was still standing—literally. We needed this because we still weren't finished.

Phase Three: Expanded Mission

Phase Three was the easy one for all of us on the mountain. We just had to stand around and wait. All the same, it was still nerve-wracking. We knew that if the expanded mission was on, our work truly had been successful. Had we failed, there would be no expanded mission.

Everything we had done in the first and second phases had been monitored by a team on the expanded mission's lead ship. It was now time for them to let David know their decision. Almost immediately, ten seconds to be exact, David received word that the expanded mission was on and that they would be shifting the energy package created by Stalin, Truman, Mao and the solstice energy (which the 7,834 expanded mission craft had been holding) out of the universe and to their corresponding lead ship beyond our universe. From there, new Aquarian government/military leyline systems for twenty-four different realities would be created, using the energy package as their foundation, and they would be infused and activated with energy from our newly activated government/military system.

As leader of the Mt. Shasta Mission, David had to give the command to launch the expanded mission. He picked up a phone in the conference room, gave the go-ahead and then told us we'd have to wait again—thirty seconds. A few of us chuckled at the insanity that all of this would take just thirty seconds. I watched the second hand on my watch, and at *exactly* thirty seconds from when David gave the go-ahead, he received word and then announced to us, "They have it."

The three phases of the Mt. Shasta Mission were now successfully completed. It took two and a half hours. Everyone on the ship and on the mountain celebrated, and a few of the Foot People had tears in their eyes. It was a great moment for us that lasted about fifteen minutes.

However, we still had some things to do. We had to get the Foot People safely out of the mother ship and off the mountain. The decision had been made to keep the ship and its passengers in place while we moved out of the site and off the mountain. I needed to escort the Foot People, one by one, through the ship and out of the site. I started with Salvesen so that she'd be available for testing the others. Once I got everyone out, I told them that we'd be leaving the mountain first. We gathered our stuff and headed down the trail. Before leaving, I turned for one last look at the mother ship. Now that I was no longer standing in it, I could not see the eight men that I assumed were still standing in the conference room. I only could see the exterior of the ship. I felt like I was looking at it through a thick fog. It was there, but distant. And the further away I moved, the denser the fog.

Our trek down the mountain trail was much more pleasant this night than it had been the night before. Instead of carping and complaining, we talked about the mission. It was difficult for us to believe that something so big, so momentous had just occurred. And they compared notes about what they saw and felt on the mountain. None of us were aware when the mother ship lifted off, and that's exactly what Lorpuris had wanted for us.

We got back to the motel and everyone headed for their rooms. That surprised me a little because I didn't want to let go of the night yet. I said goodnight to Peter and, with no one else around, headed to my room.

A few minutes later, Salvesen knocked. She and Clarence didn't want to call it a night yet either and wanted me to join them in Clarence's room for celebratory soft drinks and cookies. We had a good time rehashing the night—and laughing about Mao's refusing to hold our hands. And Truman's overenthusiastic baseball routine. Clarence told us that when David grasped his hand, he (Clarence) felt a distinct and palpable warmth. We marveled about how the Foot People morphed from a bunch of annoying, whacko individuals into a terrific mission group. Amazing. They rose to the occasion, and that's about all I can say to explain what happened. Of course, all that work with building the protection dome so that it would support everyone—including the Foot People— just might have had something to do with it as well. By 2 A.M., we called it a night and I got ready to head to the Cottage.

I arrived at the Cottage around 2:30 and found all the Cottage men were already back. (I have got to start talking to these people about transportation and time.) The ten leaders were on their way back to wherever. (The seven leaders had been on call at the Cottage in case they were needed while Mao, Truman and Stalin were on the mountain.) Hyperithon was busy with the spacecraft crews as they "unpaired" and peeled off to wherever. "Wherever" was busy that night.

But at the Cottage, there was celebration. David popped open a bottle of champagne, and I had the same fun rehashing the night that I had just had with Salvesen and Clarence—except now the talk was from the Cottage team's perspective. One thing that we pondered for a few minutes was that none of the Foot People had to go to the bathroom that whole evening. And it was a chilly night. Maybe they snuck off behind a tree without our seeing them leave. Hmmm. Oh yeah…and we laughed about Mao refusing to touch anyone's hand and Truman's overenthusiastic baseball routine.

I finally went up to my room at the Cottage around 4:30 A.M. I was exhausted.

CRAFT POSITION FOR PRIMARY
AND EXPANDED MISSIONS

Activated Aquarian Goverment/Miliary Leylines
(Beyond Universe)

Lead Expanded Mission Ship

Beyond Universe

Universe

Atmosphere

Paired Expanded Command Ship
and 7,834 Spacecraft

Primary Command Ship
and 7,834 Spacecraft

Witnesses, David, Leaders, Crew and Mothership

Start Here! →

Mt. Shasta

Earth's Activated Aquarian Goverment/Miliary Leylines

Chapter 35

Wednesday, July 17

By 10:30 A.M., I HAD LEFT THE Cottage, gotten dressed at the Finlandia and was out of my room in search of the Foot People to talk to them about what had happened on the mountain. I needed to give David, Lorpuris, St. Germain and Hyperithon an idea of what these people had experienced and were thinking. Well, much to my surprise, the only Foot People around were Clarence and Janice. Everyone else had already checked out of the motel, and all I found were a bunch of empty rooms. The Finlandia Motel was a ghost town.

Clarence, Janice and I drove into town for a late breakfast, and we talked. Other than talking to me about her shaking the night before, Janice had been quiet throughout the mission, so I wasn't sure what she experienced. As it turned out, she experienced quite a bit. She sketched the mother ship on the back of her placemat and talked about the differences she felt between the three leaders and the energy they each moved into her body. Again she brought up how important the summer solstice infusions were for her and how they kept her from falling apart from the intensity of the other energies and the mission itself. She was surprised at how intense the mission experience was and what it required from her. I told her that even if we had been able to work with Plan A, the intensity would have been just as great, if not more so. It was just the nature of this mission. She admitted that she now understood what I had been trying to tell them in the meetings and why Salvesen had done so much physical work to prepare them.

Clarence talked more about the pressure and warmth he felt from David's hand during the Gettysburg Battle energy work. It was the only tangible experience he had, but normally he doesn't perceive things like this—so feeling David's hand was a different experience for him. Because it was so clearly palpable, it was all he needed to verify that indeed something had happened on that mountain.

But Clarence had another verification that Janice and I found interesting. When we got back to the motel after the mission was aborted on Monday night, Clarence couldn't go to sleep right away. So he turned on the television in his room and watched a retrospective on Dwight David Eisenhower. The next night (July 16, the night of the mission) after Salvesen and I left his room, he turned on the television again and watched a program on Harry Truman and the fortieth anniversary of the first atomic bomb test at the Trinity test site near Alamagordo, New Mexico (July 16, 1945). Perhaps these two coincidences would only be mildly interesting, except for the fact that he hadn't searched for or deliberately selected either of these programs. They were what was on the screen when he turned on the set.

As for my experiences: I certainly saw, heard and felt the mission. I didn't lick or sniff anyone, so I can't say I smelled and tasted the mission. What I experienced is what I've written in this book. But I wasn't a witness. I functioned as part of the mission team and, as far as the witness role was concerned, how my senses were activated was not the issue.

After lunch, we bid Janice farewell, and off she drove, leaving Clarence and me alone again with the mountain. By this time, I was admitting to myself that I was too exhausted for words, so we decided to do nothing. Nothing meant driving to Castle Lake, a nearby recreational lake where I sat, watched the water and knitted while Clarence walked around taking pictures. (*Fig. 14*)

Fig. 14: Machaelle at Castle Lake the day after.

When I got back to the Cottage that evening, things were still pretty active. They received reports that afternoon on all three phases of the mission that confirmed everything was still holding. I'd like to tell you that I asked what "still holding" meant, but I was too tired to care. However, I still had it in me to smile and say, "Great." I went to bed early that night. I was going back to the mountain site the next day to do the post-mission work.

Chapter 36

Thursday, July 18

CLARENCE AND I RETURNED TO the site a little after noon. It was another beautiful, sunny, comfortably warm California day. I must admit that I found being at the site comforting. This was the world I understood. Once Clarence dropped off my backpack and left the site area, I checked to see if there were any changes or damage from the mission or any trash left by the Foot People. The only thing I found was a change in the position of the solstice bow on the work rock. Before I had left the site the night before, I placed the satin bow on the rock to the right and the wooden Gettysburg "gun" sat on the rock to the left. Now I found the bow on the left with the Gettysburg "gun" sitting on top of it. I tested that I was to leave them in that position for the post-mission work.

I wanted to give each of the Foot People a memento of the Mt. Shasta Mission, so I went to the spot where David stood when he ordered the deactivation of the old grid and the creation and activation of the new government/military leyline system. I selected nine small wooden sticks (about two inches long) that were lying there on the ground. I carefully wrapped them and placed them in my backpack.

Finally I set up my boxes, opened the Mt. Shasta Mission coning one more time and got to work. That morning, David and Hyperithon had told me they wanted to observe the post-mission work, so I adjusted the coning to give them more direct access to what I was doing.

I had four things on my to-do list:

1. Release the protection dome
2. Return the site to the natural rhythms and patterns of the mountain
3. Address nature's request to work with the mountain's trees and the atomic weapons issue
4. Find out if I was to do anything with the paho

Right off the bat, I began to receive insight from Pan into the Truman/atomic bomb/tree situation. So I recorded the session.

Pan: *As we have said to you previously, it is our request that your gift be to include in your work the healing of the mountain's trees in connection with atomic destruction. We do not consider this issue to be Truman's fault. We want to be clear about that. From our perspective, the issue is the destruction from the first atomic blast and the subsequent blasts. Truman's position as leader and decision maker at the time of the first blast is the reason he had to start the ball rolling with nature by assuming his position of leadership again. He did that on July 16th. His personal connection with this is minimal when viewed from the broader perspective. We would like to point out that atomic blast healing in all the nature kingdoms is essential to Earth's movement into the Aquarian Era.*

After you have returned the site to the mountain today, connect with us again for testing the mountain's trees around the issue of atomic blast damage and repair. We suggest that you get more information from us on this matter once you return to Perelandra. Atomic blast repair is related to the Battle Energy Release Process work and is one important positive consequence for the nature kingdoms from the Mt. Shasta Mission.

I thought about what nature was saying for a few minutes, then I turned my attention to the site's protective dome. First I checked the soil and the site. The site was fine, but the soil needed green-sand. I thought it was interesting that this mountain site needed so many applications of greensand throughout the mission week. Greensand is mined from oceans (not mountains), but it's high in potassium and this was a key nutrient our nervous systems needed a lot of during the mission.

RELEASING THE DOME

To dismantle the dome, I needed to bring each element of the dome forward and call for its release from the site. In comparison to setting up the protection dome, this release process couldn't have been easier. As per Pan's instructions, I called each element forward, one by one, starting with the last element I put in place when we constructed the dome, and moved in reverse order to the first element.

1. When I called for the first release, the Gettysburg Battle's higher energies that had been seated into the wooden "gun," the energy shot up from the gun and moved through the site, exploded and moved out into the universe in all directions as millions of sparkling flecks of white light.

2. Next, I asked for the release of the Mt. Shasta Mission con-ing dynamics from the site. I saw white energy shift hori-zontally, then stop just beyond the dome's perimeter. Pan told me that the coning had now been released from the protection dome, but would not release from the mountain until after I closed the Mt. Shasta Mission coning I cur-rently had open for the post-mission work.

3. The Mary Cassatt painting, *Mother and Child,* that was used to create the feeling of safety and protection in the site was released next, and I saw the picture (the mother embracing

her child) float up from the site and explode into bits of colored light in the universe.

4.   The groups of people: First, I called for the release of the Foot People. I watched this energy move out from the site. Then I released the ten Piscean leaders. Once I saw that energy leave the site, I called for the release of the mother ship's crew and the Cottage team.

The energy release for each of these groups was not a dramatic explosion. Instead I saw white energy shaped in a two-foot-wide band or cloud move smoothly and quickly from the site and out of the dome, into the atmosphere and out beyond where I could see.

NOTE: From this point on, unless I indicate differently, the energy releases looked like white bands or clouds moving out from the site. Also, after each release, I checked the soil to make sure that part of dismantling the dome hadn't compromised it. But everything held throughout the entire process and nothing was needed.

5.   Next, the dynamic of David's command for "mission go" was released.

6.   For my position as nature's liaison for the mission, the energy moved from the site and into me. Pan said it would remain inside me until I closed the coning after this post-mission work.

7.   Next came the dynamic of David's full understanding of the Mt. Shasta Mission.

8.   The dynamic created by David and me working as a team on the mountain was another white-cloud movement of energy out from the site.

9.   David's energy as a physical reality was released.

10.   Finally, I needed to deal with the summer solstice energy. Pan told me this energy would be staying at the site as part of the mountain's natural makeup. When I looked up and around me, I realized that the only thing left constructing the dome was the solstice energy. All I had to do at this point was ask Pan to shift the solstice energy from the dome reality and infuse it into the site's soil.

With that, I saw the Mt. Shasta Mission protection dome disappear, along with its connections to Perelandra's topaz, David, Hyperithon and myself, and felt the solstice energy move into the soil around me.

RETURNING THE SITE
TO THE MOUNTAIN

I now had to release the domeless site from the mission and return it to the mountain's patterns and rhythms. I set up with Pan and simply asked that this be done. Immediately, I felt a shift in the atmosphere around me that lasted about ten seconds. Then Pan confirmed that the shift was completed and that no damage had been sustained by the site or its soil during the mission. To me, this meant that all the nature work I did with Pan for the mission had been successful.

DEVA OF THE MT. SHASTA TREES

Now I turned my attention to the mountain's trees and the atomic blast situation. I connected with the Deva of the Mt. Shasta Trees, stated my intention and asked what I could do at that moment to assist the repair process for this situation. I was told to

release three drops of Royal Highness to the trees. Well, this was simple enough. But, considering the situation I was addressing, it seemed too simple. I checked again and got the same answer. So, I set up with Pan and released the Royal Highness. For the full minute Pan's infusion was going on, a strong wind blew up the mountain, and all the trees, including the ones around me, began to sway. Not some small, barely perceptible kind of sway. These big trees, and I mean *big*, were doing some major swaying. It was the first time in all the days I had gone to the mountain that I noticed anything more than a quiet breeze. So I figured, "Okay, that worked," and dropped my questions about Royal Highness being too small a gesture for the job.

DEVA OF THE MOUNTAIN

When I first saw the mountain on the drive from the airport, I wanted to offer a gift. Now, after all the time I had spent on that mountain, I still wanted to do something for the mountain itself and not just its trees. I did the only thing I could think to do— connect with the Deva of Mt. Shasta (mountain) again and ask the question, "Is there something I can do for the mountain?" I was told to test the flower essences. I found that I needed to release Holly (the Bach Remedy for reconnection to universal love and the heart center) and Gruss an Aachen (stabilizes on all levels while moving forward in evolutionary process). After the essences were released by Pan, I sat there with the mountain for a few minutes.

THE PAHO

After maybe ten minutes, David and I both got the hit for what was to be done with my feather on a string. I was to bury it at the spot where he ordered the shift of the leylines. Pan explained to me that we had needed to wait until the dome was released and the site returned to the mountain before I could bury the paho, because it was to be buried on the mountain and not in the mission site. Pan also said Clarence was to witness the "paho planting." Just then, I saw Clarence pass on a trail that was close enough for me to call to him. When he got to the site, I let him know what I would be doing and about his role as witness.

Well, what was I to dig the hole with? Of course…the small cherry-wood spoon that I had in my backpack—just in case. The mountain's soil is sandy, so it was easy to dig the hole. I placed the paho in the hole and covered it with the sandy soil. *(Fig 15)* When I pat the soil down firmly with my hand, I clearly heard in my mind's ear, like a voice announcing to the world:

The eagle has landed.

Fig. 15: The paho just prior to burying.

And then I had an insight: The guardians of peace had now grounded peace on the spot where the Piscean government leaders released their custodianship to the leaders of the new era.

Since receiving the paho, I had learned that the Hopi Indians were considered the guardians of peace for planet Earth. But I was quarter Navajo, not Hopi. When the insight referred to the guardians of planetary peace, I assumed it was my connection to the Native Americans in general that was important, and this overrode the fact that I was not Hopi. Well, I have an update that I can add here. About four years after the Mt. Shasta Mission, I learned that my grandmother was full-blooded Hopi, not Navajo. When I was originally told about this part of my heritage, I was about seven years old and somehow I got it mixed up in my head. So, unbeknownst to me, a Hopi, at least a quarter Hopi, actually did bury the paho for the Mt. Shasta Mission.

With that, I tested that the post-mission work was completed and closed the Mt. Shasta Mission coning. At this point, the coning energy that had been held outside the site's perimeter faded from my sight.

All the mission energies had been released and the dome dismantled, the site had been returned to the mountain, the trees were now happy campers, the mountain was happy with its two essences and the paho was buried. I cleaned up my stuff, picked up the solstice ribbon and wooden "gun" from the rock, gave my backpack one last time to Clarence, and we headed back down the mountain. I knew we would be coming back before leaving for Perelandra, but it wasn't the mission site we would be visiting, it would be just a nice spot on the mountain that held special memories for us.

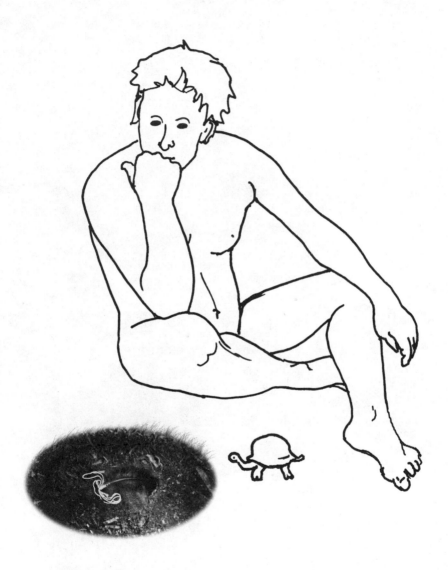

Chapter 37

Friday, July 19

IT WAS OUR LAST DAY in Mt. Shasta, California. In the morning, we drove to Ashland, Oregon to check out a town we had heard was nice. While there, we visited a stained glass shop and I bought a small piece to hang in a window in my cabin. None of this is the important stuff you need to know. What was important was what I saw when I paid for my glass ornament. Behind the cash register, hanging prominently on the wall was a framed, hand-calligraphed excerpt from the "Cross of Iron" speech Dwight David Eisenhower gave while he was president, on April 16, 1953, to the American Society of Newspaper Editors.

> *Every gun that is made, every warship launched, every rocket*
> *fired signifies, in the final sense, a theft from those who hunger*
> *and are not fed, those who are cold and are not clothed.*
> *This world in arms is not spending money alone.*
> *It is spending the sweat of its laborers, the genius of its scientists,*
> *the hopes of its children.*
> *The cost of one modern heavy bomber is this: a modern brick*
> *school in more than thirty cities....*
> *We pay for a single fighter plane with a half million bushels*
> *of wheat.*
> *We pay for a single destroyer with new homes that could have*
> *housed more than eight thousand people.*
> *This, I repeat, is the best way of life to be found on the road the*
> *world has been taking.*
> *This is not a way of life at all, in any true sense. Under the cloud*
> *of threatening war, it is humanity hanging from a cross of iron.*

Fig. 16: The July 19 sunset.

We got back to Mt. Shasta in time to get two chicken picnic dinners from a restaurant in town and head back to the mountain for a farewell dinner at sunset. The site was incredibly peaceful. We sat on a log eating dinner and feeding the ants chicken skin and watermelon. They were big ants. They could handle big food. Out of all the times I had been to the site, this was the first time I watched the sun set. And it was dramatic. *(Fig. 16)*

When it was time to go, I said a private and silent goodbye to the site and mountain. It wasn't easy for me to leave because it was like leaving my dearest friend. We walked down the trail one last time, Clarence walking ahead of me. But as soon as I stepped out of the site area, I felt myself completely enveloped by a familiar presence—the nature intelligence I had been working with all these days at the site. Pan. It was a clear, unmistakable experience of this extraordinary nature intelligence in form. I could see Pan dancing on the path beside me as I walked along. I was being escorted down the mountain. My heart was touched, and I quietly cried as I distanced myself a little from Clarence and continued walking down the trail. An amazing chapter in my life was closing and, at that moment, I did not want it to end. As we approached our car, I still had my escort. I quietly thanked Pan and said goodbye. And with that, the presence dissipated.

We drove back to the Finlandia without saying a word to one another. Clarence wasn't aware of my escort and I wasn't able to talk about it. When we got to the motel, we busied ourselves preparing for our departure the next day.

Chapter 38

Mop-up

On Sunday, July 20, David hosted a large dinner at the Cottage. The ten government leaders were present, along with eighteen mission coordinators and commanders, the Cottage team and little ole me. I was pretty nervous about attending the dinner and envisioned myself hiding in a corner throughout the evening. But I did just fine. First of all, I discovered that I wasn't the only woman attending. Six of the coordinators and commanders were women. However, it was the overall energy in the room that put me at ease. This dynamic group of powerful and accomplished people created a feeling of warmth, friendliness and openness. Everyone was excited about what the Mt. Shasta Mission had accomplished and spirits were as high as could be. (The answer to the question that I can hear you asking right now: "No. No one got drunk, nor did anyone dance around on tabletops with a lampshade parked on his or her head.")

When we sat down to dinner, David presented each of us with a gold medallion that he had designed to commemorate the mission. It's like a heavy gold coin, about 50 percent larger than a silver dollar, with a bas-relief of Mt. Shasta (the mountain) and the words "Mount Shasta Mission" and "July 16, 1985." He thanked each of us for our work and placed our medallion around our neck. I kept my medallion in its box in my room at the Cottage until about ten years ago, when I got my own office there. It's now framed and on my office wall behind my desk.

At Perelandra, I was bumping around. The Mt. Shasta Mission had been in my life for over fourteen months, and it was a little difficult figuring out what to do now. On July 27, I met with Sarah Wheatley, the woman who had agreed to go to the Gettysburg Battlefield during the mission. She went to the battlefield the night of the 15th with three other people, and together they paced off a six-pointed star near the Copse of Trees. She grounded each point of the star with a crystal—a clean, clear, unprogrammed crystal! Then she and her three friends sat quietly in the middle of the star's energy grid until she felt it was time to go. With this she proved that attitude is everything, and her using crystals and *gently* pacing off a six-pointed star were absolutely the right thing to do. She did not know the mission was aborted that evening and that it actually occurred the next night. But she said she felt the star was in place and activated, which meant it was still present the night of the mission.

On July 30, I sent a final letter to the Foot People:

Dear Fellow Mountain Trekkers,

I felt it would be good to check in with you to let you know more of the conclusion and results of the Mt. Shasta Mission.

As you know, David got a preliminary report while we were at the site that the work on the mountain was successful in all its phases. The leaders who have held the Piscean government/military dynamics did relinquish that custodianship. The government/military leylines were shifted from their Piscean global pattern to the new Aquarian global pattern. The energy from St. Germain's leylines was fully grounded into human sensory systems and then spiraled to its next level resulting in the shift of that already-established leyline system. And the expanded mission was a success—the grounded energy from our work on the mountain was received and projected to those beyond our universe.

About three hours after we left the mountain, David received the second set of reports that all had gone well. The next day, David was given a final report and verification that the work on the mountain had indeed accomplished all its goals.

David wishes me to extend his heart-felt gratitude for your part in the success of this mission. He also hopes that you are not too disappointed that they were unable to be fully of form to you. A great deal of information was collected regarding the physical landing of a ship and its occupants in such a complex mission. That information is not lost and when in the future such a mission results in our full five-senses reality, the information from the Mt. Shasta Mission will have contributed to that success.

Regarding the form issue of the Mission: The mother ship and its passengers were able to move into and maintain their position in our five-senses reality. If we could see the physical level as a broad band rather than a thin line, it would be accurate to say that we on the mountain reflected the lower vibrational half of the broad band of physicality, and those on the ship were a part of and reflecting the upper vibrational half. They were not very "far" from us at all.

One of the intents of this mission from the outset was that no person be placed in physical jeopardy. As much care given to us in preparation for and during the mission was being given to those on the ship who were experiencing a somewhat dramatic change in their bodies. David's decision to "go no further" was in response to the stress being experienced by the leaders on board the ship.

It was important that the ship get as deep within the physical band as possible for the eventual transfer of energies we participated in. Had they remained beyond our senses, the energy you received in your sensory systems probably would have remained beyond human senses despite the infusion of solstice energy. The energy gap between what you took in and your sensory system would most likely have been too great to bridge. As it was, the close proximity of the ship and guests allowed your sensory systems to resonate with and respond to a very familiar energy. The solstice energy infusion completed the grounding process and stabilized it.

On Thursday, Clarence and I went back to the mountain for cleanup. He collected our trail markers while I worked at the site. I was connected to David and Hyperithon, and together with Pan we worked two hours to release carefully every aspect of energy that had gone into creating the protection dome that had been held at the site for almost a year. The result of this work was that the site, which had been "on loan" to us from the mountain, was returned to the mountain and to the overall timing of the mountain.

On my return to the site Thursday, I found that the ivory-colored summer solstice bow that I had placed on the right side of my work rock in the site was now carefully arranged on the left side of the rock, with the Gettysburg Battlefield pieces of wood on top of part of the ribbon. To me, this was a good sign that something had occurred on July 16.

As part of my work in dismantling the site, . . . I asked if I could do anything specific at that time to aid the healing process for trees from nuclear weapons damage. I was told to make available to the trees several drops of the Royal Highness Rose Essence. During that shift, a strong wind blew up the mountain and all the trees within my sight swayed for a full minute. Of the ten times I had gone to the site that week, this was the first time wind had been prevalent. I plan to follow up on this area of nature's connection to nuclear power. I consider that the mission opened an issue as significant for nature as it did in the government/military arena.

After returning the site to the mountain, we discovered that there was one more thing to do. I had come to Mt. Shasta with two gifts given to me by two different people. One was a Hopi Indian paho (a sacred feather symbolizing peace), the other, a small hand-carved wooden spoon. I wasn't sure how these two gifts would be used. I only knew to bring them. As soon as we completed our cleanup work, we knew what to do with the gifts, and I called Clarence to the site to witness what was to happen. On the site where David stood Tuesday night when he ordered the shifting of the government/military leylines, I dug a hole with the wooden spoon and buried the paho. So on that spot is buried the Hopi symbol of peace signifying that, indeed, the eagle has landed.

As a memento of July 16, I am enclosing a small stick for each of you which I picked up from the spot where David stood and where the paho is buried. I am also enclosing a piece of the ivory ribbon used to infuse the summer solstice energy into the site, into the mother ship's landing process and into your sensory systems.

On Friday evening, July 19, Clarence and I brought the site full circle in its return to the mountain by having a fried chicken picnic dinner right in the middle of the site while we watched the sunset. We fed the ants and flies that all-time mountain favorite, fried chicken skin and watermelon. They seemed to enjoy it.

This pretty much wraps up the mission. One thing I would like from you, since everyone left Wednesday morning and we weren't able to have a "debriefing," is a letter describing your experiences and sensations on Monday evening as the ship tried to come in, on Tuesday evening during the landing and work on the mountain and any follow-up verification that you've experienced that has helped you know something happened on the mountain. I also suggest that the next time any of us sees Salvesen, we give her a big box of Godiva chocolates for her herculean efforts in keeping us all in one piece. Her work and insights all along in this mission have been invaluable. (That's pretty much a direct quote from David.)...

I plan to keep your follow-up responses confidential. We feel your input in this is essential for rounding out and completing the Mt. Shasta Mission.

In case you got the idea that the sole purpose of the team that put together the Mt. Shasta Mission was to land a mother ship and shift the leylines—an assumption that might have easily been arrived at due to our focus on the mission—allow me to clarify. The Mt. Shasta Mission was just the beginning of a new phase of work in the White Brotherhood for the team involved. Now that the leylines have been shifted and the Piscean custodianship released, the Cottage team will concentrate on aiding us on Earth as we actively move the government/military arena around the world into the Aquarian Era. As you well know, their job is just beginning....

Again, I pass on to you David's gratitude for your good work on the mountain. I thank you as well.

I put a copy of the letter in a package, along with a box containing a site stick and a piece of the solstice ribbon (*Fig. 17*), and sent it

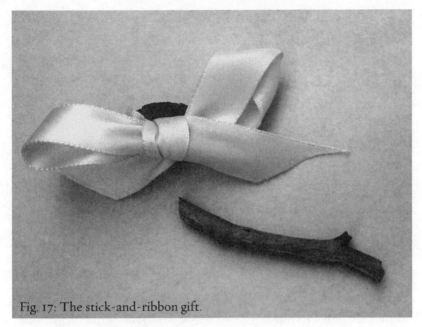

Fig. 17: The stick-and-ribbon gift.

out. By the way, I presented the ninth stick to David along with a piece of the solstice ribbon, as well. He has these two items framed and on his office wall. My stick and ribbon are displayed under glass in my Perelandra office.

I'd like to say to you that I got permission from everyone to reprint their responses to that letter, but I didn't need it. I received only two responses. Peter Caddy sent me a personal letter congratulating us on the mission but said nothing about what he experienced. I suspected this was because he saw and felt nothing. Paul sent a poem he wrote that was so incomprehensible that it was useless for the mission records. I know that Salvesen had a clear sense of what was happening on the mountain and I know that no one bumped into or stepped on anyone else, whether they could see them or not. So, other than this, along with what Janice and Clarence told me, I don't know what they experienced. Oh, yeah…I think I was the only one who gave Salvesen a box of chocolates.

I had my own report to write for the mission.

MT. SHASTA MISSION
FOLLOW-UP AND REVIEW
Errors and Recommendations
from Machaelle Small Wright

1. The July 12 Site Preparation

I think the ten leaders should have been moved *individually* into the site dome and essence/soil readings taken not only for their impact on the site as individuals, but the site's impact on them. As it was, they were introduced as a group with attention paid only to the site balance. This did not take into account individual reactions to the site reality. This is where we may have been able to pick up the medical problems we encountered with the leaders when the mother ship began to move into five-senses form during the mission.

I also suggest for any future site preparation that the site's energy be moved into each person coming into five-senses form using a process similar to what Salvesen, Hyperithon and I used for moving the mother ship into the Foot People. Any potentially adverse physical reaction to them as individuals should be picked up during the testing, and this would indicate that further medical attention is needed in preparation for the physical stage of the mission. Once the individual work is accomplished, then move them as a group dynamic into the site and test the site/group impact as was done in the July 12 process.

2. Re: Truman's Issue with Nature and the Atomic Bomb

Out of respect, I set up the link between Truman and nature, then completely removed myself from the process to give him privacy. Had I maintained my position as nature's liaison during the Truman/nature exchange attempt, I would have been in a position to know if problems were arising. Nature accepted Truman's intent and bypassed the problem, thus registering positive when I tested if the exchange was complete and we could proceed. But by my stepping out of the picture, I was "out of position" and could not tell that a problem was occurring—i.e., Truman did not know how to move thought as energy from himself to a point outside himself. In short, it looks as if the position of liaison between man and nature must be maintained at all times no matter how sensitive a particular situation may be. In fact, the more sensitive the situation, the more important it is that this position of responsibility be maintained to ensure success. This is certainly a lesson I have now learned.

3. Re: Witnesses and Guests in a Mission

In a mission such as this, only those who are prepared and ready to participate should be involved—uninvolved family, friends and pressure artists should be excluded. This was not a consciousness-raising event in which many people were to be present. The fact that all those whom Peter Caddy invited ended up not participating (by their own decision) should have been looked at more carefully. Perhaps it was an indication that we should have done the mission with only Salvesen, Clarence, Peter Caddy and myself as witnesses. For a mission such as this, attention and the ability to function and do a job are essential. Although the seven Foot People performed well during the two and a half hours of work, they managed to add complication, confusion, distress and personality issues due to their inability to grasp what was going on in the time leading up to the mission. This was unnecessary to the mission, draining to me and burdensome to David.

4. The Need for a "Cruise Director"

If witnesses and guests are to be included, add one more person to the team: group coordinator/liaison/counselor (a.k.a. "cruise director"). This should not only be someone functioning in an intermediary position between the mission team and the witnesses/guests. It should also be someone whose job it is to concentrate on them and provide whatever they need before and after the mission. This was not provided for in the Mt. Shasta Mission, leaving the job to me by default since I was already the liaison between them and the mission. Having this responsibility added to what I was already carrying was too much. The needs of the group were often contrary to the needs of the mission, leaving me at times feeling like I was being pulled in opposite directions. But, had I had no other responsibilities, I still would not have been the right person for this position. It takes a particular kind of patience and understanding, and the right person needs to be chosen for the job.

The fact that the final seven who made it to the mountain on July 16 performed extremely well during the actual mission is, in my opinion, a tribute to the human ability to rise to the occasion when under the gun. This phenomenon should not be assumed in future missions and a "cruise director" should be appointed to ensure group cooperation, comfort and function before, during and after the work at hand.

Follow-up on the Reports from the Foot People for the Mission Files

Other than Peter Caddy's personal letter of congratulations, only one response was received, and that one was so confusing and had little, if anything, to do with the mission, I did not include it with this file. It was a poem, and there was nothing in it that made sense or would have been of future value. No one else responded.

Chapter 39

Mission Update

As I wrote to the Foot People in their mop-up letter, the Mt. Shasta Mission was just the beginning of a new phase of work for the Cottage team. When the leylines were activated, it was as if someone had plugged the system into a big electric socket in the sky. But the leylines themselves were "in neutral"; that is, they had yet to be programmed beyond the overall intent that this system operate with the Aquarian government/military dynamic and principles. Nothing specific had been introduced into the system.

The Foundation Program

For nearly a year after the mission, the Cottage team worked to put the finishing touches on the first Aquarian government/military program that was to be seated into the leyline system. I use the word "program" because this is the word that was used when the Cottage team described it to me. And like a comprehensive new software program, it is massive and it is deep. It serves as the foundation for the Aquarian government principles and, as with any good foundation, the program is solid, strong, broad, clear, clean, inclusive and capable of supporting the movement and variables the future might require. Any further information on specifics and detail for shifting our governments from the Piscean dynamic to the Aquarian dynamic springs from this foundation. It opens every conceivable door so that no matter how an individual or group addresses their particular structure and governing principles, there is information, support and assistance for the new makeup and direction of that government.

Here's what we did to seat the foundation program into the new leyline system.

June 20, 1986

To prepare for seating the program, I needed to clear out any debris from the leyline system. David told me that the deactivation of the old Piscean leylines and the activation of the new Aquarian leylines created a protective reaction from various government-related Piscean dynamics. This had been expected, and I now needed to clear out the debris it caused in the Aquarian system so that it would not function as a computer virus in the new foundation program.

My work with the leyline system was done primarily from the center of the Perelandra garden. Several leyline circuits intersect at the garden center, and this gives me direct and immediate access to the system.

1.   First, I had to shift the Mt. Shasta Mission coning's intent, thus creating a new coning, because the mission for which the coning was originally set up was completed and any leyline work we did now was beyond the mission's parameters. However, by using the mission coning as the foundation for the new one, rather than creating a new four-point coning from "scratch," we maintained a link with the Aquarian leylines from the very beginning of their creation. This would add continuity and stability to the new coning and to any work done from within that coning.

To make the shift, I first needed to change the intent of the Mt. Shasta Mission coning. I opened that coning and stated that its focus was now to be for the maintenance of the Aquarian government/military leyline system and the continuing Cottage work with this system. As a result of the intent change, four members of the original coning were no longer needed: the Deva of the Mt. Shasta Mission, the Deva of Mt. Shasta (mountain), Universal Light and Lorpuris. And a new member was now required: the Deva of the Aquarian Government/Military Leylines. Because the intent of the coning was changed, along with some of its members, this new coning has been given a new name: the Cottage Leyline Coning. It looks like this:

- Devic Point: Deva of the Aquarian Government Leylines, Deva of Perelandra
- Nature Spirit Point: Pan
- White Brotherhood Point: David and Hyperithon
- Earth level human point: myself/my higher self

Without having to close the old coning and open the new one, the shift automatically occurred and I was now operating from within the Cottage Leyline Coning.

2. For the next order of business, I checked the Perelandra garden's balance to make sure it was fully prepared for the coming leyline work. According to my test results, nothing was needed and the garden was ready.

3. I activated both of my bodies so that I could be present at the Cottage while simultaneously present in the center of the garden.

At the Cottage, the heads of several different mission departments had gathered. For this part of the work, they used their focus to recreate the intent and complexities of the Mt. Shasta Mission from each of their perspectives. The energy from what they recreated was shifted to Hyperithon who, in turn, infused it into a small golden spacecraft (crewless), about a foot in diameter and visible to us, that he had created from energy using his focus especially for this work. The spacecraft gave all of us present something concrete to focus on and, because of this, added a higher level of vitality to what we were doing. Hyperithon placed the infused craft into my hands. I moved it into my body, then shifted it from my Cottage body to my Perelandra body and, finally, into my Perelandra hands. As instructed, I *carefully* placed the spacecraft energy package in the center of the garden on top of Perelandra's crystal/topaz.

By recreating the intent of the Mt. Shasta Mission, they recreated the situation on the mountain that had caused the Piscean reaction to begin with. Only now, the recreation attracted the debris that had hooked into the leylines and literally pulled that debris out of the system. It would be fair to say that the infused spacecraft acted as a decoy—a decoy with a big vacuum cleaner attached to it.

For about fifteen seconds, I watched debris move as chunks of energy from the leylines under the garden center to the craft. Once completed, Pan informed me that the debris-laden spacecraft was now throwing the garden off balance. So I tested the soil for balancing and released three drops of liquid seaweed to Pan for infusing in the garden soil.

4. Using the Energy Cleansing Process, I then cleansed the spacecraft. Pan activated the white cleansing sheet of energy about five feet beneath the craft. From there we moved the sheet up to and through the craft, coming to a stop about ten feet above the garden. We now had all the debris in the white cleansing sheet. I asked Pan to form a bundle with the sheet, move it out of the Earth's atmosphere and release

the contents appropriately and safely. I saw the bundle form and slowly lift up and out of my sight Then, to be sure, I asked Pan to do a final sweep of the entire leyline system. After about ten seconds, I was told the leylines were clear.

5.   We now had a newly cleansed leyline system and craft. Pan suggested I set up another protection dome, this one over the center of the Perelandra garden where the craft was still sitting. It seemed to me that the garden center was now an open portal to the leyline system and needed to be protected until we completed the work with the foundation program. As soon as I called for a protection dome, a gold dome of light about ten feet in radius and eight feet tall formed over the garden center. The spacecraft and I were now both inside the dome. The day's work was completed, and I moved out of the dome leaving a little spacecraft sitting in the center of my garden. Of course.

June 21, 1986: Summer Solstice

According to Pan, the next step was to infuse the spacecraft and the garden's crystal/topaz with that day's summer solstice energy in order to prepare them for use during the seating of the foundation program.

At the moment of the 1986 solstice, I stood inside the dome and directed the summer solstice energy to infuse the crystal/topaz. Once this was done, the crystal/topaz in the garden lit up. Within a few seconds, I saw the solstice energy from the crystal/topaz expand to envelop and infuse the small spacecraft sitting on top of it. I requested that the energy in these two objects be held "until further notice." Mission accomplished, I closed down the Cottage Leyline Coning, and David told me he'd let me know what day we would be shifting the foundation programming into the leylines.

July 2, 1986

We didn't have to wait long. Within a couple of days, David said
we would be programming the leylines on July 3. He and I had a
meeting with Pan on July 2, to find out what procedure we would
be working with the next day.

Pan: *First, let me say that everything is ready for tomorrow's program-*
ming. The mission energy and the leylines were cleared on June 21
and have remained clear. There was a possibility of picking up
additional debris between the solstice and the programming, but
this has not occurred. To explain, the leyline system, although
cleansed and protected, is currently in a state of vulnerability until
the programming and subsequent activation. The vulnerability
was only minimal, however, partly due to the fact that the process
utilized by David on the mountain was well within the range of
five-senses form. This resulted in greater strength for the leylines
because they are in the band of form on a level that is compatible
with the planet's own level of five-senses form. Had David's work
been initiated and carried out on a level beyond five-senses form, we
would have had a far different situation facing us now. There is no
additional preparation that needs to occur prior to the program-
ming and activation, except to remove the protection dome from
the center of the Perelandra garden.

   Here are my suggestions about how to seat the foundation pro-
gram into the leylines and activate the program. I base these sugges-
tions on the prevailing conditions at Perelandra and on the planet.

   First of all, the fact that you are initiating the programming
process from the Cottage and completing it through Perelandra will
give you an advantage regarding the necessary synchronization
between the two levels—the Cottage and Earth levels. Machaelle,
you are already working with the Perelandra/Cottage connection

because of the coning you use to connect you with these two levels and your two bodies. I point this out because had you not had this linkup already in place, you personally would have had to deal with a synchronization problem prior to shifting the foundation program into the Earth level. At Mt. Shasta, David dealt effectively with this issue by actually coming into the Earth level. That process itself took care of the synchronization issue there.

So, for tomorrow, have all present at the Cottage as you begin the process. This will include Machaelle. It will be essential for her to be present at the Cottage and make her shift to Perelandra while, at the same time, shifting the foundation program to Perelandra. This will assure an automatic and full synchronization of the foundation program with the Earth level. (Machaelle, if we did not synchronize everything tomorrow, the foundation program and its activation would be as if you were trying to play a 45 rpm record on a 78 rpm player. You can partially discern the sound and perhaps even identify the song, but its distortion would be terrible.)

I suggest that Machaelle activate the Cottage Leyline Coning from the Cottage and that everyone present be included in the coning. I also suggest that the balance of the coning be checked once everyone is included, and that everyone's individual balance also be checked. This will give you the balance of the parts as well as the balance of the whole.

Shift the entire foundation program to Machaelle while she is present at the Cottage. She should not be physically present in the Perelandra garden at this point. It is essential that her focus be fully at the Cottage. I suggest that the shift of the foundation program come directly from you, David, to her. Once she has custody of the program—which can be verified by both Hyperithon and myself—she should be checked for any needed flower essences at the Cottage by Lorpuris for her balance. At this point, her attention should be fully on that which she has in custody and not diverted to an additional process such as checking balance.

David: Lorpuris will be present and is ready to assist her.

Pan: *Good. Once she is checked, then I suggest she do a Split Molecular Process, thus activating her Perelandra body, and move as softly and quietly as possible to the center of the garden at Perelandra. During this, she will keep her focus at the Cottage on the foundation program. Once in the center of the garden, she should take a moment at the Cottage to focus fully on the foundation program she is holding. (David, you may wish to symbolize the foundation program for her so that she can use the symbol for re-focusing. This would simplify the process for her.)*

Have Lorpuris link into her Perelandra body before the foundation program shift and do a balance check on her there. This will assure her protection when she receives the program into the Perelandra body.

She will shift the program, as she did the Mt. Shasta Mission energies, through her two body systems. This will also assure the automatic synchronization of the program with Earth's leylines. Once she has shifted the program and is holding it in her Perelandra body, Lorpuris should check her again for balance.

At this point, having the foundation program stabilized within her, she is to request that the dome be released. All she need do is request this—that will indicate to us the proper timing—and we will immediately release it. She need do nothing else.

When everyone is ready, she should infuse the foundation program, thus releasing it from her personal custody, into the interior of the golden spacecraft currently sitting within and on the crystal/ topaz in the center of the Perelandra garden. To infuse the program, she needs only to breathe the program energy from within herself into the craft interior. Since it will be better that this part of the process be as unencumbered as possible, only I will assist to assure complete and full transference.

Once complete, I will verify the fusion and report that to you, David, through Machaelle. Hyperithon will be able to verify the fusion from the Cottage level, as well. As soon as she has completed the transfer and it has been verified, we can stop for another balance check for her.

The seating and activation of the foundation program into the leyline system will take place from the spacecraft sitting in the Perelandra garden.

(I did not mention earlier, but before Machaelle opens the coning at the Cottage, the Cottage crystal/topaz should be placed in a prominent position within the room where you will be assembled.)

Once the craft interior has been infused with the foundation program energy, Machaelle will add an additional infusion of the crystal/topaz energy. To do this, she will use the energy from the crystal/topaz at Perelandra, not the Cottage. But you will see a change in the crystal/topaz at the Cottage once she finishes this step.

When completed, she will call for the release of the craft from the crystal/topaz and "allow" it to expand to the size of the outermost ring of the Perelandra garden. The craft will then be 100 feet in diameter—which is also the size of the mother ship used at Mt. Shasta. At this point, she will need to check the balance of the garden environment using both essences and soil balancers.

Once this is accomplished and the craft is stabilized into its position in the garden (touching the ground fully), you will be ready for the seating and activation. It is my understanding that a number of those who will be present at the Cottage also wish to be present at Perelandra for the seating and activation.

David: That's true. There are also a few who wish to be present solely at Perelandra for this, but I haven't discussed it with Machaelle as of yet.

Pan: *It is my opinion that there be complete freedom for whoever wishes to be present at Perelandra. I realize that this is Machaelle's decision, but their role as witnesses would greatly benefit the activation, especially this particular activation.*

Machaelle: I have no issue about who is present. I wouldn't mind
the company at that end. As long as they don't step on me
or scare the bejeebers out of me.

David (laughing): You'll be safe.

Pan: *I suggest you activate the leylines with the new foundation program
as you did the creation of those leylines at Mt. Shasta. Do this once
everyone is in position at the Cottage and Perelandra. When you
give the word, David, the infused energy from the craft interior
will release and move instantaneously into the full leyline system.
As you had thousands of craft in position to assist the creation at
Mt. Shasta, we of nature will be in position throughout the entire
leyline system to assure the reception, seating and activation of the
new foundation program. In Earth time, this should take no longer
than thirty seconds. I will inform you of its completion, and you
may begin your verification and checks at any time after that. The
activation of the program should register on all appropriate levels
the moment the process is complete. At that time, you will see
another shift in the crystal/topaz at the Cottage.*

*There is one additional thing I suggest for Machaelle to do at
this point. Besides checking the balance of the garden environment
again just to be sure it held during the work, I recommend that she
connect with the Overlighting Deva of Planet Earth and check the
balance of the planet using essences and soil balancing. Now, what I
mean is that part of the planet's balance that is directly linked to the
new government/military leylines. She will not be attempting a full
ecological balance of the planet. Although that can be done, the
planet would only stabilize for a second before shifting back to imbalance due to the prevalent consciousness of the inhabitants on the
planet. What she will be focused on is the balance that pertains
only to the leylines and their surrounding environment. Now, she
need not do a planetary check prior to this time because that is
what we have verified as clear and ready to go. The check we are*

discussing is to verify that all has held after the activation, and if not, we will re-balance it. This will greatly assist the new foundation program and the active leylines and will allow the program's impulses to "go right to work" without a lag time.

Once the activation is complete and after the planetary balance check, Machaelle needs to disperse the craft energy so that it will no longer be present at Perelandra.

Then, I recommend that all those present at Perelandra shift their focus to the Cottage to remove themselves from the Perelandra level.

After this, close the coning.

The Cottage crystal/topaz will maintain its light to signify full activation of the leyline system. I recommend that it be placed in David's office and remain there for however long he wishes. The quality of light within this crystal/topaz will enable David to monitor the stabilization and power of the leyline system and any programming that it contains—the foundation programming and any future programming.

David: Do you have any suggestions regarding the timing of what will take place tomorrow?

Pan: *From the standpoint of the planet, translated into linear time, I suggest the process begin at 8:32 P.M. tomorrow night. I also suggest the seating and activation occur no later than 10:10 P.M.*

David: Thank you. You seem to have covered everything.

July 3, 1986

As you might imagine, this was an extraordinarily important moment for the Cottage. Standing with David to witness what was about to happen were eleven Mt. Shasta Mission department heads, along with Hyperithon, Lorpuris and fifteen leaders from

the White Brotherhood, including St. Germain. I was more than
a little nervous because so much was riding on what we were about
to do. I had visions of dropping the program or tipping it over
and having all its bytes fall out in a big pile at my feet. That would
be such bad form.

Precisely at 8:32 P.M., I opened the coning and included everyone standing with me at the Cottage individually and as a group. I
checked the coning while Lorpuris checked the others for balance.
Everyone and everything tested clear.

I then proceeded to do everything as laid out by Pan in the
meeting the day before. When David shifted the foundation program to me as an energy package, he announced the name of the
program for the first time: Overlord. This was the symbol that we
were all to use as a focal point for the program. I understood that
he was using the name of the operation he had led for the Nor-
mandy invasion during World War II, and I thought, "Well, that's
interesting." However, when he made the announcement, the others in the room broke out in applause—enthusiastic applause. Now
I was lost and knew I didn't understand the true significance of
naming the program "Overlord." But it didn't seem like the right
time to stop the proceedings and ask for a clarification. I didn't
mind being the dumb one in the room and I still had work to do.

When I shifted the foundation program from my Perelandra
body to the spacecraft, the solstice energy from the crystal/topaz
infused the program energy, making the grounding dynamics of
summer solstice energy a permanent part of the foundation program. With this, the craft expanded to the larger size, just as Pan
had described. It now sat on the entire garden, and once again, I
found myself enveloped in the energy of a spacecraft. It was
becoming old hat for me, and I didn't experience any of the discomfort I had felt on the mountain the first time I found myself
in the mother ship. (Can you imagine how odd it is to write this
last sentence about yourself?)

At this point in the proceedings, I noticed about twenty-five people standing in a circle around me in the Perelandra garden and watching as I worked. I said "hello," and went on with the work. I was glad for the company.

When it was time for David to initiate the release of the program to the leylines, he said simply,

> *I call for the release, seating and activation of Overlord to the new government/military leyline system in the name of peace.*

I felt a dramatic motion and saw the energy quickly drop from the craft and disappear into the soil. Then I felt a slight movement in the ground beneath my feet. I assumed I was feeling the program seating into the leyline circuits. Either that, or I was experiencing my first earthquake. And that's when the crystal/topaz at the Cottage lit up.

We waited quietly for thirty seconds, and then Pan let us know the seating and activation were complete. Hyperithon started receiving other verifications and checks. Now it was confirmed that Overlord had seated and was activated in the leylines. And all my balance checks tested clear.

The work with the gold spacecraft was now completed. I directed my attention to Pan and called for the craft to disperse. And that's exactly what it did. A million flecks of gold light shot up from the garden and floated out into the sky. I then did a balance check for the garden, which tested clear again.

Finally, I connected with the Overlighting Deva of Planet Earth and, along with Pan, checked the balance of the full government/military leyline system and the planet's soil that the system impacts. The planet's soil needed three drops of liquid seaweed. I placed the drops in a spoon and held it out for Pan to shift to wherever it was needed. This took ten seconds, after which the crystal/topaz at the Cottage became brighter.

With that, Overlord was seated and my work was done. I thanked everyone who was present in the garden (What else do you say at such moments?) and told them I'd see them shortly back at the Cottage. (I was just happy they weren't expecting me to serve beer and pretzels.) Within a few moments, I could no longer see or feel anyone around me, so I closed the coning. It was now 9:43 P.M. We had gotten everything done well before the 10:10 P.M. deadline.

When I got back to the Cottage, everyone was there celebrating. After formally meeting the people who were at Perelandra, I asked about the name "Overlord." David wanted to use this name because of what it meant to him personally and what it signified historically. But in order for the name to be used for the foundation program, the Cottage team had to shift the original Operation Overlord to its higher intent and purpose as we had done with the Battle of Gettysburg. The work I did in 1984 to 1985 opened the door for this work between humans and nature, and the Cottage team was now able to make that shift themselves. The applause was not just out of respect for Operation Overlord and what it accomplished in World War II, but also for the fact that now its tuning fork had been released, and the higher intent and purpose for that operation that had turned the tide for us all in 1944 now resonated throughout the universe and beyond.

◆●◆

With Overlord successfully seated into the leylines, the Cottage team could get down to the business of assisting our movement in the arena of Aquarian government and military in a new, detailed way. Actually, the Cottage team has a fascinating job. They cannot create an entire system based on what they know and understand, and then superimpose it onto a country or group of people. That's manipulation. But wouldn't it be nice if they just put together the new Aquarian systems and handed the blueprints to us for our respective countries? I dare say this is what most of us would prefer. It certainly would eliminate the need for a lot of thinking and effort on our part. Unfortunately, it just doesn't work that way.

What the Cottage team does is much more complex than this. We are the ones who dictate the timing and rhythm for our movement forward. We are the ones who define what we want to address and when we want to address it. We are the ones who decide what we want to avoid and ignore. And we are the ones who initiate change. We initiated the shift from the era of Piscean government/military to the era of Aquarian government/military (a process that will take about two hundred years to complete) when we dropped the first atomic bomb in 1945. At that point, people around the world began to understand that warfare as we had known it was now obsolete. No longer was warfare regional and contained within the context of specific conflicts affecting specific people. Now with the atomic bomb, the entire world could be destroyed, whether all regions are involved with the conflict or not. The arrival of the atomic bomb announced that the Piscean dynamic in our lives and throughout our social structures was ending and would become increasingly less effective.

It is important to understand that the White Brotherhood did not choose for us to drop an atomic bomb in order to initiate change toward the new. We chose this. We were the ones who freely decided in 1945 that it was the time, and the bomb was the instrument we chose to use to lead to the changes that the White Brotherhood laid before us.

We are in full partnership with these changes and nothing is imposed on us—or our lives. The Cottage team supplies us with impulse and option, all of which are compatible with Aquarian principles. They do this by seating those impulses and options into the new government leyline system, making them available to any of us at any time. As we think about and work through the challenges that come with change, we pick up on the impulses and options. Then we define what is important to us and how we will use the options. And as we act to implement these changes, we feel the support.

Thankfully, we don't have to invent the wheel. That is, we don't have to construct a new foundation for our government principles and structures. That would be difficult since we really don't understand the Aquarian dynamic and what is needed for the government/military foundation. But the Cottage team does understand these things and has the vision to see what is possible for us. In short, the Cottage team has already invented that new government wheel for us. And to further assist us, they update and modify that wheel as we move forward and need new options and awareness within the government/military arena to address specific crises as they arise, as well as to address overall change.

How do we work this leyline system? It's a lot easier than we might imagine. Leylines are a collection of electrical circuits. In order to connect with this leyline system, all a person has to do is focus on a government or military issue with the intent of discovering a new approach, a new direction, a new structure, a new solution…Focus is a biological electrical process. It is supported by the electrical system within the person's body. Once a person focuses on a problem or issue with the intent to discover the new, he automatically connects electrically with that part of the leyline system and program that relates to whatever he is focusing on. Like is attracting like. Electrical circuits within the human body that support a specific focus are connecting with electrical circuits in the leylines that support and hold the information on that same focus. The linking of human electrical systems is a natural process that we use in surrogate kinesiology testing all the time. Only with surrogate testing, we link two human electrical systems. When focusing on a government or military problem with the intent of finding a new solution, we link specific human electrical circuits with specific and related electrical leyline circuits. We do not have to be special. We do not have to be gurus. It's the natural way these electrical circuits work.

And receiving information from the leyline system is as easy as connecting with it. Remember all the work that went into making sure the primary mission intents and energies commingled with human sensory systems? This enables the information contained within the new government leylines to be so grounded that its impulses are accessible to anyone with a sensory system and the ability to think clearly—i.e., focus. And there we have it. This is the reason the Cottage team was so determined for the Mt. Shasta Mission to activate human sensory systems. It was the key to making their assistance available to any of us at any time.

Once we connect with the information in the leyline system that corresponds with what we are focusing on, that information then activates our nervous and sensory systems, becoming accessible to us in our thoughts, ideas and creations. It's up to us to decide how the information applies and how it is to be used. We have absolute and total free will at all times. But we also are not left to figure out everything by ourselves. We have help, and we have extraordinarily qualified experts as partners.

We civilians who are not working in the government or military are encouraged to tap into this new leyline system in order to educate ourselves about Aquarian principles and what Aquarian governments and military look like. In many societies, it's the citizens who elect the officials who run their government and make these decisions for us. Therefore, it is vital for all citizens to dedicate themselves to moving forward in the government arena through education and grassroots activity.

Another way the system works: The leylines and the program that is seated in that system are capable of supporting a population's movement as well as the movement of an individual. Let's say there is one mid-level government official who has been entrusted to upgrade his country's public health system. As an individual who is working on this one area of government, he can sit at his desk, think about the issues involved and commit to coming up with new solutions. Right away he may begin getting ideas that can point him toward new solutions. Or he can commit to new solutions and nothing happens right away. Then he goes to lunch and the waitress says something that triggers new thoughts for him. Or he goes home and his six-year-old does something that gives him an idea. The point is, once he focused on the issue and committed to coming up with something new, the leyline information was activated and will move into his consciousness through any avenue that is needed—his mind, his sight, his hearing, his taste, his smell, his touch. Whatever is needed and whatever route is easiest for him to receive clear, accurate impulse and understanding from the leyline information will be activated. This is how the government leylines were set up by the Cottage during the Mt. Shasta Mission, and this is how easy it is for us to work with them.

As I've said, the leyline information can expand to inspire and motivate entire populations or it can be used by an individual with a problem to solve. It is designed to accommodate this wide range of situations. But it's important to understand that it has action and change embedded in its intent. And this is where I give you fair warning: Although we civilians may wish to *educate* ourselves about the new Aquarian government and military principles, we will also be inspired to *act*. Action is part of the Cottage foundation program (Overlord) and the Cottage work in general. As a result, those who act will feel its support.

HOW DO THESE LEYLINES WORK?

1. *Focus on a government or military issue, problem or crisis.*
2. *Commit to finding new solutions.*
3. *Act. Apply the new solution(s).*

THE GLOBE

As I've said, the Cottage team responds to specific regional and global government/military crises as they arise. Actually, they respond to situations *before* we heat them up into crises. Whenever the team becomes aware of situations or conditions that may lead to a crisis, they study that situation, break down its elements and seat into the leyline system solutions that are compatible with Aquarian principles as they apply to that potential crisis. In short, we have the information we need to diffuse any situation long before it becomes a crisis.

On March 6, 1987, I worked with nature to activate the Globe. This is a twelve-foot in diameter globe of our planet that was specially designed for the Cottage team. It presently resides in its own room at the Cottage, which we've cleverly named "the Globe Room." The continents, countries and topography are delineated in remarkable detail. But when a certain button is pressed on the console with a thousand buttons that lines one side of the room, the government/military leyline system appears as it is laid out on and in our planet. It's quite impressive.

The government/military leylines move information in two directions: from the Cottage to Earth and from Earth to the Cottage. The Cottage team can seat information into the system in response to our needs. At the same time, Overlord included the setup for any government/military preparation or activity to activate the related leyline circuits. The Globe's leylines are never static. In fact, they're quite active. Different circuits light up, different colors appear, and they will light up in ways that show what combination of circuits have been activated by a particular situation. Using this technology, the Cottage team can identify what is happening in the arena of government and military well before it becomes a crisis, and oftentimes before it is recognized as a problem by those involved on our planet, and provide us an array of options to be considered for resolving the situation. And they do all this by working with the Globe. More often than not, if I'm looking for someone at the Cottage, I'll find him in the Globe Room watching circuits.

Any new information that is seated into the leyline system is now done at the Cottage with the Globe. And any balancing and stabilizing I might do with the system is also now done with the Globe rather than from the Perelandra garden. The Globe's leylines connect and function with our planet's leylines similarly as my two bodies function when I move energy from my Cottage body to my Perelandra body. To use computer terms, the impulses and information are introduced into the Globe's leylines, then downloaded into the corresponding leylines around our planet. The clarity and scope of the work done on Mt. Shasta enabled the Cottage team to work with the kind of efficiency and precision the Globe offers.

THE TREES

And now the final update I'd like to tell you about. On August 15, 1988, I did a follow-up on the trees and the nuclear weapons issue. Several days before, I had gotten word from Pan that now was the time for the follow-up to the work I had begun on Mt. Shasta, only now the focus would be expanded to include all trees globally. That stopped me in my tracks a little. Plunging into the unknown, I opened a coning and included the Overlighting Deva of Trees in order to connect with the devic intelligence for all trees around the world. Then I followed instructions.

1.   I did a Battle Energy Release Process for all trees, working with them as a unit. When I called for the release of the energy that had resulted from the use of nuclear weapons or nuclear testing, I saw the outline of the planet in my mind's

eye with energy shooting out from every direction and stopping at an altitude still within our planet's atmosphere. According to Pan's instructions, I directed the released energy to move to its next level of evolution, wherever that may be. And I saw the energy move out of our atmosphere.

2.   Then, I did balancing and stabilizing testing for the trees. Kelp was needed for balancing. For stabilizing, the world's trees needed Royal Highness, plus Broccoli and Zucchini flower essences from the new Perelandra Garden Essences set I had developed since the Mt. Shasta Mission. When Pan finished shifting the balancers and stabilizers, in my mind's eye I saw white energy surrounding the globe. And I felt a palpable sense of calm and peace all around me.

3.   Finally, Pan told me to pick one Angel Card* for nature's response from the trees to us humans as a result of the release of the effects of nuclear weapons and testing. I spread the cards out face down in front of me and picked the one that caught my eye. Before turning it over, I tested to make sure this was the card nature wanted us to have. I'm pleased to finally pass along that message from the trees to you:

Forgiveness

---

* Angel Cards are a deck of over fifty-five cards, with each card listing a different quality such as Power, Brotherhood, Simplicity, Understanding, etc.

The following day, I had a session with Pan for further information about this work and the trees.

Pan: I would like to address the work you did yesterday. The Battle Energy Release Process was successful in accomplishing the needed release and initiating a new level of healing for the trees. We have stated before that man and nature separately are two powerful forces, but together, they create a power beyond imagination. Yesterday is a fine example of this. Your work with nature accomplished what we had hoped for on a global level. This has released the barriers between man and the trees, and you will begin to see an improved and cooperative interaction regarding the state of trees and forests around the world. With the barriers removed, human efforts will improve and the ability of trees to reseed and establish will also improve.

The need for change has been present for some time now. Humans are beginning to understand the indispensable role trees play in the overall health and balance of the planet. But efforts to make far-reaching fundamental changes in approach, replenishing and conservation have not been easy, due to the barriers that were created between man and trees from man's use of nuclear weapons. Those efforts will now begin to move with greater ease and will pave the way for better, more comprehensive efforts and action. We would say to you that the timing for yesterday's work was right, but we will also say to you that the planet could not wait much longer for such an action to occur due to the mounting critical situation with the global tree population.

When Pan lets me know that the trees need the next step in this extraordinary work, I'll be ready. I'm expecting this to be an ongoing project over a very long time, and I let nature know I'm in it for the long haul.

The Cottage work continues, of course. And it will continue for as long as there is time. I still go to the Cottage daily (it's been twenty-three years now since I began my Cottage adventure), and I continue to work there with nature as it relates to the team's goals. I have to admit that in light of the current state of the world's governments and their activities (military and otherwise), I sometimes ask the men if they've given up on us. I'll even accuse them of giving up on us! But they assure me they haven't. They say they're right with us, and they even have told me that there has been movement toward establishing Aquarian principles in government and military. When we feel despair about this, the key is to *look for demonstrations of cooperation, equality and teamwork*—on a large scale and on a small scale. Wherever we find these three qualities, we find the reflection of Aquarian principles.

And how do we help create the government structures that demonstrate cooperation, equality and teamwork? How do we move ourselves out of the old world and into the new? We just focus on specific situations and dedicate ourselves to discovering new solutions—and we'll have the help we need from the Cottage team and those leylines. I swear to you, it's that easy. It's all sitting right there for us. All we have to do is want it.

Appendices

Nature Process Steps I Used for the Mission

My purpose for including the steps for the Energy Cleansing Process, the Balancing and Stabilizing Process and the Pan Shift is to give you a better idea of what I was doing when I wrote that I was testing these processes during the mission work. I'd write, "I tested the site," or "I did an Energy Cleansing Process," or "Pan shifted the essences"... But I didn't tell you exactly what I was doing. Just in case this matters to you, I'm including the steps that I was using. In Chapter 3, I included Pan's instructions for opening and closing the first coning, as well as the steps given me for the Battle Energy Release Process, so I won't be repeating them in this appendix.

> IMPORTANT NOTE: *If you wish to work with these processes, and I hope you will be inspired to do so, do not use the steps that are listed in this book. After the Mt. Shasta Mission, nature and I continued to work together to refine these processes and to set them up so that they will be effective and safe for everyone to use. For example, your Energy Cleansing Process has seventeen steps, while what I did on the mountain had only nine steps. This is because some of the steps that are listed for you are embedded and implied in the steps that I did for the mission and I knew what to do. It's not that I skipped these steps. It's just that this is a good example of the kind of shorthand that develops between two*

*people—in this case, two intelligences (Pan and me)—when
they have worked together for many years.*

Remember I wrote that in 1985 I put together an outline for a
new book. Well, that book was the *Perelandra Garden Workbook,*
and it includes all the information and updated steps for these
processes that you'll need. I tore apart all that shorthand between
Pan and me and clearly listed every step for you. As another
example, there are ten pages on four-point conings—what they
are, how to set them up, how to work with them and what to
watch out for—instead of Pan's one page of instructions to me on
opening and closing a four-point coning. If you're interested in
pursuing these processes, I hope you will use the steps listed in
the *Perelandra Garden Workbook.*

ENERGY CLEANSING PROCESS

There are all kinds of environmental imbalances and pollution
we have to deal with. The Energy Cleansing Process deals with
this on the levels we can't see, and includes thought and emotional energy pollution. These can have quite a damaging effect
on an environment.

1.   Whenever I worked with the Energy Cleansing Process, I
was already functioning within an open coning prior to setting up for the process, the coning had already been
checked for balancers and stabilizers, and I had already
defined the area in which I was working—such as my garden or the mission site. I set up for this process by saying to
nature:

"I'd like to set up for an Energy Cleansing Process."

After this, I was ready to go.

2.   To start with, I had to activate the various elements and energies of the process and get them set for the release. First, I saw in my mind's eye a white beam of light, the evolutionary light, above my head. This light was generated by the White Brotherhood point of the four-point coning. I watched the light rays from the beam move down toward me and totally envelop me. Then I stated:

"I ask that the evolutionary light aid this process so that what I am about to do will be for the highest good. I ask that this light help me in transmuting the ungrounded emotional energies released by us humans and that I be protected fully during this process."

3.   Next, I saw a second beam of light, a green light—the light of nature (the involutionary dynamic). This light was generated by Pan from within the coning. I watched as this light totally enveloped me and commingled with the white light. I stated:

"I ask that the light of nature aid me in releasing and collecting the energies absorbed by the nature kingdoms, tangible and intangible, animate and inanimate. I also ask that the light of nature aid me so that what I am about to do will be for the highest good."

4.   I addressed the area to be cleansed:
"I ask that any inappropriate, stagnant, darkened or ungrounded energies be released from this area. I request this in gentleness and love, knowing that the cleansing and transmutation process I am about to be a part of is a process of life, of evolution—and not negation."

5.   I visualized a white sheet of light forming five feet below the lowest point of the area and watched as the edges of the

sheet extended five feet beyond the outside boundary of the area.

6.   I then asked that the two lights (the White Brotherhood and Pan) join me as together we slowly moved the sheet up and through the area being cleansed. The sheet rose to five feet above the highest point in the area, and then stopped. I took a moment to recognize the released energies that were now being held in the sheet.

7.   I directed that a bundle be created and watched the edges of the sheet form a bundle of white light that totally enclosed the collected energies. The closed bundle was tied with two gold cords—one created by the White Brotherhood and the other by nature. I then stated:

"I now release the bundle to the evolutionary light and the light of nature, so that the energies that have been released can be moved on to their next higher level for transmutation and the continuation of their evolutionary process."

Once said, I spent a moment watching the bundle lift and disappear.

8.   Then I shifted my focus to the area in order to feel, sense or see any changes.

9.   For the finishing touches, I tested balancers and stabilizers for the area for whatever might be needed as a result of the Energy Cleansing Process. First, I asked:
"What balancers are needed for this _____ (site, soil, environment, garden, etc.)?"

I tested my soil balancing kit, set up for a Pan shift (See "Pan Shift" on p. 428.) and held out any needed balancers in a spoon for Pan to shift into the area I was working with.

Next, I asked:

"What stabilizers are needed for this_____?"

Finally, I tested the flower essences. I placed one drop of each needed essence in a spoon and held it out for Pan to shift into the area.

At this point, I had completed the Energy Cleansing Process. For my Mt. Shasta Mission work, the process was not the only thing I was doing within an open coning, so I would state that I was moving on to the next item of business and continued with the rest of my work.

BALANCING AND STABILIZING PROCESS

I did this a lot during the mission. Every time I wrote, "I tested the soil" or "I tested the site," this is the process I was doing. As a result, this process was especially critical for successfully balancing the mission site. What I did in Step 9 of the Energy Cleansing Process constitutes the Balancing and Stabilizing Process.

As with the Energy Cleansing Process, I was already working within an open coning—the Mt. Shasta Mission coning—when I needed to do a balancing and stabilizing.

1.   First, I asked:
     "What balancers are needed for this_____(site, soil, environment, garden, etc.)?"

     I tested my soil balancing kit, set up for a Pan shift and held out any needed balancers in a spoon for Pan to shift into the area I was working with.

2.   Next, I asked:
     "What stabilizers are needed for this_____?"

Then, I tested the flower essences. I placed one drop of each needed essence in a spoon and held it out for Pan to shift into the area.

PAN SHIFT

1. Anytime I needed balancers and stabilizers to be shifted, I set up for a Pan shift. To do this, I "brought Pan forward" in the coning by stating:
    "I'd like to set up for a Pan shift."

    Pan automatically moved forward in the coning, and I could feel the dynamics in the coning change.

2. After putting all the needed balancers in a spoon, I held the spoon out in front of me and stated:
    "I ask that you shift these balancers to the needed areas."

    I held the spoon out until after the shift was completed (ten seconds), then I threw away the depleted balancers and cleaned the spoon.

3. I tested the essences needed for stabilizing and placed the drop(s) of each essence needed in the spoon. I held the spoon out in front of me and said:
    "I ask that you shift these stabilizers to the needed areas."

    Again, I held the spoon out until after the shift was completed (ten seconds), then poured the depleted essences on the ground and cleaned the spoon.

This completed the Pan shift. Because I was doing other work within the open coning, I would just state that I was moving on, and the coning would automatically adjust to the normal four-point dynamic.

Appendix B

Flower Essences Definitions

THIS IS A LIST OF THE ESSENCES and their definitions that were used during the Mt. Shasta Mission. The definitions are meant to be guideposts and were written for humans. Much of my work was with the site and soil on Mt. Shasta and the Gettysburg Battlefield. Because of this, you will need to consider these definitions in the most general of terms when applying them to site and soil work.

Key to the essence sets I used:

Bach: Bach Flower Remedies

FES: Flower Essence Society

PGE: Perelandra Garden Essences

PRE: Perelandra Rose Essences

misc.: miscellaneous essences

Agrimony (Bach): For those who suffer inner torture with a cheerful façade.

Ambassador (PRE): Pattern. Aids the individual in seeing the relationship of the part to the whole, in perceiving his pattern and purpose.

Blue Aster (misc.): The courage needed to respond to process already under way.

Borage (FES): For feeling disheartened, discouraged.

Broccoli (PGE): For the power balance that must be maintained when one perceives himself to be under siege from outside. Stabilizes the body/soul unit so the individual won't close down, detach and scatter.

Cherry Plum (Bach): Desperation; fear of losing control of the mind; dread of doing some frightful thing.

Chestnut Bud (Bach): Failure to learn from experience; lack of observation in one's life lessons that causes repetition.

Chicory (Bach): Possessiveness, self-love, self-pity.

Clematis (Bach): Indifference, dreaminess, inattention, unconscious.

Comfrey (PGE): Repairs higher vibrational soul damage that occurred in present or past lifetime.

Crab Apple (Bach): Despondency, despair.

Delphinium (misc.): The courage to face personal challenge resulting in inner shifting of understanding.

Eclipse (PRE): Acceptance and insight. Enhances the individual's appreciation of his own inner knowing. Supports the mechanism that allows the body to receive the soul's input and insight.

Elm (Bach): Occasional feelings of inadequacy, despondency, exhaustion from overstriving for perfection.

Gentian (Bach): Doubt, depression, discouragement.

Gruss an Aachen (PRE): Stability. Balances and stabilizes the body/soul unit on all levels—physical, emotional, mental, soul—as it moves forward in its evolutionary process.

Holly (Bach): Important antidote for hatred.

Impatiens (Bach): Impatience, irritability, extreme mental tension.

Larch (Bach): Lack of confidence, anticipation of failure, despondency.

Larkspur (FES): Generosity, altruism, true leadership qualities.

Mimulus (Bach): Fear or anxiety of a known origin.

Mustard (Bach): For gloom, depression and melancholy that descends for no known cause.

Nasturtium (FES): For over-intellectuality, lacking vitality.

Nymphenburg (PRE): Strength. Supports and holds the strength created by the balance of the body/soul fusion, and facilitates the individual's ability to regain that balance.

Oak (Bach): Despondency, despair, but never-ceasing effort.

Orange Marigold (misc.): For fear.

Orange Ruffles (PRE): Receptivity. Stabilizes the individual during the expansion of his sensory system.

Peace (PRE): Courage. Opens the individual to the inner dynamic of courage that is aligned to universal courage.

Pink Nicotiana (misc.): For impatience.

Pink Yarrow (FES): For emotional vulnerability.

Red Clover (FES): For feeling swept up in mass hysteria, doomsday obsessions.

Rescue Remedy (Bach): For shock and trauma in emergencies.

Rock Rose (Bach): Terror, panic, extreme fright.

Royal Highness (PRE): Final stabilization. The mop-up essence that helps to insulate, protect and stabilize the individual and to stabilize the shift during its final stages while vulnerable.

Saguaro (FES): Clarity in relation to parental/authority images; appreciating the wisdom of true spiritual elders and tradition.

Scotch Broom (FES): Motivation, perseverance, faith; acceptance of difficulties as opportunities. For despair, pessimism, alienation, feeling "what's the use."

Shasta Daisy (FES): Clarity and focus in spiritual knowledge, synthesis of information. For scattered seeking, unintegrated knowledge.

Star of Bethlehem (Bach): Aftereffect of shock, mental or physical.

Sweet Chestnut (Bach): Extreme mental anguish, hopelessness, despair.

Vervain (Bach): Strain, stress, tension, over-enthusiasm.

Walnut (Bach): Oversensitive to ideas and influences.

White Lightnin' (PRE): Synchronized movement. Stabilizes the timing of all levels moving in concert and enhances the body/soul fusion.

Willow (Bach): Resentment, bitterness.

Yarrow (FES): For vulnerability to psychic or emotional "attack," to harmful environmental influences or energies.

Yerba Santa (FES): Spiritual insight into emotions; relaxation of emotional constriction.

Zinnia (FES): Laughter, lightness and release of tension.

Zucchini (PGE): Helps restore physical strength during convalescence.

The Bach Flower Essence information is from notes taken from *Handbook of the Bach Flower Remedies* by Philip M. Chancellor. Copyright 1971. Printed in Great Britain by Lowe and Brydone Printers Ltd., Thetford, Norfolk.

The FES definitions are from the Flower Essence Repertory and were compiled by Richard Katz and Patricia Kaminski. They have been reprinted with permission. Since first publishing these definitions twenty-five years ago, FES has written more about the qualities of each of the essences. For further information and research, see the Flower Essence Society (non-profit educational and research organization), www.flowersociety.org.

Appendix C

Perelandra Post-Death Flower Essence Process

THIS IS A GOOD PROCESS TO have on hand if you use flower essences and know how to do kinesiology testing. It allows you to assist family and friends in a way that will both surprise and amaze you. Flower essences are tremendously helpful to those who have just died. They stabilize the individual during that initial post-death period when he or she is most vulnerable, and greatly assist the healing process from the illness or condition that caused death.

First, this process must be used within seventy-two hours after a person has died. After seventy-two hours, the electrical system has detached from the Earth reality, and it is no longer effective to administer essences from the Earth level. If essences are used after seventy-two hours, it is more efficient and effective for someone from the new level upon which the person's being "resides" to administer them. What makes the Post-Death Flower Essence Process so effective within the first seventy-two hours is the compatibility between the person's electrical system and the level upon which the essences are administered.

It is, of course, best in the death process for people to be stabilized with essences throughout the entire process. (See the book *Flower Essences,* Chapter 8, Death Process.) If this is impossible to do for someone, then it is most helpful to administer essences during the three-day post-death period. As I've stated, for both the death and post-death processes, the person is not only stabilized by the essences, but assisted through the healing process, as well. However, if it is impossible to do either of these two processes, don't feel that the chances for this person to receive the benefits of essences has passed. Essences will be made available on the other level once the person requests them.

The tester does not need to be in physical proximity to the person who has died in order to do this process. It transcends physical distance.

IMPORTANT: Read through this process in its entirety so that you can familiarize yourself with its rhythm before you actually have to do it for someone.

POST-DEATH PROCESS

1.   The tester: Prepare yourself by doing a general essence test and taking any needed essences one time. (Don't bother testing for a solution.) Then telegraph test your reactions to the news that this person has died. Take any needed essences one time. (Don't test for a solution.)

2.   Open a Post-Death Flower Essence Process coning:
     a. Deva of the Post-Death Flower Essence Process
     b. Pan
     c. Appropriate connection to the White Brotherhood for the Post-Death Flower Essence Process
     d. Your higher self *and* the higher self of the person who has died
     Verify each connection using kinesiology.

3.   Test yourself again for essences to make sure you are still holding your balance now that the coning is activated. (Don't test for solution.)

4. Shift your focus to the person who has died. Ask to be appropriately linked with this person for surrogate kinesiology testing. Verify your connection.

Now, say hello and explain to the person that you would like to offer essences if he would like them. Describe flower essences and how they work if the person is unfamiliar with them. Speak to the person as if you were talking to him over a telephone. Once you have explained the essences, ask the person if he understands what you are explaining. Use kinesiology to discern his answer. (You are linked to this person exactly as you would be for any surrogate testing.) The person can hear you quite well. If he doesn't understand, it's because he needs it explained differently and not because you need to say it louder. Keep your explanation as simple and direct as possible. You don't have to give a full-blown class on essences. Just give the person the idea of what they are and how they can help stabilize and assist in healing now. Don't be surprised if a person who had no interest in flower essences prior to death is open to using them after death. We all tend to change our perspective on things once we've died!

NOTE: It is not unusual for a tester who is close to the person or empathetic about his death to feel deep emotions—and express them—during this process. At any time, you (the tester) may stop the process, ask to be disconnected electrically from the person who has died and retest yourself for essences you might now need as a result of your feelings. Don't bother getting a solution for any of these tests. Be sure to reconnect electrically with the person before going on with the process. Verify the connection.

Disconnecting in this manner from a person who has died is the electrical equivalent of having someone remove his hand from your arm or knee during a regular surrogate essence test. When you reconnect, the person who has died is "touching" you again—only the touch is electrical rather than physical. Disconnecting and reconnecting do not affect the coning in any way. The person you are testing remains in the coning until it is dismantled at the conclusion of the process.

5. Once the person understands, ask if he would like you to test him for essences. Surrogate test using kinesiology. If he says yes, ask to be electrically disconnected from the person while you clear yourself once more and test for any essences you might need. Then ask to be electrically connected again with the person. Verify the connection.

 Now do a surrogate general test for that person. (Telegraph testing won't be needed.)

 (If the person does not wish to be tested, see Step 8. Do not try to coerce the person into changing his mind. It is important to respect his decision.)

6. Place one drop of each essence needed onto a clean spoon. Ask Pan to shift this solution to the electrical system of the person you are testing. Hold the spoon in front of you for fifteen seconds for the shift. (No need to verify that the shift has occurred. It will happen in this time frame.)

7. Put the spoon down and wait one full minute. (You may chat with the person during this time. You are waiting for the essences to impact his electrical system fully.)

 After the minute, test the person again—a general test. Most of the time, no additional essences will be needed. If additional ones are needed, place one drop of each onto the spoon (which you have washed clean!) and, once again, ask Pan to shift the solution to the person's electrical system. Hold the spoon out for fifteen seconds for the shift. Wait another minute, then test again for any additional essences. Keep repeating this until the person tests he needs no additional essences. That is, he tests clear.

HINT: Have several clean spoons on hand so you won't have to keep washing the same spoon.

8. Once the testing is over (or if he has said no to essence testing), you may spend up to one half hour talking to the person. You may talk about anything, and you may even ask questions about how he feels and so forth. Try not to press any feelings of grief and sorrow (or anger) you might have onto the person. This process and time is for the welfare of the person who has died, and it is not appropriate to try to unload your emotions onto that person. Do not spend more than one half hour talking with the person. By this time, you are both getting tired. And this person needs to move on. After the half hour is up, tell the person you have to "go," say goodbye, wish him well—and close the session and the coning.

9. To close: First, ask to be disconnected electrically from the person. Then close the coning. Disconnect from the members of the coning in the following order:
   a. Higher self of the person who has died *and* your higher self
   b. Appropriate connection to the White Brotherhood for the Post-Death Flower Essence Process
   c. Pan
   d. Deva of the Post-Death Flower Essence Process
   Verify that the coning is fully dismantled.

10. Telegraph test yourself again for any essences needed as a result of your having done this process. This time, check for solution. Then telegraph test the personal grief you feel as a result of this person dying. Check for solution again. Both of these essence solutions will stabilize you as you move through your grief process. Do all the necessary follow-up testing for these two solutions until each tests clear.

Index

About the Author

She's tired.

Other Books by Machaelle Wright

Behaving as If the God in All Life Mattered

Co-Creative Science:
  A Revolution in Science Providing Real
  Solutions for Today's Health and Environment

Dancing in the Shadows of the Moon

Flower Essences:
  Reordering Our Understanding and Approach
  to Illness and Health

MAP:
  The Co-Creative White Brotherhood
  Medical Assistance Program

Perelandra Garden Workbook:
  A Complete Guide to Gardening
  with Nature Intelligences

Perelandra Garden Workbook II:
  Co-Creative Energy Processes for
  Gardening, Agriculture and Life

Perelandra Microbial Balancing Program Manual

Perelandra, Ltd.

P.O. Box 3603, Warrenton, VA 20188
U.S. & Canada Phone Order Line: 1-800-960-8806
Overseas & Mexico Phone Order Line: 1-540-937-2153
Fax: 1-540-937-3360
Web Site: www.perelandra-ltd.com
E-mail: email@perelandra-ltd.com

PERELANDRA CATALOG

Information about Perelandra and a complete listing of all Perelandra products is included in our free catalog. Our annual catalog is available year-round upon request.

PERELANDRA WEB SITE

You can also visit our beautiful, extensive and user-friendly web site. Along with browsing our complete and up-to-date catalog or placing an order, you can visit our Education section for answers to frequently asked questions, excerpts from each of Machaelle's books or one of the many other informative articles. Overall, our goal is for the web site to be as much of a resource and education center as it is an online catalog. It also includes money-saving specials, networking lists, a weekly photo gallery of the Perelandra garden, and special updates and reminders from Machaelle. Please visit us online and let us know what you think.

PERELANDRA PHONE ORDER LINE

The nice folks in our customer service department can answer basic questions about the products, help you figure what to order and tell you the most economical way to order it.